D1035188

MEDIA AND REVOLUTION

Media
and
Revolution

Comparative Perspectives

Jeremy D. Popkin, Editor

THE UNIVERSITY PRESS OF KENTUCKY

Copyright © 1995 by The University Press of Kentucky

Scholarly publisher for the Commonwealth,
serving Bellarmine College, Berea College, Centre
College of Kentucky, Eastern Kentucky University,
The Filson Club, Georgetown College, Kentucky
Historical Society, Kentucky State University,
Morehead State University, Murray State University,
Northern Kentucky University, Transylvania University,
University of Kentucky, University of Louisville,
and Western Kentucky University.

Editorial and Sales Offices: Lexington, Kentucky 40508-4008

Library of Congress Cataloging-in-Publication Data

Media and revolution / Jeremy D. Popkin, editor.
    p.   cm.
Papers of a conference held 1992 in Lexington.
Includes bibliographical references and index.
ISBN 0-8131-1899-9
1. Press and politics—Congresses.   2. Revolutions—Congresses.
I. Popkin, Jeremy D., 1948-
PN4751.M43   1995
070—dc20   94-31808

This book is printed on acid-free recycled paper meeting
the requirements of the American National Standard
for Permanence of Paper for Printed Library Materials.

♾ ⊕

Contents

Acknowledgments

The essays in this volume were first presented at the conference "Media and Revolution" held at the University of Kentucky on 15-17 October 1992. The conference was supported by a major grant from the National Endowment for the Humanities, along with funding from the Kentucky Humanities Council; the University of Kentucky's Graduate School, College of Arts and Sciences and College of Communications; and the United Nations Association of the Bluegrass, to all of which I express my thanks.

It has not been possible to include in this volume the papers delivered at the conference by Orville Schell on China in 1989, by Robert Darnton and Michael Richards on East Germany in 1989, by Javier Garciadiego Dantan on the press in the Mexican Revolution of 1910, and by Majid Tehranian on how communications scholars have used the concept of "media revolutions." They all nevertheless contributed to the development of the essays published here both by the issues they raised in their own talks and by their active participation in the discussions that marked the conference. So did several scholars who participated in the conference as discussants, thanks to the generosity of the National Endowment for the Humanities: Mohammed Alam, Lisa Holstein, Laura Mason, Abraham Miller, and Giles Richter. Special thanks to John Stempel for his invaluable assistance in preparing the 1992 conference; to my administrative assistant, Delia Pergande, for her help in organizing the conference and assembling the contributions for the volume; and to François Le Roy, who translated Professor Rétat's contribution. The readers for the University Press of Kentucky offered many helpful suggestions to all the individual contributors. Jack Censer's advice and encouragement were indispensable to the compilation of this volume, as they have been to so much of my work on the history of the press.

Jeremy D. Popkin

1

Lessons from a Symposium

JEREMY D. POPKIN and JACK R. CENSER

The historical essays included in this volume take us from the opening stages of the Puritan Revolution in 1640 to events in China and Czechoslovakia in 1989. They range in approach from a detailed case study of a single journal and its author to broad considerations of the media as a whole over the course of long and complex revolutionary events. They also indicate that scholars who share a common interest in the problem of media and revolution can come to very different conclusions about the significance of the connection between the two.

Contributors took a wide degree of latitude in constructing their essays. Authors were selected because of their knowledge about one of the major revolutionary crises of the last three and a half centuries. Some, such as Jeffery Smith and Pierre Rétat, have published extensively on the history of the press during "their" revolution.[1] Others, including Jonathan Sperber and Jeffrey Wasserstrom, are experts on a particular revolutionary crisis who had not previously devoted special attention to media issues in their own work but who were intrigued by the invitation to do so. Each contributor chose to emphasize some particular aspect of the larger issue of the role of the media in revolutionary situations. The resulting volume can hardly pretend to exhaust all the possible approaches to the problem; some fundamental issues, such as the economics of financing a revolutionary "press explosion," are not addressed in any of these essays. But the contents of this volume do serve to exemplify the variety of ways in which the subject can be studied.

To some extent, the range of issues addressed proved surprising. Jonathan Sperber's case study of an obscure periodical from the German revolution of 1848 is the only contribution dealing with a specific paper and a specific journalist. The great names in revolutionary journalism—Tom Paine, Marat, Lenin—are evoked only in passing. Except for Jeffery Smith, none of the contributors attempted to survey the overall media landscape during any of the revolutionary crises dealt with. Absent here are the long lists of titles and attempts to classify them by political tendency that are characteristic of the history of the press. None of the contributors to this volume took what is probably the most common approach to the subject in the overall literature: that of choosing a particular journalist or title and arguing that the messages articulated by that person or media organ guided events. Instead of this "intentionalist" approach, contributors generally took a structuralist view of their subject, seeing the media system as one of the contexts in which the outcome of "their" revolution was shaped. Whereas the intentionalist structure of much media history has often emphasized "precursor" media organs, whose content is seen as having inspired subsequent revolutionary movements, the studies here focus primarily on what happened *after* the moment of revolutionary rupture and institutional breakdown.

The intention of this volume, as of the conference out of which it has grown, was to look at the role of the communications media in specific revolutionary situations with an eye toward suggesting possible frameworks for comparison. Understandably—although regrettably—few scholars, particularly in the discipline of history, have single-handedly undertaken comparative research in this area. In general, comparative studies of revolutions have more often been the work of sociologists rather than historians, who, by training and disciplinary inclination, tend to specialize in a single national history. Journalism historians, located in schools of journalism or communications, are often more ecumenical in their interests, but they too are limited by the problem of learning multiple languages and mastering disparate bodies of sources. The comparisons suggested by reading these essays are thus more often implicit than explicit. Paths pursued in one contribution may well incite readers versed in the history of other revolutions to think about new aspects of their "own" revolution. Only an initial approach to a vast subject, this volume aims to stimulate recognition of the important questions raised more than to propose a firm framework for their resolution.

The contributors to this volume take a broad view of the concept of revolution. Most deal with crises that are generally included in any list of major revolutions in the modern world: England in 1640, the North American colonies in 1776, France in 1789, Russia in 1917, China from 1911 to 1949. In general, conference participants agreed that the events in Eastern Europe in 1989 deserved to be considered under the rubric of revolution. In the extensive discussions that followed delivery of the original drafts of these papers at the 1992 Lexington conference, comparisons with the events of 1989 were frequent and served to demonstrate how powerfully these occurrences have already begun to reshape understanding of the past. Some selections in this volume—such as the second half of Timothy Harris's contribution on seventeenth-century England, Jonathan Sperber's essay on Germany in 1848, and Jeffrey Wasserstrom's analysis of China in 1989—deal with failed revolutions: upheavals that destabilized or threatened to subvert existing state structures but that ultimately ended without achieving their desired results. Thomas Leonard stretched the notion of revolution farthest by applying the label to episodes in United States history in which the definition of race relations, but not the entire political structure, was put into question. Finally, Mark Summers's contribution on American political cartoonists' representations of revolution deals not with a specific revolutionary crisis but with media images of revolution in a distinctly nonrevolutionary society.

Just as these essays do not share any rigid definition of revolution, they differ greatly in their use of the concept of media. Many of the authors limit their discussion to the classic instrument of mass political communication, the newspaper press. It is true that the two contributions on seventeenth-century England focus primarily on pamphlets rather than periodicals. Although weekly "mercuries" were an important feature of English political literature in the 1640s, the periodical press had not yet truly established its primacy. By the second half of the eighteenth century, newspapers had become much more common, but it is not necessarily obvious that they had become the only important medium of political communication. Their leading role in the essays presented here may in part reflect a bias in historical research, which has long had a special relationship with this particular form of publication.

Newspapers are among the richest sources of the specific kinds of information historians look for. They also offer the enormous advantage of presenting that information already printed in an orderly chronological sequence. Collections of pamphlets, caricatures, or videotapes of television broadcasts—to name a few of the other media referred to in at least some of these essays—rarely possess the same helpful structure, and it is not always clear whether newspapers feature so largely in historians' accounts because of their intrinsic importance in the shaping of events or because they are already structured, at least in part, as historical narratives. Certainly it has often been argued that special features of the newspaper make it a uniquely powerful means of communication, especially in a revolutionary situation. Surely it is no accident that all the contributions presented here that concern revolutionary crises between the time of the American Revolution and the mid-twentieth century are about newspapers. Even Summers's essay on cartoons deals largely with illustrations that first appeared in the press. But none of these essays presents a clear theoretical argument that would justify this concentration.

On the other hand, those that focus on history since the electronic media became widespread—Leonard's essay on the United States in the 1950s, Wasserstrom's on China in 1989, and Owen Johnson's on Czechoslovakia in the same year—make it clear that the primacy of the newspaper in revolutionary situations has been broken and suggest that, as a result, it may now be much more difficult to conceptualize the connection between media and revolution. Indeed, in a recent book on postmodernist thought, historian Mark Poster has argued that in the decentralized world of the modern electronic media, classical revolutions are no longer possible.[2] If this proves to be so, it would be powerful grounds for asserting that revolutions are (or were) indeed essentially linked to the printed periodical press, and that the age of Gutenberg and the age of revolution were coterminous.

Implicit in most of the following essays is the assertion that revolutionary crises coincide with sudden changes in the media system of the society in which they occur. The mere assertion that communications media are widely employed during revolutionary crises would not necessarily distinguish these periods from the calmer epochs that precede and follow them. Typically, the essays here describe a sudden multiplication of competing publications or media organs, a rapid shift from one dominant medium to another (from pamphlets to newspapers, for example), a marked change in the form or substance of media content, or a major alternation in different groups' access to the media. The central issue at stake is simply the question of whether the media do in fact have a real influence on the unfolding of revolutionary crises. To the general public, the power of the media's influence, even in normal times, seems obvious. Best-selling books like David Halberstam's *The Powers That Be* propagate the notion that American journalists stopped the Vietnam War and forced Richard Nixon from office.[3] Scholars have often demurred, however. Recent studies have questioned the extent of the press's role in the Watergate crisis, for example.[4]

Although, as noted, none of the essays in this collection take an "intentionalist" approach, they argue for the importance of the media in several different ways. Pierre Rétat, whose contribution is a succinct summary of themes he has developed at greater length in his French-language publications, is perhaps the most forceful in arguing that the revolutionary journal and the revolutionary journalist are absolutely central to the revolutionary process. As Rétat writes in his essay in this volume, referring to one of the leading revolutionary journals of 1789, the *Révolutions de Paris*: "Much of the effect that it produces comes from the intervention of a spectator who is simultaneously a reporter, from the presence of a central consciousness—both vocal and visible in the text—whose intervention gives the event its passionate strength and its exemplarity. The Revolution instigates a type of journalism destined to perpetuate it, a text that becomes the consciousness of the revolution, at once representation of and reflection on what a revolution is, what it will become, what it must be."[5] For Rétat, the press does not bring about the Revolution, but it is one and the same with the revolutionary process. Scholars familiar with the whole corpus of Rétat's writing on the eighteenth-century and revolutionary periodical press know that he is a meticulous scholar, not given to broad pronouncements about the relationship between discourse and reality. By his own route, however, he seems to come close to asserting that the French Revolution is first and foremost a creation of journalistic rhetoric.

Rétat's essay is part of a broader trend in recent research on the French Revolution that emphasizes the importance of discourse, symbolism, and the media of communication that transmitted both words and images. Jeremy Popkin, another contributor to this body of research, shares Rétat's conviction that changes in media praxis are essential symbols of the nature of revolutionary upheaval. His essay explains how developments in the historiography of the French Revolution have made a media-based approach central to the understanding of that event. He further argues that a model of "media revolution" based on the French experience can be useful in understanding other revolutionary crises.

Jeffrey Wasserstrom occupies the opposite extreme from Rétat and Popkin. His essay argues that the extensive attention paid to the effects of worldwide television coverage of the demonstrations in Tiananmen Square masked the fact that the Chinese students were essentially reworking elements from a repertoire of political behaviors rooted in their country's history. Those protest rituals, many of them derived from official forms of celebration, developed prior to the modern media era. Wasserstrom sees their real efficacy as coming from the symbolic message they conveyed to those in power, rather than from the images they generated for transmission to the general public. Wasserstrom's analysis, which draws on ideas from historians of the French Revolution such as Lynn Hunt and Mona Ozouf and on Charles Tilly's concept of protest repertoires,[6] suggests that the presence of the media does not really alter the behavior of participants in revolutionary dramas. Their scripts are laid down in deep-rooted cultural traditions, and comparative studies ought to focus on the differences in collective memories that make for different habits of collective action.

Ironically, in view of the way the world events of 1989 focused new attention on media images of revolution, Owen Johnson's essay on the Czechoslovak press in the "Velvet Revolution" parallels Wasserstrom's in downplaying the role of the media, although Johnson's approach is more empirical than theoretical. His historical survey shows that this had not always been the case: for example, the Slovak press in the period after 1918 was central in developing a sense of national identity. But in Johnson's view, disillusionment after the failure of the "Prague Spring" in 1968 and the weight of government controls up to the eve of the 1989 events had essentially discredited the whole Czechoslovak media system. Johnson says little about the possible role of extraterritorial media in the events of 1989, and he does not follow the story after the sudden collapse of the Communist regime. It does appear, however, that the situation in the Soviet Union during the years of Gorbachev's *perestroika* and in Russia during the current phase of post-Communism has been somewhat different. A recent essay by American journalist Jamey Gambrell describes a dynamic and conflictual media landscape quite different from that pictured by Johnson.[7] The contrast between Johnson's and Gambrell's views indicates the danger of treating the events in the Communist world in 1989 as part of a single, uniform process.

The remaining essays occupy various positions in the space between Pierre Rétat's and Jeremy Popkin's sweeping claims for the media and Wasserstrom's and Johnson's relegation of them to the margins. Jeffery Smith has no doubt that the press provided essential "reassurance and inspiration" to the American revolutionaries. Newspapers publicized American military successes and popularized political ideas that legitimated the struggle against England. Rather than representing competing parties in a wide-open competition to control the new revolutionary state, the American press, in Smith's presentation, appears to have moved almost immediately to promote the process of state reconstruction, to use a term made familiar by recent students of comparative revolution. The apparent absence of a phase of utopian fantasy and violent verbal conflict after 1776 could be interpreted either as proof that what happened in the North American colonies was not a true revolution (this is the position of the sociologists Theda Skocpol and Jack Goldstone, who both break with a long tradition of comparative analyses of revolution by omitting the American case from consideration)[8] or as evidence for the effectiveness of the press and other factors in promoting an uncharacteristically rapid process of postrevolutionary consolidation.

The American and Russian Revolutions had very different outcomes, but Jeffrey Brooks's essay on *Pravda* in the 1920s suggests that the impact of the press on state reconstruction was an equally important theme in both cases. Much of the literature on the media in the Russian revolutionary era, such as Peter Kenez's excellent study *The Birth of the Propaganda State,*[9] has emphasized the role of propaganda directed at the general mass of the population. Brooks's essay directs our attention to the impact of the press in shaping the mentality of the men and women who made up the state and party apparatus. By helping to provide this elite with a common language and a sense of participating in a common effort, the press had a major impact on Soviet society even if, as sociologist Alex Inkeles long ago suggested in his classic analysis of the Soviet media, the state-controlled media were "far from completely successful" in persuading the general population.[10]

Michael Mendle's detailed essay on press controls in the early phase of the English Revolution focuses on a revolutionary process of state breakdown rather than reconstruction. His is also the only contribution to bring into the picture not just the wordsmiths of revolutionary propaganda but also the producers and distributors without whom these printed messages would never have circulated. Mendle's essay echoes work by Jeremy Popkin, Carla Hesse, and others that has underlined the importance of this media-industry background in shaping the press in revolutionary France.[11] His essay also underlines the fact that even revolutionaries whose causes profit from the collapse of constraints characteristic of the onset of a revolution can be hostile to the concept of press freedom. The babble of conflicting discourses unleashed by the "media revolutions" that accompany these crises unsettles even the most avid opponents of the old order and seems to be experienced by all parties as a disquieting phenomenon that needs to be liquidated.

In Stephen MacKinnon's essay on twentieth-century China, the emphasis is also less on the press's role in the period of state reconstruction that followed the Communist triumph of 1949 than on the press between the collapse of the old order and the installation of a new one. MacKinnon shows the conditions that briefly permitted the development of an ideologically diversified press in the 1930s. His description of the Chinese situation suggests many parallels with the early years of the French Revolution. There, too, newspapers served as surrogates for political parties, and journalism was a risky profession. In France, however, political patrons of the sort MacKinnon describes played a minor role, and no symbiosis equivalent to that between Chinese journalists and the Western media covering China existed in France in the 1790s. MacKinnon's attention to this phenomenon suggests a fertile field for further research. Like Mark Summers in his treatment of American political cartoonists' representations of foreign revolutions, MacKinnon reminds us that the media and their personnel are crucial intermediaries in determining how revolutions are judged outside their home countries.

Tim Harris's study of the press in two seventeenth-century English crises and Tom Leonard's contribution on the media's role in two crises concerning race relations in the United States both compare different episodes in the history of a single country. Both emphasize that history does not simply repeat itself, even in situations with many similarities. Almost alone among the contributors to this volume, Harris takes seriously the notion that media *content* may have a major effect in determining the outcome of propaganda campaigns. His suggestion that appeals to the "middle ground" of general opinion were most successful echoes the conclusion of Robert Scribner in his classic study of German Reformation propaganda.[12] Paradoxically, the media may be most successful in spreading revolutionary messages when these are presented as defenses of tradition and the status quo, rather than as incitements to sudden change. Harris reminds us that, as every advertising writer knows, there are successful media strategies and unsuccessful ones, and his essay points to the necessity of paying close attention to what is actually said in the media as well as analyzing, as Pierre Rétat does, the new ways in which it is said. On the whole, Harris downplays the effectiveness of media propaganda; it must resonate with its context to be effective, and it can be successfully combatted by an offsetting campaign.

Leonard's study looks at two occasions when changes in media conduct generated a belief that the media themselves had provoked a revolution in race relations. The attacks on northern abolitionist newspapers in the 1830s and on reporters and photographers covering civil rights issues in the 1950s indicate that the media had a central impact in these situations, not necessarily because their content changed minds but because newspaper offices and media personnel became the targets of organized violence that had important social consequences. Indeed, in the short run, the violent southern reaction against pro-civil rights reporting in the national media may have strengthened resistance to integration, rather than hastening acceptance of new values propagated by the media. Leonard's essay suggests that communities normally have certain expectations about how the news media should function, and that when the rules change, reactions up to and including physical destruction of newspaper offices and assaults on journalists are likely. Numerous similar examples could be cited from revolutionary crises in other societies, such as France and—as Stephen MacKinnon's statistics on murdered journalists remind us—China.

Aside from Pierre Rétat's, Jonathan Sperber's is the only essay to focus on the figure of the journalist—in this case, a specific and highly atypical figure, the master-baker-turned-editorialist Mathias Wessel. Sperber's case study reminds us that the existence of the mass media opens opportunities for truly marginal figures to carve out roles for themselves in the midst of revolutionary crises, independent not only of the institutional frameworks of the old regime but also of the main political groupings in the new revolutionary situation. Wessel's career cannot be compared to such cases of loners-turned-leaders as those of Jean Paul Marat and Gracchus Babeuf in the French Revolution of 1789, but the phenomenon does seem to be characteristic of revolutionary crises.

Mark Summers's intriguing essay on American political cartoonists is the only piece in this volume to focus on visual images. Although caricature is often treated as an inherently subversive and destabilizing form of representation, Summers shows that it can also be employed in the interests of preserving an established order. His sampling shows that the visual image of revolution in the nineteenth- and early twentieth-century American press was an overwhelmingly negative one, consistently portraying the phenomenon of revolution as both foreign and destructive. The cartoonists, guided by newspaper owners hostile to radical ideas, thus reinforced notions of American exceptionalism and contributed to the rejection of revolutionary ideologies that has consistently characterized American society since the consolidation of the republic.

Taken as a whole, the essays in this volume suggest that current approaches to cultural and social history have had a strong effect on the way scholars conceptualize the issues that history raises. Like mass mobilization and the breakdown of state authority, the sudden alteration of media systems does indeed appear to be one of the defining characteristics of revolutions. For the most part, however, the contributors to this volume no longer see that relationship as causal, one in which the media diffuse radical ideas, which in turn provoke revolutionary upheaval. Instead, they generally see a revolutionary media structure emerging as preexisting institutions—including media institutions—crumble, and they tend to focus either on how the new media structure shapes conflicts in the chaotic periods that follow the overthrow of established authority or on the media's role in the reconstruction of new institutions. Most contributors are skeptical about voluntarist schemas that attribute to particular media organs a decisive capacity for changing minds and directing events. Many draw attention to the perverse or unintended effects of certain kinds of media content or to the way recipients resist the messages the media tries to impose on them. Those who focus on periods of revolutionary confusion are likely to emphasize the conflicting effects of the pluralistic media and the unpredictability of media influence on the outcomes of such crises.

On the whole, the essays presented here reflect a certain skepticism about the results of revolutions themselves. The abuse of revolutionary rhetoric by twentieth-century Communist regimes has discredited the claim that revolutionary ruptures necessarily lead to progress. Jack Goldstone, the most recent theorist of comparative revolution, concludes that the association of revolutions and democracy is no more than an "illusion."[13] Immersion in media sources can easily incline scholars to see the actors in a revolution as manipulators consciously distorting the truth.

And yet the comparative survey of the media's role in revolution sketched in this volume suggests that this pessimistic perspective is incomplete. For better or for worse, revolutions are moments when freedom can truly be acted out in the media. If freedom of expression in the media is indeed part of the general notion of liberty whose triumph over totalitarianism we now celebrate, it is only just to remember that it is a principle first imagined and articulated in the revolutionary crises of 1640, 1776, and 1789. Perhaps the principle would have triumphed even without those upheavals, and certainly it was violated in the course of those three revolutions as well as in many others. Nevertheless, historically, media freedom and revolution were intertwined until the Bolshevik tradition supplanted earlier revolutionary ideologies.

Ironically, the Communist regimes of the twentieth century rejected freedom of expression in part because of their exaggerated respect for the power of the media. Convinced that propaganda could transform people and societies, Lenin and Mao could not imagine tolerating the pluralistic media that had eventually emerged after the English, American, and French Revolutions. One way of understanding the events of 1989, which loomed so large in the discussions out of which the essays in this volume emerged, is to see them as evidence that the pluralistic global media system of our own day is now strong enough to undermine the monolithic media of totalitarian societies. It is certainly too soon to predict the outcome of the various revolutionary movements that have shaken the world since the mid-1980s, but it is at least possible that they will, in the main, demonstrate that "media revolutions" can have a genuinely liberating potential.

NOTES

1. See Jeffery A. Smith, *Printers and Press Freedom: The Ideology of Early American Journalism* (New York, 1988).

2. Mark Poster, *The Mode of Information* (Chicago, 1990).

3. David Halberstam, *The Powers That Be* (New York, 1979).

4. Gladys Engel Lang and Kurt Lang, *The Battle for Public Opinion: The President, the Press, and the Polls during Watergate* (New York, 1983).

5. See below, pp. 93-94.

6. Lynn Hunt, *Politics, Culture, and Class in the French Revolution* (Berkeley, Calif., 1984); Mona Ozouf, *La fête révolutionnaire* (Paris, 1976); Charles Tilly, *The Contentious French* (Cambridge, Mass., 1986).

7. Jamey Gambrell, "Moscow: The Front Page," *New York Review of Books*, 8 Oct. 1992.

8. Theda Skocpol, *States and Social Revolutions* (Cambridge, Mass., 1979); Jack A. Goldstone, *Revolution and Rebellion in the Early Modern World* (Berkeley, Calif., 1991).

9. Peter Kenez, *The Birth of the Propaganda State* (Cambridge, 1985).

10. Alex Inkeles, *Public Opinion in Soviet Russia* (Cambridge, Mass., 1950), 319.

11. See esp. Jeremy D. Popkin, "The Business of Political Enlightenment in France, 1770-1800," in John Brewer and Roy Porter, eds., *Consumption and the World of Goods* (London, 1993), 412-37; and Carla Hesse, *Publishing and Cultural Politics in Revolutionary Paris, 1789-1810* (Berkeley, Calif., 1991).

12. Robert Scribner, *For the Sake of Simple Folk* (Cambridge, Mass., 1981).

13. Goldstone, *Revolution and Rebellion*, 483.

2

Media and Revolutionary Crises

JEREMY D. POPKIN

O n 17 November 1830, a company of New York printshop workers
gathered to celebrate the recently concluded July Revolution in France and
to proclaim: "It is acknowledged, that principally through the Press, and
those immediately connected with it, was the recent important and glorious Revolution in France effected—a Revolution which is destined ultimately to shake to its center every despotism in the old world."[1] For the
New York printers, the intimate connection between the phenomenon of
revolution and the media of mass communication appeared unmistakable.
So were the crucial roles of both the journalists whose words appeared in
print and the printers who made their production possible.

The New York printers of 1830 understood the role of the communications media in revolutionary crises better than many modern historians.
More often than not, the study of the media has been relegated to a secondary status in the historiography of modern revolutions. But the time is ripe
for a reassessment of this question. The revolutionary crises of the 1980s
have drawn renewed attention to the roles the communications media play
in such situations. The Philippine "People Power" revolution of 1986, the
Chinese student occupation of Tiananmen Square in 1989, and the disman-
tling of the Berlin Wall later that year were in part "media events" whose
significance and worldwide impact owed much to the power of the media
images they generated. Modern communications technology has often
played an unanticipated part in the revolutionary processes of our own

day—think of the circulation of the Ayatollah Khomeini's speeches on au-
dio cassettes, or the Chinese students' employment of fax machines to reach
the outside world in 1989—which has become part of the folklore surrounding these events. After the cease-fire that ended the civil war in El
Salvador, a book about the *Radio Venceremos*, the insurgents' broadcasting
service, became a nationwide bestseller. The book's success testifies to the
important symbolic role that the revolutionaries' ability to create their own
mass medium played in their movement.[2] The interest in the media aroused
by these recent events suggests the value of looking at the role of the media
of communication in a comparative perspective. Our current situation
makes it more than usually likely that such comparison across cultures and
centuries will generate what historian William Sewell has called "plausible
and illuminating analogies" that will broaden our understanding of both the
past and the present.[3]

That the media of communication do affect revolutionary processes
has always been evident, both to participants in such movements and to
historians. From the seventeenth-century English pamphleteer Marcha-
mont Needham to the Bolshevik agitators Lenin and Trotsky, the history of
revolutionary militants throughout the world is also a history of media specialists. What a French historian has written about the revolutionary Paris
Commune of 1871 can be applied also to many other revolutionary crises, in
that country and elsewhere: "If a great historical movement such as the Reformation can legitimately be said to have started as 'a quarrel of monks,'
the Commune was also, in a certain sense, a tumult of journalists."[4]

Both revolutionaries and their opponents have recognized the importance of the mass media in precipitating crises and determining their outcome. When Lenin set out in 1901 to promote revolution in Russia, his first
step was to create a newspaper. It was in the article justifying that project
that he made his often quoted statement that "a newspaper is not only a
collective propagandist and a collective agitator; it is also a collective organizer," which became one of the clichés of Communist discourse after
1917. In his article, however, the future Bolshevik leader sketched out a
broader argument that showed how intimately thinking about the medium
through which revolutionary ideas were to be spread was tied to his larger
vision of the revolutionary process. He argued that a change in the medium of communication employed for spreading the revolutionary message
would in and of itself change the nature of the revolutionary movement:
"Never has the need been felt so acutely as today for reinforcing dispersed
agitation in the form of individual action, local leaflets, pamphlets, etc., by
means of generalized and systematic agitation that can only be conducted

with the aid of the periodical press." A newspaper, Lenin argued, would be both substance and symbol of the revolutionary cause: "It may be said without exaggeration that the frequency and regularity with which a newspaper is printed (and distributed) can serve as a precise criterion of how well this cardinal and most essential sector of our militant activities is built up." Even more, the activity of producing a newspaper would transform the revolutionary militants themselves: "The mere technical task of regularly supplying the newspaper with copy and of promoting regular distribution will necessitate a network of local agents of the united party. . . . this work will train and bring into the foreground, not only the most skillful propagandists, but the most capable organizers, the most talented political party leaders, capable, at the right moment, of releasing the slogan for the decisive struggle and of taking the lead in that struggle."[5]

Lenin's article is just one example of how strongly the available media of communication have shaped both revolutionary imagination and revolutionary practice. One could equally well cite Mirabeau, a leader of the French Revolution of 1789, who made freedom of the press one of his most pressing demands. Among his publications on the eve of the revolution was a paraphrase of a text in favor of press freedom emanating from an earlier revolutionary crisis, John Milton's *Areopagitica*, and he coupled his oratory in the Estates-General with the launching of a newspaper, a project he justified on the grounds that only such periodicals could "propagate instruction and reflect its influence, . . . unite all good spirits and all dedicated citizens; they establish communications that cannot fail to produce a harmony of sentiments, of opinions, of plans and of actions that constitutes the real public force, the safeguard of the constitution."[6]

Indeed, it was a politician and journalist of the French revolutionary period who may be said to have offered the first substantial analysis of the differences in impact among the various means of communication in a revolutionary situation. Pierre-Louis Roederer's remarkable "Analytic Essay on the Different Means of Communication of Ideas, Among Men in the State of Society," published in 1796, makes a clear and convincing distinction among books ("whose consumption requires, besides the price of the purchase, the expense of attention, and a significant amount of time"), pamphlets, periodicals, and wallposters. Roederer noted that "in a time of agitation and faction, and among a poorly educated people," wallposters could be "the most powerful of writings," but in general, he concluded from the experience of the French Revolution that newspapers were the most influential political medium: "Having a much larger number of readers than works sold through bookstores, having them all, every day, at the same time, having them in all classes of society, in all public places, being the almost obligatory diet of daily conversation, [they] not only act on a larger body of men, but they act more powerfully than any other form of writing."[7] Like Lenin a century later, the author of this essay recognized that certain forms of communication had a special relationship to the revolutionary process.

Activists have thus always been conscious of the close relationship between communications media and the crises by which they have striven to change society. Among historians, however, only a few scholars have taken this issue seriously. Many have been put off by the claims of a few theorists, most notably Marshall McLuhan, who have argued that the communications media are so fundamental to the structure of the social world that the only true revolutions are those brought about by changes in communications technology. Although McLuhan did not use the world "revolution," the concept certainly underlay his description of the two radical shifts which, he contended, structured all of modern experience: the invention of printing in the fifteenth century, and the spread of the electronic mass media in the twentieth. He saw both as sudden and all-encompassing ruptures that profoundly transformed social and political structures and ways of thinking—in other words, as what most of us would call revolutions.[8]

A few historians, such as Mark Poster in *The Mode of Information*, a recent work on the connection between the computer age and postmodernist philosophy, have been tempted to follow in McLuhan's footsteps and posit that changes in the forms of communication must necessarily bring fundamental changes in consciousness in their train.[9] In general, historians have found McLuhan's version of communications revolutions too simplistic for their taste. Those who have been most "McLuhanite" in approach, such as Elizabeth Eisenstein in *The Printing Press as an Agent of Change*, have nevertheless been far more nuanced in their arguments; even if they describe the shift from one form of communication to another as a "revolution," they depict it as a complex of changes spread over a long period of time, rather than a historical cataclysm.[10] Recent historians of communications technology have tended to steer away from grand theories in the McLuhan mode. French historian Pascal Griset's *Les révolutions de la communication* is a good example.[11] By "revolution," Griset essentially means the introduction of new forms of technology. He discusses the political contexts within which these changes have occurred, but he makes no effort to link these changes with broader social and cultural upheavals. His book provides a striking illustration of how different groups of scholars can use the terms "communications" and "revolution," yet end up discussing totally different subjects.

Most of the historians who have written about the media in connection with revolutionary crises have started from an interest in revolutions themselves rather than from a focus on communications methods and technology. James Billington, whose *Fire in the Minds of Men* is one of the few recent attempts by a historian to study the general phenomenon of revolution in the western world, is also one of the few who has highlighted the importance of the link between revolution and the media of communications, which, he argues, "may even validate the hypothesis 'that every revolutionary change in the means of communication is followed by a change in the entire structure of society.'" Billington notes that for many of the leading French, German, and Russian revolutionaries of the nineteenth and early twentieth centuries, "journalism was the most important single professional activity" through which they expressed their faith.[12] Certainly it would be hard to find many studies of the revolutionary crises of the past five centuries that make no reference to journals, pamphlets, caricatures, and speeches generated by these events, and to the journalists and others who articulated these texts and images. Historians are, after all, dependent on media sources for much of their data about revolutionary crises, because such crises disrupt the generation and preservation of such "normal" sources of data as official records and oblige the scholar willy-nilly to turn to the media for basic factual information. This necessity shows that one characteristic of revolutionary crises is that they force into the public sphere—and therefore into the media of mass communication—a great deal of discourse that would normally be conducted behind closed doors.

Nevertheless, in the vast scholarly literature devoted to revolutionary phenomena, studies of the communications media usually occupy a modest place, compared with the attention given social structures, political leaders, the history of doctrines, and the role of parties and movements. Since the 1970s, there has been a revival of interest among sociologists in the comparative analysis of revolutions, but neither of the two major books that have attracted the most attention in this connection, Theda Skocpol's *States and Social Revolutions* and Jack A. Goldstone's *Revolution and Rebellion in the Early Modern World*, devotes any discussion to the problem of the media per se. In fact, there are no index entries in either book for "journalism," "media," "press" or "propaganda."[13] Indeed, because they both reject the idea that the diffusion of subversive ideologies has much significance for the understanding of how revolutionary crises originate, Skocpol and Goldstone downplay the one aspect of the revolutionary process where earlier analysts were most likely to accord a major role to ideas and texts. Readers of their books will find hardly any mention of Puritan pamphleteers, French philosophes, or Russian radical intelligentsia. Goldstone does briefly allude to the role of the media in what he calls the phase of "state breakdown," when competing groups strive to gain power and "revolutions characteristically see a flood of pamphlet literature and wildly shifting postures and alliances,"[14] and he does grant some role to revolutionary ideology in the consolidation of new regimes. But it is clear that he does not see the question of the media through which revolutionary ideological messages are propagated as a central one.

Goldstone's neglect of media issues is surprising because his treatment of the role of ideology describes phenomena that could be said to result as much from ruptures and innovations in the media of political communication as from the actual content of revolutionary discourse. The multiplication of competing media organs and the shift to those that convey messages most rapidly and with the greatest emotional impact, which he does mention, do indeed seem to be common characteristics of most revolutionary crises, at least those within the sphere of Western civilization. Goldstone does eventually argue that the content of ideology accounts for the difference in outcomes between European and non-European revolutions: only Western revolutions have produced an eschatological "ideological framework" within which permanent change could be consolidated.[15] But is not the absence of a print culture in the cases of seventeenth-century Turkey and China—the non-Western cases he compares with England and France—an equally striking difference, and one that may well have shaped the difference in outcomes? Goldstone's own analysis suggests that the possibility deserves consideration.

Although the comparatist students of revolutionary phenomena have tended to omit the media from their purview, the experts on particular revolutionary crises have usually paid them somewhat more attention. There are well-documented monographs on the press in the English, American, and French revolutions, as well as on some of the more recent movements in various parts of the world. In most cases, however, these works are not in the mainstream of historiographical debate. Drawn on as sources of information, they have rarely had much influence in shaping overall interpretations of the revolutions they deal with.

The historical literature devoted to the French Revolution provides a good illustration of the reasons why the history of the press and the mass media generally have only recently emerged as central issues in the understanding of the subject. From early in this century until the 1970s, the most influential interpretation of the event was one derived from a Marxist model, in which social conflicts generated by the evolution of the modern capitalist economy were seen as the moving forces of history. These social conflicts achieved intellectual expression in the form of political movements, which were associated with ideologies, or systems of discourse. In turn, these were disseminated through various media of communication. In this scheme of things, then, the study of communications media themselves occupied a tertiary role, as an ancillary aid to the analysis of texts which, interpreted as superstructural reflections of a deeper social reality, could be decoded independently of the material form and immediate social circumstances in which they were produced and distributed.

Daniel Mornet's classic study, *Les origines intellectuelles de la Révolution française*, which dominated the literature on the ideological background of the revolution for half a century, devoted considerable attention to the lesser authors whose tracts and periodicals vulgarized the ideas of the century's great thinkers. For Mornet, however, shifts in the media of communication served at best to simplify and popularize ideas. Books, the noblest genre of print literature, were the sources of all genuinely important ideas, which then gradually filtered into pamphlets, plays, and salon conversation. Furthermore, Mornet followed a classic pattern in implying that revolutions have ideological origins, but that once they spill over into the streets, they become political or social events in which ideas play little part. He ended his study in 1787, when the overt revolutionary crisis began. The fact that revolutionary crises are most unfavorable environments for the writing of books helps explain why French literary historians long neglected the period from 1789 to 1799, when ephemeral genres dominated the scene.

It is hardly necessary to retrace in detail the stages of the "paradigm shift" that has led the social interpretation of the French Revolution to be contested and largely replaced, and its cultural dimension to be reassessed in ways that go beyond the framework suggested by Mornet. Of the various books associated with these transformations, the most influential was undoubtedly François Furet's *Interpreting the French Revolution*, whose impact on historians of the French Revolution could be compared to the effect the abbé Sieyès's pamphlet *What Is the Third Estate?* had on the revolutionaries themselves. Furet challenged the notion that the decisive actors in the revolutionary drama were social groups. But if the real actors of the revolutionary crisis were not social classes, who were they? Furet suggested that they were words: the revolution was a conflict of discourses, a struggle for the control of the meaning to be assigned to key phrases such as "liberty" and "the people"[16] Soon thereafter, Lynn Hunt added a convincing demonstration of the centrality of symbols and images to the understanding of the revolution, while Keith Baker pursued in detail Furet's agenda of liberating the study of revolutionary-era political discourse from the secondary position it had long occupied.[17]

In this new approach to the French Revolution, concepts such as "public opinion" and "the public sphere" soon came to occupy a central position. These concepts were drawn from the work of the German social philosopher Jürgen Habermas, whose *Strukturwandel der Öffentlichkeit*, originally published in German in 1962, came out in French translation in 1979.[18] Habermas suggested that the process of change that culminated in the creation of liberal parliamentary regimes in Western Europe was not simply the result of the "rise of the bourgeoisie." He analyzed it as the outcome of changes in the way members of society exchanged opinions about political issues or, as he put it, as the result of the emergence of a "public sphere" in which private individuals could come together to debate the actions of their rulers. The eighteenth century was thus marked by the shift from an absolutist framework, in which only the sovereign could speak publicly about political issues, to one in which members of civil society—by virtue of their status as owners of property and therefore as bearers of rights—could engage one another in a reasoned dialogue about such affairs. The French Revolution, in Habermas's schema, could be understood as the moment when "public opinion could dictate laws to the lawgiver": that is, when public opinion "was transformed into the sovereign itself."[19]

Habermas did not use the notion of "media revolution," but he did emphasize the importance of new forms of communication—particularly the periodical press, whose development of "explosive power" was one of the major cultural phenomena of the eighteenth century—in changing the nature of the public sphere of political discourse. Without the periodical press and the active, ongoing exchange of ideas that it made possible, public opinion could not have taken on the importance that it did in the late eighteenth century.[20] By stressing the importance of the nature of the dialogue in which members of the public engaged, rather than the sociological identity of the participants or the specific content of their debate, Habermas adopted a perspective that implied a need to understand the media in which that dialogue was conducted.

Rather than adopting such a perspective, however, the most prominent historians associated with the discourse- or culture-oriented approach to the era of the French Revolution generally followed a different course and failed to give the media much attention. François Furet, in *Interpreting the French Revolution*, did refer to the importance of "the specialists" who rose to power by their expertise in manipulating the language of the revolution, "those who produce it and hence find themselves, as a result, possessors of its legitimacy." Nevertheless, his own discussion deals only with the orators of the revolution's assemblies and clubs.[21] Lynn Hunt saw the issue as sufficiently significant for her to make clear that she wanted to separate her interest in "symbolic practices, such as language, imagery, and gestures", which she saw as the essence of revolutionary political culture, from the media through which they were expressed. Since periodicals already existed prior to 1789, she argued that "the large number of newspapers, . . . however dramatic the contrast with pre-revolutionary times, did not make the politics of the Revolution revolutionary."[22] Keith Baker's main interest has been in the *concept* of public opinion, as opposed to the institutions through which it expressed itself.[23] What may be loosely labeled as the new-cultural-history approach to the French Revolution has thus tended to separate the content of revolutionary language from the form in which it appeared, at the risk of turning the revolution into an abstract and disembodied conflict of discourses and symbols.

The major exception to this tendency among the Habermas-influenced practitioners of the new cultural history is the French historian Roger Chartier, who has made an elaborate effort to keep the cultural and the social history of communication tied together. Chartier has defined the basic thrust of his work as an effort to "understand how, in Old Regime societies between the sixteenth and the eighteenth centuries, the increased circulation of printed texts transformed forms of sociability, authorized new ideas, modified relationships with authority."[24] Chartier consistently rejects what he sees as technological determinism: he has criticized Elizabeth Eisenstein, for instance, for overemphasizing the rupture between the manuscript and the printed book.[25] He has emphasized instead the importance of changes in forms of reading and has seen a revolution in reading practices that resulted in a "new mode of reading" associated with "a critical attitude freed from ties of dependence and obedience" as the essential precursor of the French Revolution.[26] At the same time, he has strongly underlined the importance of studying the form in which specific texts are circulated, rather than resting content with an analysis of the ideas they contain. "There is no text independent of the material form in which it is read (or heard), and . . . no way of understanding anything written, whatever it is, that is not dependent on the forms in which it reaches its reader."[27]

Chartier's simultaneous insistence on the importance of the active role of the reader or audience in giving meaning to texts and on how readers' reactions are always mediated by the form of the message is particularly appropriate to the reconstruction of the role of the media in revolutionary situations, in which traditional social roles and traditional media forms are both thrown into question. Although Chartier's own work has been focused on the prerevolutionary period, it offers many suggestive insights for students of the French Revolution and other revolutionary crises.

The shift from a social-historical to a cultural-historical perspective on the French Revolution has opened up new theoretical possibilities for an appreciation of the importance of the mass media and the representations of ideas and events that they convey. As a result, recent empirical research on the communications media in the French Revolution has brought the subject into the mainstream of scholarship and illustrated many ways in which the issue might be pursued in the context of other revolutionary crises. The growing attention to the subject is exemplified by the recent publication of numerous books with titles linking the concepts of revolution and the media, such as *Revolution in Print, La naissance du journal révolutionnaire* (The birth of the revolutionary newspaper), *La révolution du journal, Revolutionary News, Die Bildpublizistik der Französische Revolution* (Illustrated Publications during the French Revolution), and *Publishing and Cultural Politics in Revolutionary Paris.*[28]

Out of this work has come a general consensus that the French Revolution was related to a revolution in France's system of communications media, that what took place in 1789 could not have occurred as it did without a "press" or "media revolution." Rolf Reichardt has stressed the multiplicity of the revolutionary media, speaking of "the new form of publicness and its communication system—a network of assemblies and clubs, newspapers, pamphlets, broadsides, songs, and other media . . . that had never before existed in such numbers and never been so closely and intensely tied to events."[29] Other scholars have put particular emphasis on the periodical press. As Pierre Rétat has written, "The birth of the [revolutionary] newspaper coincides with that of a new era; it has the vocation of measuring it and defining its rhythm."[30] Whether they emphasize the whole range of media created to convey the revolutionary message or concentrate on the press, scholars who have contributed to this new approach generally identify a number of related phenomena that indicate the media's central role in the revolutionary process. These include the sudden and dramatic appearance of large numbers of new organs of political communication directly concerned with the events of the revolution, the tremendous acceleration in the rhythm of communication and the resulting sense that events themselves were proceeding more rapidly, and the institution of new relations between the articulators of revolutionary messages, their audiences, and events.

Pierre Rétat and Claude Labrosse have charted with precision the sudden explosion of newspapers in mid-1789, providing a firm statistical basis to show that France was flooded with new media organs; they have also demonstrated the rapid shift from weekly and monthly rhythms of publication toward triweekly and daily schedules.[31] The production of political engravings cannot be dated with the same precision, but Klaus Herding and Rolf Reichardt show that it certainly surged after the fall of the Bastille.[32] Rétat and Labrosse have analyzed the appearance of new forms of narrative and rhetoric in the revolutionary press, and new forms of journalistic self-presentation, which made the revolutionary journalist both a stand-in for the sovereign people and a prophet summoning them to action. Many scholars have documented the diffusion of these new media, which exhorted readers to be not merely passive consumers of messages but activists who translated into reality the scripts for action outlined in newspapers and caricatures.

Those who have been most explicit in arguing that the revolution as a whole cannot be comprehended without reference to the transformation of the public sphere brought about by the communications media are thus arguing that the "press revolution" of 1789 is not merely a secondary consequence of the abrogation of censorship, the creation of the National Assembly, and the storming of the Bastille but one of the preconditions for those events having taken on the significance that they did. It is not merely that the media conveyed new messages and new symbols after 1789; this group of scholars—in which I include myself—stresses the importance of the new ways in which this content was presented and received. We argue that the transformation of the media is one of the defining characteristics of what happened in France in 1789 and afterward. Claude Labrosse and Pierre Rétat have asserted that the speeding up of history and the sense that human action could reshape the world, key features of what Keith Baker has analyzed as the new consciousness of revolution produced by 1789,[33] are conditioned by the sudden shift to daily newspaper publication in 1789. I have maintained that it was the purported capacity of the printing press to unite the entire population of a large country in common political discussion that emboldened the revolutionaries to try to recreate the conditions of classical democracy in the modern world.[34] Elizabeth Eisenstein has underlined the significance of the emergence of the modern political journalist, the "tribune of the people," who took advantage of the printing press to update and redefine a role derived from classical models.[35] In their path-breaking work on revolutionary symbolism, Hans-Jürgen Lüsebrink and Rolf Reichardt have shown that media images foreshadowed the storming of the Bastille and then made representations of the event a powerful force for spreading revolutionary ideals.[36]

The recent wave of scholarship on media and revolution in the France of the 1790s has succeeded to a large degree in putting the role of communications media on the agenda of all serious discussions about that event. It thus suggests a model against which both theories of media action and analyses of other revolutionary crises can be measured. Above all, this model suggests that in France the drastically altered media were both symbol and substance of the revolutionary process. The greatly increased flow of pamphlets, newspapers, and caricatures, the creation of a new culture of ceremonies and of revolutionary theater spectacles, altered the basic framework of daily life for much of the population and created new frameworks for social interaction.

Although there has as yet been little interaction between historians of the media in revolutionary France and social science and communications theorists with special interests in the media, such as Benedict Anderson and James W. Carey, the historians' work both confirms certain of their insights and offers new perspectives on them. Anderson has pointed to the importance of the press in creating the "imagined communities" that structure collective behavior in the modern world. When geographically dispersed individuals come to read the same journalistic texts at the same time on a regular basis, Anderson argues, they develop a sense of common identity that allows them to become historical actors.[37] Similarly, Carey emphasizes the role of newspapers and other media "in the construction and maintenance of an ordered, meaningful cultural world that can serve as a control and container for human action." In his view, the most important effect of newspaper reading is not that the reader acquires factual information but that he or she "joins a world of contending forces as an observer at a play."[38]

Historians of the revolutionary press in France can find much of use in these insights. The historical process we observe in France in the years following 1789 is indeed the constitution of a new "imagined community" in Anderson's sense, one constituted in good part through the medium of the press. And we can indeed see that the citizens of this new community relied on the press to guide and structure their political activity. But the historians also have new insights to contribute to the theorists. The examples cited in Anderson's book, for example, highlight gradual processes of identity formation. Study of the French Revolution directs attention to sudden processes of identity *transformation*, suggesting the power of the media to restructure identities and redefine community boundaries with unexpected suddenness. Carey's discussion of what he calls the ritual function of newspaper reading emphasizes the maintenance of social stability, whereas the example of the French Revolution shows how a ritualized reading of revolutionary texts can destabilize an existing order.

The recent literature on the media and the French Revolution thus confirms and enriches a theoretical literature suggesting that the form in which information and ideas are disseminated is as important as their content.

The contributions in this volume indicate that this insight can be fruitfully applied to other revolutionary situations, but they also show that the work done on the French Revolution in recent years is far from exhausting the possible approaches to the subject. There is much here in many of the contributions to validate the notion, suggested in the work of François Furet and Jack Goldstone, that the competition of revolutionary discourses is most intense—and, by implication, the role of the mass media most central—not *before* the outbreak of a revolution, as the classical model of the search for revolutionary origins would have it, but during the phase of what Goldstone calls "revolutionary struggle and state reconstruction."[39] The explosion of new voices in the media, the invention of new forms of presentation, and the search for ways to enlarge the potential audience and shorten the time necessary for reaching it—all so evident in France in 1789—certainly seem to be characteristic as well of crises from England in the 1640s to Eastern Europe in the 1980s.[40] Characteristic, too, is the episodic nature of this phenomenon and the tendency toward establishment of renewed controls over the media in a phase of stabilization.

In addition to the multiplication of media outlets, revolutionary crises do generally seem to be characterized by a shift toward forms of communication that can be produced and distributed most rapidly and hence have the fastest impact: from books to pamphlets or broadsheets, from oil paintings to engravings, nowadays perhaps from newspapers to television. This sudden shift in the media mix also tends to result in an economic crisis for enterprises linked to the "old" media. Carla Hesse's work on book publishing during the French Revolution illustrates a phenomenon that may well be characteristic of other revolutionary crises, although the study of the economics of media production in periods of revolutionary upheaval is one of the most neglected aspects of the subject.

This shift in the weight of the different media available in a revolutionary crisis seems to go along, however, with an increased intensity of direct, face-to-face oral communication. Historians are in part retracing the path by which communications scholars discovered the "two-step flow of communication" and the role of strategically placed readers in interpreting and validating media messages for their communities.[41] But scholars of the French Revolution, at least, are also proposing the hypothesis that the revolutionary crisis was characterized by what Pierre Rétat labels a "regression" toward forms of oral discourse even in the printed texts of the French revolutionary period, and what Roger Chartier and Daniel Roche call the "return of orality" accompanying the flood of print after 1789.[42] If revolution is not a dinner party, it nevertheless finds one of its fundamental expressions in an intensification of direct interchange, and the more structured media find their importance in the influence they exercise on this stream of spoken words. Is this favoring of media genres that mimic living speech and public discussion—as opposed to private meditation—perhaps a common characteristic of revolutionary crises? In any event, there are enough suggestive similarities in the evolution of the media in different revolutionary crises that one can plausibly argue for the existence of a common anatomy of media revolution exhibiting substantial regularities.

The comparisons suggested by the contributions in this volume caution against an excessively schematic model of "media revolution," however. It is clear that there are substantial differences between the great revolutionary crises of the past four centuries. For one thing, they occurred in very different technological environments. From the time of Gutenberg to the twentieth century, the products of the printing press—both texts and easily reproduced images—have held pride of place among the media in revolutionary situations. Before the development of mechanized printing machinery in the nineteenth century, however, printed materials were relatively rare, and the sudden increase in their production that characterized 1640 in England or 1789 in France was in itself a revolutionary phenomenon. By the middle of the nineteenth century this was much less the case, at least in Western Europe and the United States. Even Russia in 1917 had a mass press on a scale completely different from what existed in France in 1789.[43] The Utopian dream of blanketing a society with ideological messages, so difficult to achieve in the premodern world, had become a practical possibility.

After the First World War, technological change opened up new possibilities. The supremacy of the printing press was no longer unchallenged. The spread of the broadcast media offered new possibilities for enlarging audiences and speeding up the transmission of news, images, and slogans.

But this process has produced paradoxical effects. On the one hand, as Todd Gitlin has noted in his study of the American "New Left" of the 1960s, radicals now faced new problems in getting their messages across in a society "saturated with mass media" even under normal conditions.[44] On the other hand, the modern electronic media made it possible for news of the revolutionary movements of the late 1980s to be reported in "real time" all over the world.

The twentieth century has seen the development of "big" media capable of reaching audiences on an unprecedented scale, but it has also been characterized by the spread of "small" media that can be wielded by individuals or small groups: the mimeograph machine (essential in the development of the Resistance press in occupied Europe during World War II, for example),[45] the photocopier, the cassette tape recorder, the fax machine. The notion of a single public sphere unified by a single system of mass media may no longer be applicable to modern societies, and any model of "media revolution" derived from the printing-press era is likely to prove outdated today. Mark Poster, in *The Mode of Information*, goes so far as to suggest that "new and unrecognizable modes of community are in the process of formation" in the age of computerized, electronic information and that "the image of the people in the streets, from the Bastille in 1789 to the Sorbonne in 1968 and Tiananmen Square, Beijing in 1989, may be the images that will not be repeated in the forms of upheaval in the twenty-first century and beyond."[46]

Technology is not the only variable that complicates a comparative approach to the role of the media in revolutionary crises. The media are themselves an important subject of revolutionary discourse. Movements for revolutionary change tend to incorporate new possibilities for the use of the mass media into their overall projects for transformation, while anti-revolutionary movements—Catholics in the Reformation crisis, Prussian Junkers in 1848—sometimes see the very resort to new methods of communication as a dangerous concession to evil.[47] Milton in the 1640s and the proponents of the liberal revolutions of the eighteenth and nineteenth centuries argued that a pluralistic media landscape was an essential aspect of freedom. Restrictions on the press were synonymous with abandonment of the proper goals of the revolutionary movement. The twentieth century, however, has seen the Leninist revolutionary tradition explicitly reject the notion that freedom for the media symbolizes and gives concrete form to freedom in general. The Russian Revolution of 1917 and the triumph of the Chinese Communists in 1949 gave rise to tightly controlled media systems designed to further the revolutionary transformation of society, rather than libertarian media systems seen as marking the victory of freedom over tyranny. Jean-Paul Marat's *Ami du Peuple*, with its pervasive hostility to all organized political power, is obviously a revolutionary journal in a very different sense from *Pravda*, with its devotion to the "building of socialism."

The institutional framework within which revolutionary crises occur is another important variable in determining the extent and importance of the "media revolution" that accompanies them. The comparison of the American and French Revolutions immediately reminds us that the revolutions we are setting out to compare took place in very different societies with different media systems and traditions. The North American colonies that revolted against England in 1776 had, as Jeffery Smith has shown, a tradition of an outspoken local press;[48] still, they were on the periphery of the world communication network of their day, and the American press had little impact in the rest of the world. The French press of 1789, by contrast, marked a sharp break with the censored journals of the prerevolutionary period, and the "press revolution" in France had immediate consequences for the entire European journalistic system.

The attempt to "make the great revolutions speak to each other"[49] with respect to the issue of the media, then, is intended not to impose a single model of "media revolution" on a variety of phenomena but to stretch our imagination with regard to the many ways in which this theme can be employed to deepen the understanding of revolutions and of the communications media. Whatever their differences, revolutionary upheavals are defined in part by the accelerated circulation of words and images that characterizes them. Since Gutenberg, this intensified communication has implied the use of means of reproduction that allow the same message to be disseminated in many places at the same time. It has also required the activity of specialists who prepare information to be circulated through the available media. Just as the recognition that mass violence, major shifts in elite composition, and other phenomena are common to revolutionary upheavals has inspired creative new approaches to investigation, so the realization that the media are always centrally implicated in these great historical dramas should lead to profitable new paths of inquiry.

NOTES

1. Myer Moses, *Full Account of the Celebration of the Revolution in France, in the City of New-York, on the 25th November, 1830: Being the forty-seventh anniversary of an event that restored our citizens to their homes and to the enjoyment of their rights and liberties* (N.p., n.d. [1830]), 22.

2. José Ignacio Lopez Vigil, *Las Mil y Una Historias de Radio Venceremos* (San Salvador, El Salvador, 1992).

3. William Sewell, "Assessing Structural Approaches to Comparative Revolution," paper delivered to the Comparative Revolutions Workshop, Indiana University, Sept. 1992.

4. Aimé Dupuy, *1870-1871: La guerre, la commune, et la presse* (Paris, 1959), 13. Unless otherwise indicated, all translations in the text are my own.

5. V.I. Lenin, "Where to Begin" (1901), in *Collected Works*, trans. Joe Fineberg and George Hanna (Moscow, 1964), 1:21-24. I owe thanks to Peter Kenez, whose work drew my attention to this article.

6. Mirabeau, prospectus to *Etats-généraux* (Paris, 1789).

7. Pierre-Louis Roederer, "Essai analytique sur les divers moyens établis pour la communication des pensées, entre les hommes en société," *Journal d'Economie Publique*, 30 brumaire IV (Dec. 1796). Roederer, a moderate revolutionary, was an experienced pamphleteer and journalist, and part owner of a daily Paris paper during the Directory period.

8. Marshall McLuhan, *The Gutenberg Galaxy: The Making of Typographic Man* (Toronto, 1962); and McLuhan, *Understanding Media: The Extensions of Man* (New York, 1964).

9. Mark Poster, *The Mode of Information* (Chicago, 1990).

10. Elizabeth Eisenstein, *The Printing Press as an Agent of Change*, 2 vols. (Cambridge, 1979), 1:39.

11. Pascal Griset, *Les révolutions de la communication XIXe-XXe siècle* (Paris, 1991).

12. James H. Billington, *Fire in the Minds of Men: The Origins of the Revolutionary Faith* (New York, 1980), 306, 308.

13. Theda Skocpol, *States and Social Revolutions* (Cambridge, 1979); Jack A. Goldstone, *Revolution and Rebellion in the Early Modern World* (Berkeley, Calif., 1991).

14. Goldstone, *Revolution and Rebellion*, 421.

15. Jack A. Goldstone, "Ideology, Cultural Frameworks, and the Process of Revolution," *Theory and Society* 20 (1991): 405, 411, 413-14, 443.

16. François Furet, *Interpreting the French Revolution*, trans. Elborg Forster (Cambridge, 1981); originally published as *Penser la révolution française* (Paris, 1978).

17. Lynn Hunt, *Politics, Culture, and Class in the French Revolution* (Berkeley, Calif., 1984); Keith Baker, *Inventing the French Revolution* (Cambridge, 1990).

18. Jürgen Habermas, *Strukturwandel der Oeffentlichkeit* (Berlin, 1962); trans. Thomas Burger, as *The Structural Transformation of the Public Sphere* (Cambridge, Mass., 1989).

19. Jürgen Habermas, "Naturrecht und Revolution," in *Theorie und Praxis*, 4th ed. (Frankfurt, 1971), 96, 106.

20. Habermas, *Strukturwandel*, 34-41.

21. Furet, *Interpreting the French Revolution*, 50.

22. Hunt, *Politics, Culture, and Class*, 13, 56.

23. Keith Baker, "Public Opinion as Political Invention," in Baker, *Inventing*

the French Revolution, 167-99; and Baker, "Defining the Public Sphere in Eighteenth-Century France: Variations on a Theme by Habermas," in Craig Calhoun, ed., *Habermas and the Public Sphere* (Cambridge, Mass., 1992), 181-211.

24. Roger Chartier, "Le monde comme représentation," in *Annales E.S.C.* 44 (1989): 1509.

25. Roger Chartier, "L'ancien régime typographique," in *Annales E.S.C.* 36 (1981): 191-209.

26. Roger Chartier, *The Cultural Origins of the French Revolution,* trans. Lydia G. Cochrane (Durham, N.C., 1991), 91. This notion of a "reading revolution" was first articulated by the late German scholar Rolf Engelsing in his *Der Bürger als Leser* (Stuttgart, 1974).

27. Chartier, "Monde," 1512-13.

28. Robert Darnton and Daniel Roche, eds., *Revolution in Print* (Berkeley, Calif., 1989); Claude Labrosse and Pierre Rétat, *Naissance du journal révolutionnaire* (Lyon, 1989); Jeremy D. Popkin, *Revolutionary News: The Press in France, 1789-1799* (Durham, N.C., 1990); Klaus Herding and Rolf Reichardt, *Die Bildpublizistik der Französische Revolution* (Frankfurt, 1989); Carla Hesse, *Publishing and Cultural Politics in Revolutionary Paris, 1789-1810* (Berkeley, Calif., 1991). Other major publications on the subject include Hugh Gough, *The Newspaper Press in the French Revolution* (London, 1988), and several volumes of conference papers and essays, esp. Rolf Reichardt and Eberhard Schmitt, eds., *Die französische Revolution als Bruch des gesellschaftlichen Bewusstseins* (Munich, 1988); Michel Vovelle, *Les images de la révolution française* (Paris, 1988); Harvey Chisick, ed., *The Press in the French Revolution* (Oxford, 1991); Pierre Rétat, ed., *La révolution du journal* (Paris, 1989); and the special issue "Pamphlet Literature of the French Revolution," *History of European Ideas* 17, nos. 2-3 (1993). For an overview of the literature on the revolutionary newspaper press, see Jeremy D. Popkin, "The Press and the French Revolution after Two Hundred Years," *French Historical Studies* 16 (1990): 664-83.

29. Rolf Reichardt, "Die städtische Revolution als politisch-kultureller Prozess," in Reichardt, ed., *Die französische Revolution* (Frankfurt, 1988), 30.

30. Rétat, "Forme et discours d'un journal révolutionnaire: Les *Révolutions de Paris* en 1789," in Claude Labrosse and Pierre Rétat, *L'instrument périodique* (Lyon, 1985), 142.

31. Labrosse and Rétat, *Naissance,* 22, 24.

32. Herding and Reichardt, *Bildpublizistik,* 20-24.

33. Baker, in *Inventing the French Revolution,* 203-23.

34. Claude Labrosse, "L'événement," in Labrosse and Rétat, *Naissance,* 126; Jeremy D. Popkin, "Citizenship and the Press in the French Revolution," in Renée Waldinger, ed., *The French Revolution and the Meaning of Citizenship* (Westport, Conn., 1993) 123-36.

35. Elizabeth Eisenstein, "The Tribune of the People: A New Species of Demagogue," in Chisick, *The Press in the French Revolution,* 145-60.

36. Hans-Jürgen Lüsebrink and Rolf Reichardt, *Die 'Bastille': Zur Symbolgeschichte von Herrschaft und Freiheit* (Frankfurt, 1990).

37. Benedict Anderson, *Imagined Communities,* 2nd ed. (New York, 1991), 33-35, 77.

38. James W. Carey, *Communications as Culture: Essays on Media and Society* (Boston, 1988), 18-20.

39. Goldstone, "Ideology," 354.

40. Jamey Gambrell, "Moscow: The Front Page," in *New York Review of Books*, 8 Oct. 1992, indicates that many of these phenomena have repeated themselves in the former Soviet Union since the collapse of Communism.

41. Elihu Katz, "The Two-Step Flow of Communication," in Wilbur Schramm, ed., *Mass Communications* (Urbana, Ill., 1960), 346-66.

42. Roger Chartier and Daniel Roche, "Les livres ont-ils fait la révolution?" in Frédéric Barbier, Claude Jolly, and Sabine Juratic, eds., *Livre et révolution* (Paris, 1988), 16.

43. See Louise McReynolds, *The News under Russia's Old Regime* (Princeton, N.J., 1991).

44. Todd Gitlin, *The Whole World Is Watching: Mass Media in the Making and Unmaking of the New Left* (Berkeley, Calif., 1980), 1.

45. The memoirs of French historian Annie Kriegel, active in the Communist Resistance during World War II, include an eloquent description of the "veritable love affair" her group maintained with its cranky but indispensable Gestetner duplicator (*Ce que j'ai cru comprendre* [Paris, 1991], 211).

46. Poster, *Mode of Information*, 154.

47. Robert Scribner, *For the Sake of Simple Folk* (Cambridge, 1981), 229-39; Hermann Wagener, *Erlebtes* (Berlin, 1884).

48. Jeffery Smith, *Printers and Press Freedom: The Ideology of Early American Journalism* (New York, 1988).

49. This phrase is taken from the title of a conference on the comparative study of revolutions held at Indiana University in September 1992, codirected by Jeffrey Wasserstrom and William B. Cohen.

3

Grub Street and Parliament at the Beginning of the English Revolution

MICHAEL MENDLE

When rules and systems collapse and no one is sure they will not return, there may be a moment when fear, hope, and the ridiculous commingle. Such a twinkling of time occurred at the beginning of 1641, when England's reform-minded Long Parliament set about to dismantle Charles I's apparatus of personal rule and to undo the damage it thought Charles had done to England's Protestant church. Soon the Parliament's members found more on their plate than had been expected, as a new politics of crowds, religious passion, and vulgar opinion both unnerved them and served their interests.[1]

Perhaps nowhere was the new order—rather, disorder—of things more apparent than in the press. For a century before 1641 the monarchy and the London Stationers (a guild of booksellers, printers, and others in the book trade) had held to a bargain that suited them both. As its *quid* the state supplied the force and authority that guaranteed copyright and the company's formidable powers of search and seizure. The Stationers returned their *quo*, generally adhering to the rules themselves and occasionally serving as investigative and enforcement agents of the church-state's censorship of printed matter. Copyright and prior censorship thus went hand in hand.[2] This partnership had always been based on prerogative power, rather than full and explicit parliamentary sanction. Its last redaction, the Star Chamber decree of 1637, was the most intimate; violation of the Stationers' book registration rules (by which copyright was secured

and allowance was duly noted) was for the first time a *direct* violation of
the Court of Star Chamber. The decree also sought to limit the number of
official printers to twenty—a fiction of sorts even at the moment of its
promulgation, but one that indicated a crucial congruence of interest between state and Stationers.[3]

The arrangement had withstood occasional windstorms of religious
dissent, smuggling, interloping, and the Stationers' own internal dissen-
sions. The most recent episode, Archbishop William Laud's successful if
messy Star Chamber prosecution of the Puritan writer-smugglers Henry
Burton, William Prynne, and John Bastwick in 1637, had not been a public
relations success: there was a backlash against the ear-cropping mutilation
imposed by the upstart Laud upon the trio.[4] The system had functioned,
though, and only a fanatic would have thought that this time was different
from similar moments before. Yet within a few months of the Long Parliament's assembling on 3 November 1640, the system was in disarray, albeit
with results the zealots as well as the Stationers and quondam authorities
could not have predicted.

Star Chamber was high on the Long Parliament's agenda, and the mutilated
authors at the top of the list of its misdeeds. John Pym, whose views carried
great authority in the Commons, pointedly made his first action in the Long
Parliament the presentation of petitions from the wives of Burton and Bastwick.[5] Laud was soon under arrest; Burton and Prynne made triumphal
returns to London, welcomed by the faithful in their thousands, candles in
their hands. But while the old order's status was at best uncertain, there
was scant sense of the locus of emergence of a new regime. Spasmodically
individual Stationers, who did not know what else to do, used the old licensing and copyright arrangements.[6] Nevertheless, most licensers and
many Star Chamber and High Commission officials, threatened with or under parliamentary investigation, were in no mood to make their problems
worse. The Stationers, as will be seen, lost their nerve as they realized that
their ancient partnership with the prerogative courts was now a liability.
The Commons, under the rubrics of parliamentary privilege, redress of
grievances, and legislative remedy, entered indirectly into the province of
press regulation. The Lords, unilaterally operating as an alternative to the
quasi-moribund Privy Council, pursued a course that amounted to interim
governance of a press suddenly grown unruly.

Early in March 1641 the Stationers and the Lords' Committee on Printing
held meetings on the new disorder.[7] A few pamphlet mills (the most notorious located in Grub Street) had been spewing out a surprising volume of

unlicensed, frequently hostile, and scurrilous pamphlets. These were distributed by a new, largely informal network of street hawkers outside the jurisdiction of the company and by shadowy elements within, especially the straitened bookbinders, who by informal arrangement had often been paid in copies and who now were becoming significant distributors of the new little tracts. The perpetrators showed a stunning disregard for the hitherto all but inevitable consequences. Humiliated and desperate, the Stationers confessed they could not act under the aegis of the prerogative-based old regime; the new crew of culprits (whether interlopers or delinquents in their own midst) no longer obeyed them. They pled with the Lords for an interim order authorizing their search-and-seizure activities until a proper legislative solution could be found. They also presented the Lords with a cull of miscreants, notably an irrepressible interloping Puritan zealot, Henry Walker,[8] and a pair of officially sanctioned printers, Thomas Fawcett and Bernard Alsop, found in Grub Street "neare to the Flying Horse." These old partners matched a wretched stock of ancient type with a long history of poverty and indiscipline.[9] The Lords responded to the Stationers with disheartening reserve. While enjoining the Stationers to perform their traditional functions, they also required the company to act "according to law" (which the Stationers had confessed to be an impossibility under the new dispensation); the troublesome printers, writers, and hawkers either escaped unpunished or were handed token, utterly undeterring penalties in the name of "exemplary punishment." Most were soon at it again.

Meanwhile the lower house entered into its own arrangements with the Stationers. Prominent members and clerks became licensing agents (and copyright dispensers) for the Commons' own flow of print: speeches, orders, fast sermons, and a few special-interest items.[10] That in turn led to a moment of truth for the Stationers. In mid-May 1641 the two houses sent contradictory directives to the Stationers about publishing documents from the recently concluded treason trial of the Earl of Strafford, Charles's trusted adviser whose death was a sine qua non among the parliamentary faithful. The Commons wanted to print John Pym's and Oliver St. John's trial arguments; the peers ordered nothing printed without their leave. The Stationers decided to obey the Commons, which was about to grapple with a printing bill, and which also held the fate of key Stationers and even the company itself in its hands, since the house could either punish or ignore the company's misdeeds in the 1630s.

The Commons chose the latter course, to the Stationers' relief. But the company now faced a novel and embarrassing dilemma. On the one hand, they hoped to provide their new masters with the customary services in return for legislative refoundation of their prerogative-based privileges. For their part the Commons' leadership was too shrewd to abandon this apparatus of control; moreover, Presbyterian clergy were waiting for an occasion to impose their own species of intolerance.[11] On the other hand, counterpressures impelled the Stationers to tolerate unregulated printing, which to this point had served the leadership's interests, joining the pulpit in molding a metropolitan parliamentary constituency. The old regime's excesses had also lingered in the mouth; few leaders cared to resort to unsavory methods if they could be avoided. Momentarily equal, these opposite vectors resolved into a standoff. When a Stationers-backed printing bill stalled in July 1641, the house made an interim order requiring printers to supply authors' names upon demand, substituting the threat of ex post facto action for the older course of prior restraint.[12] Though the Stationers were unsatisfied, they had escaped a worse fate and could press for a better day. But the house's course also simply recognized that for the moment, prior restraint was not a realistic possibility.

For most of us the 1640s and 1650s are the years of the Presbyterians and Independents, Baptists and Quakers, Milton and Hobbes, Levellers and Diggers. The astonishing creativity seems so inseparable from the uncontrollable press that we do not question Milton's argument in *Areopagitica* (November 1644) that only a press unfettered by prior restraint would exercise the muscular virtue of the "noble and puissant Nation rousing herself like a strong man after sleep." Milton's virtue *needed* to wrestle with vice.[13]

But in 1641, the first days of de facto freedom, the press provided the English Samson a less daunting fight card: a very few tracts, a great many parliamentary speeches (some authorized, others leaked or feigned), a long Puritan backlist of sermons and controversial divinity, a growing body of miscellaneous but mostly worrisome news and rumor, and—especially in spring and summer 1641—a flood of public-affairs trash. This last was concocted by often inebriated university dropouts and other literary lowlifes, printed by the trade's down-and-outs (Alsop and Fawcett being the most notorious), and usually sold by street hawkers without other employment prospects.[14] In two senses this tabloid journalism *avant la lettre* was voyeuristic: it created a public to gaze on the nakedness of its betters; and often this public was wooed by pictures (usually crude woodcuts) as much as by words.

Spring and summer 1641 was the heyday of this new political culture.

The topics, apart from generic exposés of papists (and, later, separatists and assorted sectaries), were usually personal, the style mocking or railing. Strafford naturaly came in for a goodly share of abuse, as did Laud and a menagerie of haplessly named bishops, officials, and courtiers: Matthew Wren (the bishop of Ely), Sir John Lambe (a Laudian agent who had worked with the Stationers in formulating the 1637 decree), the civil lawyers Arthur Duck and Sir Nathaniel Brent (the latter also a book licenser), and the royalist judge Sir John Finch. Sir John Suckling was reviled as the archetype of the loose-living cavalier.[15] The crooked wine patentees Aldermen Abel and Kilvert (who naturally attracted the enmity of the besotted balladeers) and Doctors' Commons (the organization for civil lawyers, including those who practiced in the ecclesiastical courts) provided metropolitan interest.

Laud drew the bitterest bile, possibly because his own modest origins made him fair game for those whose own were little different. He was shown in the tower of London, with towers behind him as a background, or with a chain.[16] His dreams or, by anticipation, his words from beyond were used to express others' sadistic hopes. By autumn, all reserve was lost. *A New Play Called Canterburie His Change of Diot* in four acts, five pages, and three different woodcuts took the archbishop from the halcyon days when his table "dainties" were the "tippets of mens eares," to a carpenter's yard where a carpenter held the archbishop's nose to a grindstone while his boy turned the wheel. In the third act the carpenter, egged on by his wife, put Laud and a Jesuit in a bird cage.[17] Others suffered similarly vulgar vilification. *Wrens Nest Defild* was accompanied by a suitably coarse woodcut.[18] *The Sisters of the Scabards Holiday* examined the fall of Doctors' Commons for its effects upon the receipts of the local prostitutes.[19] *The Brothers of the Blade* (which took the customer's perspective) and *The Pimpes Prerogative* were the predictable sequels.[20] The new order had its press critics. *Sion's Charity Towards her Foes in Misery* condemned the name calling and "bitter words" but also recognized that "such Bookes hath been a meanes to help many a poore man in London in these dead times of trading."[21] The notorious Thomas Herbert noted the sadism of Laud's moralizing pamphlet nemeses: "But man triumphs his brother being in thrall, / Naught more doth joy him than his brothers fall."[22]

There were other aspects to England's first encounter with tabloid journalism. Ritual scourgings of papists, Arminians, and Caroline courtiers were soon matched by the exposés of sectaries and irregular preachers, reflecting a genuine popular (and populist) protoroyalism. Henry Walker's arch-antagonist John Taylor led the way with *A Swarme of Sectaries, and*

Schismatiques, "discover[ing]" in verse the "strange preaching (or prat-
ing)" of "Coblers, Tinkers, Pedlars, Weavers, Sow-gelders, and Chymney-
Sweepers." The cobbler was Samuel Howe, whose pulpit was the Nag's
Head Tavern in Coleman Street and whose message was that God "gives
his Spirit to unlearned men."[23] The title page showed Howe in a tub, with
the sign of the Nag's Head out the door. The woodcut traveled along with
the subgenre. *New Preachers, New* masked the Nag's Head and cut out the
part of the block bearing Howe's name, allowing it to be updated with the
names of "Greene the Feltmaker" and a sectary with a future, Praisegod
"Barebones."[24] The name of the "prophet" James Hunt was substituted in
his *Sermon and Prophecie*.[25] Without a name, the same cropped version
closed out *Lvcifers Lacky*, now embellished with a caption: "When Women
Preach, and Coblers Pray, / The fiends in Hell, make holiday."[26] While anti-
sectary pamphlets contemned the pretensions of the lowly, their manner
was often indistinguishable from the vulgarity of the anti-Laudian railings.[27]

The press also fed on itself. Ideological differences exacerbated the poets' rivalries, already heightened by cut-throat competition. With the con-
formist Taylor and the zealous Henry Walker, the rivalry easily turned from
the verbally violent to the obscene.[28] Thomas Herbert's enemies emerged
after he turned religious moderate in an attack upon one of Laud's most
zealous tormenters.[29] One accuser claimed that before Herbert had donned
his halo, he was as much a railer as any other; another, later, said that any
store clerk could recognize "*Harberts* Lye."[30] The "moneylesse youngster"
cut a figure. It was said he "r[a]n away from *Cambridge* when he should
have been whipt for his knavery."[31] In London our dropout holed up in an
alehouse with a "crew of roaring Ballad-singers." "Poore [and] threadbare,"
"ragged" like a "dunghill raker," dressed in "tatter'd coat" and topped with
"long shag'd locks," the young Bohemian *avant la lettre* drank his half a
crown as soon he wrote a pamphlet for it.[32] Probably Herbert was the model for "Red-nose the Poet," who never had "money two dayes together."[33]
He or another of the poets extolled sack as a "preparative to studie." If the
cup spilled onto the manuscript, no matter: "I will / Dipping in this diviner
Incke my pen, / Write myself sober, and fall too't agen."[34]

Perhaps the writers, printers, and hawkers were protected by their puerility.
How seriously could one take these eccentrics and postpubescent inebri-
ates, and the luckless crew of perpetually poor printers, Bible-binders-
turned-newsmongers, and hawkers (many women among them), "the Bac-
chanalian Society of most reverend wandring Stationers"?[35] Yet tastes
change, markets saturate, and boys grow up. The political situation turned

from hopeful to menacing, the appetite for hard news overwhelmed the taste for self-indulgent frivolities, and the denizens of Grub Street adapted. After Strafford's execution and the flagging of interest in Laud, new pictures were needed, not for new villains but for new heroes; the obverse to the shaming aspect of political voyeurism was basking in the admiration of the *canaille*. John Pym and Henry Burton were the subject of woodcuts, and, surprisingly, the future Leveller Leader John Lilburne's bust was taken to steel.[36] The hottest product, though, was fear; with good reason, many parliamentary supporters suspected that Charles's new-found public moderation and legislative concessions masked secret plans to resort to force. While the Army Plot of May 1641 received little notice, a dripping spigot of rumors and innuendos attendant upon the king's journey into Scotland in August 1641 metamorphosed into an open hydrant of plots with the outbreak of Catholic rebellion in Ireland late in October 1641. Added to the opportunities afforded by fear were those of mass politics. The respite from the crowds and tumults of May 1641 (when Strafford's fate had led to ugly demonstrations) came to an end in November with the House of Commons' Grand Remonstrance. That indictment of the Caroline regime, with its appeal to the country and the petitioning campaign that followed, gave Charles and his supporters their own reasons to fear. As winter's every week seemingly brought forth a new emergency, printed diurnals (or newsbooks) joined occasional pamphlets in a flood of news.

More urgently than with the sophomoric pamphlets against the villains of the Caroline regime, the parliamentary political leadership had choices to make. What was to be winked at, what suppressed? The Stationers continued to try to demonstrate their utility to their new masters: how badly did the de facto interim freedoms harm the ability of the company to govern the trade? What signals did the houses' actions send to Grub Street— especially when those actions were inconsistent, even erratic? A few examples illustrate the contradictions. When George Digby (a weak parliamentarian who turned into a rabid royalist) published his speech against the attainder of Strafford, the Commons responded with Laudian fury. Digby escaped through hasty elevation to the peerage, but his associates and the printer were declared delinquents, and the printed speech itself was to "be burnt publickly, by the Hands of the common Hangman," the Stationers' Company having been instructed to gather the copies with "their uttermost endeavours."[37] The Commons also moved swiftly to track down the publication route of a worrisome letter read in the House of Lords on 19 August 1641. By 24 August the source of the leakage (a servant of a house official) had been identified and the printer summoned as a delinquent. In a separate case, the houses also tried to shore up the authority of the Stationers, one of whose officers had been "abus[ed]" by a renegade printer while the officer "was in Execution of the Order of this House."[38] If such measures might have caused illicit printers and writers to worry and mainstream Stationers to take comfort, other actions did not. A pamphlet proposing a scheme of modified episcopacy was referred to Sir Edward Dering's committee on printing for investigation; no report ever emerged, the author of the scheme being none other than Sir Edward Dering![39]

The Irish rebellion provided a test case for the relation of Parliament and press. London printshops fabricated dozens of plots and atrocity stories from November 1641 to January 1642, raising antipopish hysteria and fear of Charles's deviousness. Both attitudes were advantageous to the parliamentary leadership. The leadership and the Stationers always knew very well who was involved; the pamphleteers themselves acknowledged their culpability.[40] The prime contractors were none other than Alsop and Fawcett and their new bookselling associates, John Thomas (who once described himself as Fawcett's servant) and John Greensmith. The writers were also well known; according to John Bond, they included Herbert, Walker, and Thomas Bray, an Oxford scholar who had already had a run-in with the Commons.[41] In fact, twice in the winter before the climacteric on 26 January 1642, Alsop and Fawcett found themselves attracting unwelcome attention from the two houses—a good indication that their other illicit productions were winked at.[42] The old rascal had his uses. By the end of November, though, there were rumblings about the need for "making some severe examples of some of those Printers."[43]

Tolerance of the de facto freedom of the press depended upon its utility to the powers that would be, and the insecurity and internal conflict of those powers. As the houses transmuted their own de facto power into claims of right (particularly with respect to their ability to assume in an emergency the executive authority normally vested in the king), their inhibitions about press control evaporated. In the emergency month of January 1642—when the king's failed attempt to arrest Pym and four other members of the Commons led him to flee London, and when Pym and his associates began to assert control of the city—the entire situation changed. Charles made a last-ditch effort to exert some control over the press.[44] But London now belonged to King Pym, and the real contest was for control of the rest of the kingdom.

One of Pym's activities was an intense campaign, coming to a peak on 25 January, to browbeat the House of Lords into full compliance with his program; a slew of petitions from the country to the Lords were solicited with this aim in view. Unfortunately, at the Sign of the Antelope, Thomas Herbert and another Cambridge dropout, Martin Eldred, accepted the half a crown John Greensmith offered for their own version of a petition from Hertfordshire. Greensmith took the text to Alsop. Someone proffered the false Hertfordshire petition to the real petitioners as they made their way toward the Parliament.[45] The gods did not smile. Alsop beat the rap one last time, but Herbert, Eldred, and Greensmith were sent, though briefly, to the Gatehouse.[46] Nevertheless, the episode was a hinge in the relationship of Parliament to the publishing crew. The diarist D'Ewes fantasized luxuriantly the penalty appropriate to these "beggarly fellows": first the Gatehouse, then "whipping, standing in the pillory, and the like." By week's end the Commons revived Dering's printing committee and required the Master and Wardens of the Stationers to take "special order" that nothing be printed without the name of the author.[47]

Both houses became more involved with the daily manifestations of the press than they had been in many months. The publishing tribe's nerve began to crack. In his *Poets Knavery Discovered*, John Bond, yet another Cambridge dropout, named some sixty or so false pamphlets and enumerated others—about forty, all told—about the Irish rebellion, and fourteen "shamefull lyes" masquerading as "Orders from the House of Commons."[48] Naturally, he did not expose his own efforts. His day came soon enough. At the printers' instigation Bond wrote what purported to be a letter from the queen, then in the Netherlands, to the king at York, mentioning invasion threats from Denmark, France, and Spain. Though a transparent fabrication, the pamphlet fit in rather too well with recent information.[49] The Lords fairly leaped upon this "false and scandalous Letter." Bond decided to drag his enemies down with him, naming his former associates and, for good measure, the dramatist-journalist Richard Broome and his printer, "Bernard Alsop . . . living in Grub-Street." While Bond's ready tongue put Alsop away for weeks, it bought Bond no mercy. The letter was burnt, and Bond was placed in the pillory for two days wearing a sign ("A Contriver Of False And Scandalous Libels"), then sent to the House of Correction.[50] Making his literary farewell (or so he claimed), Bond apologized in *The Poets Recantation* for being "too sawcy" and having cast his "Vulgar eye . . . upon superiour Maiestie." He retained his self-pity, claiming that the bigger fish had escaped the net.[51] Alsop and Fawcett were not yet able to learn from the example, spending several months in the Fleet in 1643.[52] Eventually, newsbooks provided Alsop with a legal business in the middle 1640s.

Meanwhile, the Stationers and the Parliament had recast the old prerogative-based relation of state and company in the more modest mold of "ancient Custom." On 26 August 1642 both houses cracked down on un-authorized publication of parliamentary materials and, indeed, all books or pamphlets false or scandalous to the Parliament. To ensure compliance, approved books were to be "entred in the Register Book" of the Stationers, who were "authorized and required" to work with the parliamentary offi-cers in search and seizure. Like the old prerogative courts, the houses would take "such Course . . . with the said Offenders as shall be just."[53] Supposedly only an interim measure, the order's provisions and logic were absorbed in the June 1643 ordinance. This was also true of a severe order from the Commons in March 1643 that turned its Committee for Examina-tions into a virtual Star Chamber for the governance of the press. The com-mittee and its agents (presumably including the Stationers) could search, seize, and imprison, and those imprisoned were not to be released until "the Parties employed for the Apprehending of the said Persons . . . be sat-isfied for their Pains and Charges."[54]

The Stationers intensified their lobbying. *The Humble Remonstrance of the Company of Stationers, London,* was the work of Henry Parker, sec-retary to the Parliament's Committee of Safety, confidant of the Puritan Lords Say and Essex, and the Parliament's most aggressive pamphleteer.[55] Parker argued that only lately had the press spun out of control. The com-pany's recent decay had led to "enormous disorders." Interlopers "in div-ers obscure corners" forced even legitimate stationers into "trespasses" and "unlawfull shifts." In principle, Parliament's interim orders were adequate, but the Stationers, the natural agents of "prosecution," lacked "full authori-ty" and "true encouragement."[56] That could be remedied legislatively; a more difficult problem was excess capacity.[57] While Parker spoke directly to the state's interest, *The Humble Remonstrance* also sought to justify the Stationers' private interest.[58] "Propriety of copies" was a necessary, benefi-cial monopoly. Fear of piracy now kept entrepreneurs from chancing ex-pensive projects of "singular use and esteem." Instead, "the Printing of Pamphlets is the utmost ambition of Stationers in *England.*"[59]

The printing ordinance of June 1643 marked the full parliamentary as-sumption of authority to control the press by means of prior restraint. It began where the order of 26 August 1642 left off, borrowing some of its language and logic (particularly in claiming license and registration to be "ancient custom"). But it went well beyond, establishing a comprehensive licensing regime. The detailed search-and-seizure arrangements, which recognized the company as an agent of the houses, made the same provi-sions for imprisonment until satisfaction to the "Parties imployed in their apprehension" as did the Commons order of March 1643.[60] The new licensing arrangements were as tight as anything the Laudians had devised. Among the new divinity licensers was Edmund Calamy, an arch-Presbyterian who had been working for two years not to dismantle but to take over the old censorship apparatus.[61] One licenser, Sir Nathaniel Brent, crossed the divide to serve the new regime as had the old.[62] The printed imprimatur, which Laud could not successfully impose, became common. The ordinance, it is true, did not address the trade's excess capacity, but it stacked the deck so heavily in favor of the established Stationers that arguably it did not matter. In some respects the company's insiders even bettered the hand they held in 1637. They were no longer required to attend to their own weaker members, nor were printers expected to post compliance bonds. Instead, the ordinance waxed tearful over the fortunes of the company's best connected members, "whose most profitable vendible Copies of Bookes" were pirated by rogue operators "by way of revenge" for their zeal in suppressing unlicensed books.[63]

Such arrangements were certain to drive a high-minded moralist to fury. While professing to respect copyright and the company's provision for its widows and orphans, John Milton regarded both as "pretenses to abuse," the "fraud of old . . . *monopolizers.*"[64] Conflating the arrangements of 1637, which insisted upon the twenty licensed printers, and those of 1643, which were mute on that point, Milton charged the houses with having set "an *Oligarchy* of twenty ingrossers" over the "new light sprung up . . . in this City."[65] Catering to the Stationers was only part of what made the ordinance the "immediate image of a Star-chamber decree."[66] While Presbyterians "by their unlicenc't books" had brought the Laudian "*imprimatur*" to the ground, latterly they had mastered "the Episcopall arts" to "execute the most *Dominican* part of the Inquisition over us." In matters of the press as in other respects, "Bishops and Presbyters are the same."[67]

Milton rose to *Areopagitica*'s cold rage only after *The Doctrine and Discipline of Divorce* had fallen afoul of the censors. Yet Milton's fears, like his opponents' hopes, were unfounded. The licensing ordinance proved unequal to the "strong and healthfull commotions" of de facto freedom.[68] Though a potent symbol of the company's resurgent power and the parliamentary state's authority, the ordinance managed to be more repressive than effective. In fact, in this area the parliamentary leadership was notably less successful than in others (such as finance and taxation, standardizing military service, and bypassing expansive notions of individual rights) in bringing England into congruence with the most advanced continental practice.

Why? One reason, perhaps by itself decisive, is revealed in one of Milton's rhetorical misrepresentations: the twenty oligarchs, twenty licensers, twenty capacities, twenty licensing forges, the prelatical commission of twenty. Even in 1637, the sum of twenty London printers was a fiction. While Alsop and Fawcett showed what mischief a single printshop could do, the Stationers in 1641 were discountenanced even more by the appearance in London of two renegade presses. Throughout the 1640s, presses continued to spawn. By 1649, they had probably doubled, and some were geographically beyond the Stationers' reach.[69] Henry Parker, using his insider's information, had adverted to this problem in 1643; had Milton been less quick to score easy points against monopolists, he might have seen as far. Scarcely less important, the trade was overstocked with human resources. Within the company there were too many apprentices and too little opportunity for the free; the company's internal history throughout the 1640s is a contentious one. Largely beyond its reach was a considerable new human infrastructure of female and male hawkers, writers, and printer-interlopers, few of whom had much to lose by getting caught (at least the first time), and who may even have enjoyed the romance of the risk. Finally the new disorder found unlikely partisans and in the process became normal, part of the system.[70] Henry Parker, the company's spokesman, published outside official channels when it suited his purpose. Royalists participated in the rogue culture, sometimes joining with Levellers. The spectacle was so fascinating that even those who condemned it did not avert their eyes. Few readers accepted Milton's arguments, or wanted to reserve seats in paradise for engaging rascals like Alsop and Herbert. Yet the lot of them—readers, reprobates, idealists—incanted the abracadabras of an accidental alchemy that would transmute the de facto freedom of 1641 into the gold of enduring right.

NOTES

1. An extended and more fully annotated version of this essay is Michael Mendle, "De Facto Freedom, De Facto Authority: Press and Parliament 1640-1643," *Historical Journal*, forthcoming. I am indebted to *Historical Journal*'s editors for their kind permission to use this material.

2. For a survey of the increasingly vexed issue of the extent and effectiveness of censorship in England before 1640, see Mendle, "De Facto Freedom." The most vigorous dissent to prevailing orthodoxy is provided in a series of studies by Sheila Lambert, of which the most recent and important is "State Control of the Press in Theory and Practice: The Role of the Stationers' Company before 1640," in Robin Myers and Michael Harris, eds., *Censorship*

and the Control of Print in England and France, 1600-1910 (Winchester, 1992), 1-32.

3. *A Decree of Starre-Chamber, Concerning Printing* (London, 1637) [Short Title Catalogue (STC) 7757]. For the hypocrisies of the supposedly exact number of twenty printers, see Sheila Lambert, "The Printers and the Government, 1604-1637," in Robin Myers and Michael Harris, eds., *Aspects of Printing from 1600* (Oxford, 1987), 11.

4. Stephen Foster, *Notes from the Caroline Underground* (Hamden, 1978), remains the authority.

5. Sir Simonds D'Ewes, *The Journal of Sir Simonds D'Ewes from the Beginning of the Long Parliament to the Opening of the Trial of the Earl of Strafford*, ed. Wallace Notestein (New Haven, Conn., 1923), 4-5.

6. See the entries in G.E. Briscoe Eyre, H.R. Plomer, and C.R. Rivington, *A Transcript of the Registers of the Worshipful Company of Stationers from 1640 to 1708*, 3 vols. (London, 1913-14), vol. 1. The licensers concerned are Undersecretary of State Weckerlyn (in the spring of 1641), and John Hansley and Thomas Wykes, ecclesiastical licensers at work even in 1642. See also Sheila Lambert, "The Beginning of Printing for the House of Commons, 1640-42," *The Library*, 6th ser., 3 (1981): 40 and n. 20.

7. Stationers' Company Records, Liber A (from British Library MS Room, Microfilm M/455/8), fol. 130a-b, 4 March 1641; House of Lords Record Office, Main Papers, 4 March 1641 (complaint of Stationers' Company concerning unlicensed books [*sic* in Hist. Manuscripts Commission, *4th Report*, 1874]), 10 March 1641 (draft of resolutions against the sale of unlicensed books), 12 March 1641 (draft report from the committee concerning printers and stationers); *Lords' Journal* 4:180, 182.

8. A later episode would earn Walker general notoriety; see Ernest Sirluck, "*To Your Tents, O Israel*: A Lost Pamphlet," *Huntington Library Quarterly* 19 (1955-56): 301-5.

9. On Alsop's and Fawcett's earlier scrapes with authority, see William A. Jackson, ed., *Records of the Court of the Stationers' Company, 1602-1640* (London, 1957), 259, 260, 293, 305-6, 481, 483. See also the entry in Henry R. Plomer, *A Dictionary of the Booksellers and Printers . . . from 1641 to 1667* (London, 1907; rpt. 1968); Lambert, "The Printers and the Government," 8-9; Edward Arber, *Transcripts of the Registers of the Company of Stationers of London, 1554-1640*, 5 vols. (London, 1875-84), 3:700-701, 704.

10. Lambert, "Beginning of Printing'" and Mendle, "De Facto Freedom", 30-30.

11. See their plea to the Lords for a licensing scheme to their liking: House of Lords Record Office, Main Papers, 12 March 1641 (petition of ministers). The signatories included the arch-Presbyterian Edmund Calamy, who later joined other ministers in supporting the Stationers' desires for strong copyright protection (Liber A, f. 131b).

12. *Commons' Journal* 2:218, 220, 222.

13. John Milton, *Complete Prose Works*, vol. 2, ed. Ernest Sirluck (New Haven, Conn., 1959), 558; cf. 515, 517.

14. Simonds D'Ewes's remark that the writers were "certain loose beggarly

scholars . . . in alehouses" is confirmed by other evidence; see *The Private Journals of the Long Parliament, 3 January to 5 March 1642*, ed. Willson H. Coates, Anne Steele Young, Vernon F. Snow (New Haven, Conn., 1982), 165. (hereafter *Private Journals I*).

15. See esp. British Library (BL) 669 f. 4 (17), *The Sucklington Faction* (1641).

16. For example, BL E. 156 (15) [also used in BL E. 169 (9)], BL E. 158 (13), BL E. 160 (13), BL E. 165 (1) [also used in BL 669. f. 4 (20)].

17. *A New Play Called Canterburie His Change of Diot* (1641). By all appearances, this is a product of the Alsop-Fawcett press. The woodcut of Laud at table with a dish of ears provides surprisingly detailed and accurate likenesses of the principals, and reflects detailed knowledge of the "martyrdom," probably obtained from the standard puritan account, *A Briefe Relation* (1638). The cut was reused, wholly inappropriately, for the title page of John Crag, *A Prophecy Concerning the Earle of Essex that Now Is* (1641) [BL E. 181 (18)].

18. *Wrens Nest Defild* (1641), title page. This woodcut is a good example of the use of dialogue bubbles to permit re-use: with different captions, the illustration was recycled in *Articles Ministered by His Majesties Commissioners . . . against John Gwin* (1641). Allegedly, Gwin was guilty of "lascivious wenching" and other manifestations of a "wanton life."

19. *The Sisters of the Scabards Holiday* (1641). The sisters rejoiced, because they would no longer be forced to provide free services to the personnel of the bawdy courts.

20. *The Brothers of the Blade* (1641) [BL E. 238 (5)]; *The Pimpes Prerogative* (1641) [BL 669 f. 4 (18)].

21. *Sion's Charity Towards her Foes in Misery* (1641), 4, 5.

22. Thomas Herbert, *The Answer to the Most Envious, Scandalous, and Libellous Pamphlet, Entituled, Mercuries Message* (1641) [BL E. 157 (7)], 3.

23. John Taylor, *A Swarme of Sectaries, and Schismatiques* (1641), title page and 9-10.

24. *New Preachers, New* (1641) [BL E. 180 (26)], title page.

25. *The Sermon and Prophecie of Mr. James Hunt* (1641) [BL E. 172 (26)], title page.

26. *Lvcifers Lacky* (1641) [BL E. 180 (3)], last page.

27. See the title page illustration of Samoth Yarb [Thomas Bray], *A New Sect of Religion Descryed, Called Adamites* (1641).

28. See the appalling woodcuts on the title pages of John Taylor, *A Reply as True as Steel* (1641) [BL E. 160 (23)], and Voluntas Ambulatoria, *Taylors Physicke has purged the Divel* (1641). The relation of this "Will Walker" to Henry is not clear. Taylor turned obscenity into a political statement, a contempt-laced refusal to be "religiously correct." In *A Reply as True as Steel* (6), he obtruded into his attack on Walker an entirely gratuitous little tale of a "sister" who thought the "Priap" of the lion rampant in the royal arms in her church "mov'd unlawfull motions." Her husband the churchwarden had the offending "whim wham" painted out. This side of Taylor, the friend of bishops, is not to be divined from the charming portrait of him in Wallace Notestein, *Four Worthies* (New Haven, Conn., 1957), 169-208.

29. Herbert, *The Answer*, answered the sharp-tongued *Mercuries Message* (Wing M1748), which was "Printed in the yeare of our Prelates feare, 1641."

30. *Mercuries Message Defended*, 13, 20, claiming that Herbert wrote the anti-Laudian *Romes ABC* (1641) [BL E. 156)]; John Bond, *The Poets Knavery Discovered* (1642) [BL E. 135 (11)], sig. A2.

31. *Mercuries Message Defended*, 3, 10; *Commons' Journal*, 2:396 (25 Jan. 1642); Cooper, *Annals Cantabridgensis*, III, reports Thomas Herbert, matriculated sizar Trinity, 1639. In *Vox Secunda Populi* (1641) [BL E. 164 (21)], 1, a poem in praise of Phillip Herbert, earl of Pembroke, Herbert was careful not to claim any connection to the earl but the name. He was a Kentishman: see *The Answer*, 5.

32. *Mercuries Message Defended*, 2, 3, 4, 10, 16; *A Second Message to Mr. William Laud . . . With a Postscript to the Author of that Foolish and Ridiculous Answer to Mercury* (1641) [BL E. 169 (9)], sig. A4.

33. *The Downefall of the Temporizing Poets, Unlicenst Printers, Upstart Booksellers, Trotting Mercuries, and Bawling Hawkers* (1641) [BL E. 165 (5)], 5. Bond, *Poets Knavery Discovered*, sig. A2, also notes Herbert's "froathy Muse."

34. *A Preparative to Studie; or, The Vertue of Sack* (1641) [BL E. 158 (7)], 5, attributed to Thomas Heywood and Richard Braithwaite. There were a fair number of other pamphlets in this vein.

35. The phrase is from *Downefall of the Temporizing Poets*, 2.

36. John Pym, *A Damnable Treason, By a Contagious Plaster of a Plague Sore* (1641) [BL E. 173 923)]; Henry Burton, *A Divine Tragedie Lately Acted* (1641) [BL E. 176 (1)]; John Lilburne, *A Christian Mans Triall* (1641) [BL E. 181 (7)]. A false likeness of Essex also made the rounds: *A True Coppie of Divers Letters* (1641) [BL E. 180 (21)], and John Crag, *A Prophecy Concerning the Earle of Essex*, sig. A2r.

37. *Commons' Journal* 2: 209 (13 July 1642).

38. *Commons' Journal* 2:268-69 (24 Aug. 1642). For the significance of the letter, see Michael Mendle, "The Great Council of Parliament and the First Ordinances: The Constitutional Theory of the Civil War," *Journal of British Studies* 31 (1992): 141.

39. *Commons' Journal* 2:221 (13 July 1642). The version at issue was *The Order and Forme for Church, Government* (1641) [BL Burney 11. a. (25)]. For the setting and other editions, see Michael Mendle, *Dangerous Positions* (University, Ala., 1985), 146-47, 218 n. 38.

40. *No Pamphlet, But a Detestation Against All Such Pamphlets As Are Printed Concerning the Irish Rebellion* (1641) [BL E. 134 (3)], sig. A2v, joined these efforts with false reports of parliamentary proceedings. See also Bond, *Poets Knavery Discovered*, for a detailed rundown of false pamphlets during this period, most of which can be traced. The Irish printer William Blayden protested the false reports: *Historical Manuscripts Commission, 4th Report*, 113.

41. Bond, *Poets Knavery Discovered*, sig. A2v. For Bray, *Commons' Journal* 2:269, for complaint against *The Anatomy of Et Caetera* (1641) [BL E. 169 (1)].

42. Charles complained to the Commons of an inaccurate version of one of

his speeches; see *The Journal of Sir Simonds D'Ewes from the First Recess of the Long Parliament to the Withdrawal of King Charles from London*, ed. W.H. Coates (New Haven, Conn., 1942), 249 and n. 1. In the other episode the Alsop-printed *A Great Discovery of a Damnable Plot* (1641) [BL E. 176 (13)] bungled into implicating the current French ambassador (who was a Pym confidant) in a plot hatched by the papist Marquis of Worcester; see D'Ewes, *Journal* (Coates), 164 and n. 2, 176-77, and *Lords' Journal* 4:443.

43. House of Lords Record Office, Main Papers, 24 Nov. 1641 (order of the House of Commons to the Committee for Printing).

44. On 6 Jan. 1642 Charles used the Privy Council to "require" the King's Bench to act against the producers of one printed version of the articles of treason against the five members and Lord Kimbolton: *Privy Council Registers Preserved in the Public Record Office*, vol. 12 (London, 1968), 209. He also attempted to use the King's Printer, Robert Barker, as a kind of alternative Stationers' Company to assist the court: House of Lords Record Office, Main Papers, 6 Jan. 1642 (warrant to Robert Barker and the Assigns of John Bill). Later Charles tried unsuccessfully to engage the House of Lords in a similar role.

45. *Commons' Journal* 2:396; *Private Journals I*, 160-61, 165-66. See also the account in BL Burney 11 a. (5), 22, which is suspiciously authoritative, since it was appended to the warranted and registered text of Pym's speech of 25 Jan. 1642.

46. Greensmith was released on 1 Feb., Eldred on 7 Feb. 1642 (*Commons' Journal* 2:408, 415). See also Eldred's petition: House of Lords Record Office, Main Papers, 7 Feb. 1942 (petition of Martin Eldred to the House of Commons).

47. *Commons' Journal*, 2:402; *Private Journals I*, 216; *An Order Made by the Honorable House of Commons Die Sabbati, 29. Januarii. 1641* (1642) [BL E. 207 (2)].

48. Bond, *Poets Knavery Discovered*, sigs. A2-A3. Bond repeatedly identified himself as a St. John's scholar; see, e.g., *King Charles his Welcome Home* (1641) [BL E. 177 (18)], title page.

49. *A Copie of the Qveens Letter From the Hague in Holland to the Kings Maiesty Residing at Yorke* (1641) [BL 669. f. 3 (62)]. BL Harl. 163 f. 37.

50. *Lords' Journal* 4:674, 678, 680, 681, 699, 708, 721, 722.

51. John Bond, *The Poets Recantation, Having Suffered in the Pillory* (1942 [*sic*]) [BL E. 142 (13)], 1, 3, 5.

52. House of Lords Record Office, Main Papers, 7 Jan. 1643 (petition of Bernard Alsop), April 1643 (petition of Bernard Alsop and Thomas Fawcett).

53. *Commons' Journal* 2:743.

54. *Commons' Journal* 2:1000-1001 (9 March 1643). The logic for the order is unclear, but may be related to a search-and-seizure episode in Oct. 1641 that was still causing ripples in 1642: House of Lords Record Office, Main Papers, 21 Oct. 1641 (petition of the Masters and Wardens of the Company of Stationers), and 14 May 1643 (petition of Joseph Hunscott).

55. *The Humble Remonstrance of the Company of Stationers, London* (n.d.) [BL E. 247 (23)]; Thomason attributed the tract to Parker and dated it simply April 1643. The reprint in Arber, *Transcripts*, 1:584-88, has a few inaccuracies. For Parker's career at this point, see Michael Mendle, "Henry Parker: The Pub-

lic's Privado," in Gordon J. Schochet, ed. *Religion, Resistance, and Civil War* (Washington, D.C., 1990), 158-59.

56. *Humble Remonstrance*, sigs. A1v, A2r.

57. Ibid., sig. A2v.

58. Ibid., sig. A1v; Parker actually praised the papists' ability to control the press.

59. Ibid., sig. A3v.

60. *An Order of the Lords and Commons Assembled in Parliament. For the Regulating of Printing* . . . (1643) [BL E. 106 (15)], 7. "Ancient custom" is used twice (pp. 5, 6-7). The licensers were named on 20 June (*Commons' Journal* 3:138); recognizing the long-term informal practice of the company, "small Pamphlets . . . and the like" could be licensed by the company's clerk. See also the explanation of the search provisions: House of Lords Record Office, Main Papers, 14 June 1643 (explanation of the ordinance of 14 June 1643).

61. See note 11.

62. *Commons' Journal* 3:138. John Downame and Calybute Downing, who signed the Stationers' solicitation, were also named licensers for works of divinity.

63. *Order of the Lords and Commons*, 4. Parker's *Humble Remonstrance*, sig. A4, included an apology for the English stock.

64. Milton, *Complete Prose Works*, 2:491, 570 (Milton knew that the line pursued in *Humble Remonstrance* underlay the ordinance).

65. Ibid., 161-62, 558, 570, and n. 309; see also 524 ("twenty licencers"), 535 ("twenty capacities"), 536 ("twenty licencing forges"), 541 ("a Prelatical commission of twenty").

66. Ibid., 569.

67. Ibid., 539, 541, 568. See also 504-5 on how popish imprimaturs became the Laudians' "deare Antiphonies."

68. Ibid., 566.

69. Cyprian Blagden, *The Stationers' Company* (London, 1960), 16.

70. See esp. Keith Lindley, "London and Popular Freedom in the 1640s," in R.C. Richardson and G.M. Ridden, eds., *Freedom and the English Revolution* (Manchester, 1986), 111-50; and Lois Potter, *Secret Rites and Secret Writing: Royalist Literature, 1641-1660* (Cambridge, 1989), 1-71.

4

Propaganda and Public Opinion in Seventeenth-Century England

TIM HARRIS

Ⅰt is well known that from the eve of the English Civil War there was a sudden and dramatic surge in the output of the press.[1] As censorship controls broke down following the meeting of the Long Parliament in late 1640, there was a great explosion of pamphlet and other printed materials, discussing a wide range of political, constitutional, and religious topics, and it is probably not too controversial to assert that the English Revolution of the mid-seventeenth century was accompanied by a concomitant media revolution. That said, it is remarkable how little scholarly attention has been paid to the impact of the media at this time.[2] The confidence with which the revisionist historians of the 1970s and early 1980s downplayed the ideological component to the outbreak of the Civil War always struck me as odd, when they largely ignored precisely those sources where the ideological dimension was most likely to be found: the pamphlets, broadsides, prints, and sermons that abounded in this period.

One of the main reasons why little has been done on the media during the English Revolution is that scholars have been unsure how to use such materials as a source. Admittedly, historians such as Christopher Hill and Brian Manning have used pamphlet literature extensively but chiefly as a descriptive source, as a way of getting at the actions and aspirations of the "common people" during this time—an approach that has been shown to be fraught with problems.[3] Pamphlets, broadsides, newspapers, and the like have to be treated for what they were: propaganda, designed to persuade, convince, cajole, even mislead. Yet it is extremely difficult to determine the impact such propaganda had; we can analyze the content of printed material, but it is not easy to gauge how the "consumers" reacted to what they read.[4]

The media revolution surely did play a highly significant role in the English revolution—not just once the Civil War had broken out but even in the process leading to the outbreak of armed conflict. In the state of existing research, however, we are still far from sorting out exactly what that role was. The aim of this essay, therefore, is fairly limited: to suggest some ways of thinking about how propaganda worked in the seventeenth century in England. I intend to do so by drawing on my own preliminary research into the media in the 1640s and offering comparisons with what I have found for the early 1680s, when a second revolutionary situation threatened. The purpose is to examine how and why the Parliamentarians were so successful in rallying public opinion in support of their cause in the early 1640s (if, indeed, that is a fair assumption to make), whereas the Tories were able to stave off the challenge of the Whigs in the early 1680s through a successful counterpropaganda campaign that helped mobilize public opinion behind the Crown. I suggest that propagandists, in order to win public support for their position, needed to appeal to the middle ground—to commonly held values and principles—and try to convince people that the holding of such principles should lead them to support their (the propagandists') particular cause. As a result, much propaganda, even that put out by the most committed opponents of the Crown, was (ostensibly) of a nonrevolutionary nature, since propagandists, in order to be successful, had to claim to be defending traditional values rather than making any radical or revolutionary demands. I argue that a combination of existing political circumstances and experience made the Parliamentarian representation of its own position plausible enough in the early 1640s to rally considerable support for its cause against the Crown. Nevertheless, Royalist propaganda was also quite successful, so that the effect of propaganda at this time was to polarize the two sides that would eventually go to war. In contrast, by the early 1680s the experiences of the previous forty years made the Tories' claim to be the true defenders of the best interests of English subjects plausible enough to discredit the Whig position and rally public opinion behind the Crown. Finally, I argue for the need to expand our definition of the media, suggesting that we should look not just at printed materials or sermons but also at such things as petitioning campaigns, public spectacles, and demonstrations, for in order to discredit the Whigs it became important for the Tories to show that they too had popular support, and that popular opinion was not overwhelmingly behind the Whigs.

Before looking at the impact of the propaganda produced on the eve of the Civil War, it is important to emphasize that we should not regard public opinion before 1640 as a tabula rasa. We are not dealing with a politically unaware populace who as a result of the media explosion after 1640 were suddenly and for the first time given a political education. People's political education was achieved first and foremost by the direct experience of being ruled, by the experience of how the government's policies impinged directly on their lives. For the period of Charles I's rule prior to the meeting of the Long Parliament, we can point to things such as ship money, enclosures, Laud's rule of thorough, the imposition of "Arminianism," and the clampdown on various religious practices perceived as nonconformist as helping to shape people's attitudes toward the Crown and the government. Research has shown that the implications of such policies cut quite deep into society.[5] The audience for the propaganda produced in the 1640s, in other words, was a population that had already become politicized to some degree.

What effect, therefore, does propaganda have on people who have already (partially) formulated their attitudes about politics? Communications research has shown that a propagandist cannot run counter to the assumptions and prejudices of the audience he is trying to reach. A person confronted with views hostile to the ones he or she already holds is likely to ignore or reject them, or even interpret them in a way that confirms (rather than challenges) his or her existing prejudices.[6] A person who has a deep sense of loyalty to the Crown and to monarchical rule is unlikely to respond sympathetically to propaganda that insists on the necessity of challenging royal sovereignty and calls for Parliament to make war on the king. To be effective, propagandists must know the sentiments, opinions, and prejudices of the audience they are trying to reach, and appeal to people in such a way as to win them over. That is the reason successful propaganda tends to appeal to the middle ground: the advocacy of extreme positions—either overtly revolutionary or ultrareactionary—is likely to be counter-productive because it runs against deeply embedded values and assumptions. This does not mean, however, that successful propaganda cannot have radical or even revolutionary implications, nor does it mean, certainly, that in appealing to commonly held values we are dealing with a consensual political culture. For example, throughout the crises of the seventeenth century most English people exhibited a deep anxiety about the possible threat from popery and arbitrary government. Parliamentarians argued that to stave off this threat required certain reforms in both the church and state, which might indeed radically alter the existing constitution of the government and the structure of the church. Royalists, on the other hand—and we see this particularly during the Exclusion Crisis—argued that the threat of popery and arbitrary government came from those people who were advocating reforms in the church and state. People shared common concerns about popery and arbitrary government but at times became bitterly divided over how best to avert the dangers.[7]

Yet how easy was it for a propagandist to reach a mass audience at this time? Surely low levels of adult literacy (30 percent for men, even lower for women) must have meant that the output of the press had a limited impact on seventeenth-century English society.[8] Perhaps the prime function of propaganda, most of which was produced in London, was to appeal to the members of the political elite and the articulate (and economically important) middle classes of the metropolis. A number of observations suggest that we should not be too skeptical about how wide an audience propagandists might have been able to reach. Not all propaganda was solely dependent upon a literary medium. Political messages were preached in sermons or conveyed pictorially in satirical prints. Moreover, our conventional test for measuring literacy, the ability to sign one's name, probably grossly underestimates the number of people who could read—since people normally learned to read before they learned to write.[9] Then there were all sorts of ways of bridging the gap between the literate and oral cultures, and we often hear reports that during the Stuart period printed material was read aloud for the benefit of those who could not read. The latest research suggests that the circulation of printed material was fairly widespread (geographically). Tessa Watt and Tamsyn Williams have shown that cheap printed works published in London were sent to provincial market towns and then hawked about the surrounding countryside by peddlers. On the eve of the Civil War thirty-three deliveries left London each week for Buckinghamshire, roughly nine weekly delivery services traveled from the capital to Yorkshire, and seven to Devon. Even the remotest village alehouse could have its walls adorned with religious prints, and sermons, of course, were preached in all parts of the country. Some printed material might have been too expensive for the lower classes to purchase, but against this economic impediment to reaching a mass audience we have examples of pamphlets and broadsides being given away or strewn about the streets, and of people reading (or having read to them) printed materials deposited in alehouses or coffeehouses for common consumption.[10]

A final point to consider is whether people would go out of their way to read or hear propaganda to which they knew they would be unsympathetic. Were propagandists merely preaching to the converted? To some extent perhaps they were, although titles of tracts were usually carefully worded in order to appeal to as wide an audience as possible. The staunch Anglican-Royalist Sir Roger L'Estrange, for example, produced a tract anonymously in 1678 titled *Liberty and Property Lording it over the Lives, Liberties and Estates of Both King and People*. The title must surely have enticed many people who differed strongly from L'Estrange's political beliefs to read the tract. Yet even preaching to the converted could have a significant effect; the aim here was to furnish one's own supporters with more sophisticated arguments so that they could go away and convince others of the merits of their particular position. As John Nalson, Tory pamphleteer of the Exclusion Crisis, advised his readers: "If you think, and find I have told you a plain truth . . . inform the ignorant, confront the impudent, satisfy the doubtful and staggering, and unite the loyal." [11]

Let us turn our attention now to the role of the media in the outbreak of the English Civil War. Here, I suggest, we see a self-conscious attempt by propagandists on all sides to appeal to the middle ground, although the effect of the propaganda was to create a process of polarization, thus helping to generate two sides and make civil war possible. For obvious tactical reasons, parliamentarians liked to portray their intentions in a conservative light: they sought to represent themselves as struggling against the attempt to subvert traditional English freedoms and introduce arbitrary and tyrannical government, and as seeking to uphold the true reformed religion against various innovations and superstitions that had been brought into the church.[12] But despite this conservative posturing, there was a radical potential within parliamentary propaganda, its ultimate aim being to shift the middle ground and point to the necessity of reaching a new position in both church and state.

Although the new vogue is to stress the religious origins of the English Civil War, it is important not to lose sight of the political, constitutional, and economic grievances voiced in parliamentary propaganda. As late as 1642 a tract in defense of Parliament could still emphasize issues such as ship money, coat and conduct money, monopolies, and the economic burden these placed on the people so that "the subjects might have been drained to the utmost penny they had." "The root of all these wrongs," this pamphlet complained, "was an arbitrary power pretended to be in his Majesty, of taxing the subject, and charging their estates without consent of

Parliament." To make the constitutional argument even stronger, the author also complained about the use of the prerogative courts of the Star Chamber and High Commission.[13] If we look at political prints that appeared in the opening months of the Long Parliament, we see that many were preoccupied with the grievances of monopolies and with attacking those who had been the chief architects of the personal rule, such as the Earl of Strafford.[14] One woodcut shows Strafford, the minister who (as the accompanying text says) had sought to "untie three realms" and "unground the foot of justice, and the laws," being rowed across the Styx to be welcomed in Hades by Charles I's former attorney general William Noy, himself castigated as the promoter of patents and monopolies and the originator of ship money.[15] A striking engraving by Wenceslas Hollar, *The Picture of a Pattenty*, shows a man with a wolf's head and fishhook fingers that pull strings attached to moneybags; his legs are screws. On his arms and body are things that had been the subjects of monopolies: tobacco (represented in the form of tobacco pipes), wine, pins, coals, playing cards, salt, and butter. The accompanying verse describes this patentee as a "wolf-like devourer of the Common Wealth / That robs by patent, worse than any stealth . . . Strong screws support him that hath screwed us all, / And now we live, to see this strong man fall."[16]

Undoubtedly the strongest concern expressed in parliamentary propaganda, however, was fear of popery. Many tracts and broadsides harked back to various popish plots to subvert Protestantism in England, from the Armada (1588) and Gunpowder Plot (1605) to the Irish Rebellion (1641), while during the months of crisis all sorts of minor popish plots surfaced. A tract of May 1642, for example, catalogued a number of "wonderful, bloody and dangerous plots": papists in Norwich going on the rampage after refusing to surrender their weapons; a Catholic rebellion in Cheshire; and the attempt at a more general, nationwide rising.[17] Parliament, therefore, was repeatedly praised as the savior of England from popery.[18]

During the early months of the Long Parliament, fear of popery and arbitrary government came to coalesce in the hatred of one man, Archbishop William Laud. Laud was condemned as a great monopolist, particularly for his involvement in the wine and tobacco monopolies.[19] He was also closely associated with the excesses of the personal rule: the use of the prerogative courts to punish enemies of church and state, and the mutilation of the "Protestant martyrs" John Bastwick, Henry Burton, and William Prynne. One print shows Laud at a table with "a doctor of physic, a lawyer, and a divine"; once everyone is seated, Laud is brought "a variety of dishes to his table," which are the ears of Bastwick, Prynne, and Burton.[20] But the

main charge against Laud was that he was leading the church back to
Rome. One interesting print shows three ecclesiastics named Sound-head,
Rattle-head, and Round-head. Rattle-head is a double-headed figure, half
bishop, half Jesuit (with the bishop clearly being recognizable as Laud).
Rattle-head is shown rejecting truth from Sound-head (a Puritan, "whom
atheists call a round-head"), preferring instead to receive a crucifix from
the true round-head, who is a monk.[21] With Laud, the whole Arminian faction in the church was attacked. "We see that . . . Arminianism is a bridge
to popery," argued one author in 1641. "Some have past over it . . . and had
not God of his great mercy undermined the chief arches of that bridge . . .
we have cause to think that the greater part of this Land would also have
followed the rest."[22]

The press campaign against popery and arbitrary government was
couched in the language of conservatism. It was Laud who was the innova-
tor: "Your aim was always to have alterations," one rhymester accused the
archbishop, "And by your altars thought to alter nations."[23] In the early days
of the Long Parliament many members, even those who were to side with
Parliament after the outbreak of hostilities, could maintain that the need to
obliterate Laudianism did not require a fundamental restructuring of church
government. In a speech in the House of Commons in November 1640, subsequently printed in pamphlet form, Sir Benjamin Rudyerd alleged that
many of our clergy "think the simplicity of the Gospel, too mean a vocation
for them to serve in: they must have a specious, pompous, sumptuous religion, with additionals of temporal greatness, authority, negotiation. . . .
This Roman ambition will at length bring in the Roman religion." Nevertheless, he argued, we must "restrain the bishops to the duties of their function" rather than abolish them: "Whilst we are earnest to take away Innovations, let us beware we bring not in the greatest innovation that ever was in
England."[24] For obvious reasons, care was always taken not to hold the king
personally responsible for the misfortunes that had befallen the church and
state during the 1630s but rather to lay the blame on evil counselors.[25] Indeed, the attack on the Arminian faction within the church was represented
as a defense of the Crown, for those who upheld *iure divino* episcopacy, it
was argued, were challenging the king's supremacy over the church established by the Henrician Reformation. One illustrated pamphlet shows the
ghost of Cardinal Thomas Wolsey visiting Laud; the cardinal wears a miter
and carries the archiepiscopal crosier. The text describes Wolsey lamenting
to the archbishop the downfall of others who, like themselves, had attempted to set the miter on a "parity with the Crown."[26] Sir Benjamin
Rudyerd believed that "histories will tell us, that whensoever the clergy

went high, monarchy still went lower."[27] John Bastwick claimed that he had always supported and respected the bishops as long as they were appointed by and answerable to the king. But when they claimed to hold office by divine right, they became agents of Rome and guilty of treason by placing themselves above the king: "There was never such an affront put upon regal dignity."[28] The Laudian "cries no bishop, no king," observed one pamphleteer in 1641, "thereby professing episcopacy to the chief handmaid of monarchy; and yet exercises contrary to the law, regal jurisdiction in his own name, and his own courts. Is not this to supplant monarchy?"[29]

But during 1641 and early 1642 we see a definite radicalization process taking place. John Morrill has shown that as Parliament began its cleansing exercise in the church, many came to feel that it would not be enough just to root out Arminianism, that the institution of episcopacy itself was rotten.[30] We see a similar process reflected in propaganda, and what is interesting to note is how the appeal to the middle ground was redirected in a more radical direction, as the campaign against Arminianism and popery became linked with the demand for root and branch reform. As the Presbyterian Robert Baillie, put it: "That government whereby heresies, prophaneness, idolatry, and superstitions, has great opportunity to creep into the church, is the ruin and misery of any church, nation, or kingdom: but prelatical government gives great opportunity for heresies, prophaneness, idolatry, and superstition to creep into the church; therefore prelatical government is the church's ruin and misery."[31] Another author, asserting that the bishops "would soon reduce the land to popery, and (we may justly fear) bring us under as much cruelty as ever Queen Mary's prelates," therefore concluded, "If thou wilt banish Antichrist, and the Pope out of this realm, thou must fell down to the ground those rotten posts the bishops . . . and utterly abolish all and every his [sic] ungodly laws, decrees, traditions, and ceremonies without significations."[32]

Ultimately, the Parliamentarians had to justify taking up arms against Charles I, and the media played a crucial role in helping to delegitimize the authority of the king so that armed resistance could become conceivable. Space does not permit a full exploration of this issue here, but I would suggest we need a more subtle reading of propaganda to see how that process of delegitimization took effect. For example, although we do not see the king attacked directly in satirical prints, neither do we see a positive image of the monarchy represented, whereas all those people closely associated with the king are portrayed in a very negative light. In the prints of the 1640s the primary victim of popish tyranny is not the Crown, as had been the case in 1588 or 1605, but rather the Protestant nation threatened by disintegration from within by evil counselors surrounding the monarch.[33] Satire could be an effective way of undermining the king's prestige. One highly amusing pamphlet describes a place called Antipodes, where people in outward features, language, and religion resemble those in England "but in their manners, carriage, and condition of life [are] extremely contrary." Thus in Antipodes people rule magistrates, women rule men, maids woo bachelors, men are whores (the tract is full of images of gender inversion), and lawyers charge no fees; then, we are told, "the king of this country of Antipodes is a prince so full of virtue, that he is beloved and admired [by] most of his subjects . . . an example to all princes whatsoever." [34] We could count this as a personal attack on Charles I rather than on the institution of kingship, and it is well known that Parliamentarians made a clear distinction between the person of the king and the authority of the Crown when justifying their position: though they might be opposing the person, they denied ever seeking to challenge kingly authority.

Henry Parker, among others, developed this argument, and Parker could even deny that he was "in favour of any alteration in England," since he was "as zealously addicted to monarchy, as any man" could be. But at the same time, Parker denied that kings' power came from God (asserting that their royalty came from the people) and argued that kingship was a trust, that *salus populi* was the supreme law, that the law of the prerogative was subservient to this law, and that kings were accountable to Parliament.[35] Clearly this was a different image of monarchy from that held by most Royalists. The Parliamentarians' claim not to be challenging regal authority cannot be accepted at face value, since the exalting of what Parliament was doing encouraged people to develop a different perception of the constitutional balance within this body politic than had been the norm prior to the meeting of the Long Parliament. In these sorts of ways, perhaps, the media may have helped radicalize people's views of the constitution, or shift the middle ground—if that is a better way of putting it—more effectively than by coming out bluntly and arguing that "monarchy needs to be changed in England in the following ways because . . ."

How did the Royalists meet this challenge? Some did so by asserting that the king's authority could not be challenged in any way.[36] Thus one author vehemently denied that power was originally in the people: the king's power was derived immediately from God; the people could not justify using force to regain their liberty; and not "*salus populi* alone . . . but *salus regis et populi*" was "the true end of monarchical government." [37] Another author rehearsed scriptural arguments directing that kings were to govern and that subjects had to obey, even "though he were a tyrant." [38]

But we also see an attempt in Royalist propaganda to recapture the middle ground. Thus we see Royalists coming to develop their own theory of mixed monarchy and professing their attachment to the rule of law.[39] Charles I's *Answer to the XIX Propositions,* written by Sir John Culpepper and Lord Falkland, is the classic and most famous example.[40] Another tract argued that a mixed government of king, Lords, and Commons was best but nevertheless maintained that government, according to law, was vested in the king. The House of Commons had no share in the government but was solely entrusted with the introduction of bills for the raising of taxes and with impeaching those who had violated the law, and the House of Lords was the judicatory power.[41] One author, writing on the eve of the war, maintained that Parliament's claim to sovereignty meant that it was setting itself up as an absolute and arbitrary power that would threaten the liberties of the subjects. Although the king was "willing to govern his subjects according to the known laws," Parliament was claiming that it could judge of public necessity without the king and dispose of any thing in times of emergency. In other words, "the life and liberty of the subject, and all good laws made for the security of them, may be disposed of, and repealed by the major part of both Houses, at any time. . . . And His Majesty shall have no power to protect them. They see nothing, that see not the misery, which may follow upon such a vast transcendency of arbitrary power, if it were invested in the Parliament. . . . Every (the meanest) subject has such a right and propriety in his goods, that without law, they cannot be taken from him, though to be employed for the public good."[42] Charles I himself repeatedly insisted that "for our part, we are resolved not only duly to observe the laws our self, but to maintain them against what opposition soever."[43]

The breakdown of religious unity and the rise of separatist groups enabled the Royalists to pose as defenders of the Protestant church and the social order. Much of the antisectarian literature was produced by John Taylor, the water poet, who repeatedly complained not only of the sects' erroneous and heretical opinions but also of their impudence and turbulence. "Hence," he said in one tract, "come those violent outrages, and sacrilegious disorders committed in the church, even in the time of divine service, and hubbubs and strange tumults raised, where reverend silence ought to be used, by laying violent hands upon the minister, rending his hood from his neck, and tearing the surplice from his back . . . as likewise rending the rails from before the communion table, chopping them in pieces, and burning them in the church yard, and this to be done without authority, commission, or order, in a riotous manner."[44]

Opposition to the sects became linked with a defense of the Book of Common Prayer and episcopacy. As Taylor put it in another tract: "We acknowledge that some parts of our public liturgy, may be very well corrected . . . but the clamors now go very high . . . [so] that it is confidently expected by many, that all forms of public worship should be utterly abrogated, and that our book of Common-Prayer should be quite abolished, as they would have episcopacy everlastingly extirpated."[45] Taylor also attempted to identify the sectarians with the Puritans or Parliamentarians more generally. In the same tract he asserted, "They are the separatists, or Brownists; the libertines or Anabaptists; who are grown to a great head, . . . a giddy-headed multitude, and are so common amongst us, that they are commonly called the Round-heads."[46] Other authors came to defend the bishops as essential bulwarks against such disorders. One claimed that time was wise and that time vindicated the bishops, which he attempted to prove by praising their actions throughout history.[47] At the same time, most Royalists sought to distance themselves from Laud and the Arminians, and thus by championing episcopacy and the prayerbook they were able to represent themselves as defenders of tradition and the true religion against innovation of whatever kind. In one pamphlet John Taylor listed sixteen "sorts of religions" that had "crept into the very bowels of the kingdom" and threatened "to destroy both church and kingdom." Among those he condemned were Arminians, Anabaptists, separatists, Puritans, and Roundheads.[48] Another tract rehearsed the testimony of Bishop George Carleton (James I's Bishop of Llandaff and then Chichester) against Presbyterian discipline in the Low Counties, in which the bishop first states that he is an enemy of Rome and has also written against Arminianism; then he defends episcopal government as the true way set down by the Apostles, maintaining that the Presbyterians in the Low Countries wished they had "the good order and discipline of the Church of England."[49]

Royalist propaganda also sought to turn the charge of popery against their opponents. One author, alleging that Parliament's claim to be "the universal unerring and impervertibly just body of the kingdom" came close to the Roman church's claim to infallibility, concluded that "men that so much detest popery, should not borrow the ground of their reasoning from them."[50] Anti-Puritan polemicists repeatedly equated the sectaries with Catholics, because they shared similar antimonarchical tenets.[51] As Taylor lamented in 1642, "The Papist and the schismatic, both grieves [*sic*] / The church, for she's like Christ between two thieves."[52] In another pamphlet Taylor claimed to have uncovered a plot by the "hellish Parliament" to make "a perfect league . . . between the two hellish factions, the Papists and the Brownists."[53] Elsewhere, Taylor wrote that "these our sectarists [*sic*] will abide no degrees in schools, all human learning must be laid by, academies are to them abominable" and that "herein they comply with the Papists, whose doctrines they pretend utterly to abhor, who hold that ignorance is the mother of devotion."[54] Similar arguments were made from the pulpit. The Anglican vicar of Stepney, preaching before the king at Christ Church, Oxford, in 1642, exclaimed, "The Zealous sectary . . . is now Jesuit enough."[55]

Although we still do not know enough about the impact such propaganda had, there is a tendency to think that the Parliamentarians had the better of things and that Royalist propaganda was largely ineffectual.[56] This assumption needs to be challenged. Royalist propaganda probably did have a very powerful effect, and their attempt to recapture the middle ground, I would suggest, helped establish a body of support for the Crown which defined its position in terms of a defense of mixed government (where the king was still sovereign), the rule of law, and the traditional Church of England of bishops and prayerbook against the innovations of both Laudians and Puritans.[57] The Royalist position had considerable popular purchase; not just members of the elite but also many more humble subjects could feel that their interests and concerns were best protected by the traditional establishment in church and state so defined.[58] Parliamentarian polemicists certainly believed that Royalist propaganda was effective, and their own tracts of 1642 often express a concern that they were losing popular support because of the efforts of "friends to the Popish party" to stir up people against Parliament.[59] In that sense, the effect of propaganda in the early 1640s was probably to create a polarization in allegiances between those who were against popery and arbitrary government but saw the need for further reform, and those who were also against popery and arbitrary government but saw the need to defend the traditional establishment in church and state. As others have said, the achievement of the supporters of the Crown between the meeting of the Long Parliament and the outbreak of war was to create a Royalist party and thus make it possible for them to fight a war.[60]

But we do need to recognize limitations to the effectiveness of Royalist propaganda; it certainly failed to bring about the sort of conservative reaction that the Tories were able to encourage in the early 1680s. A number of reasons may be suggested for this. First the course of events up to the actual outbreak of hostilities lent more plausibility to Parliament's position. The events of the 1630s together with the tactical mistakes and blunders made by Charles I in 1640-42—such as the attempted arrest of the five members,

and his mishandling of the Scottish Crisis and the Irish Rebellion—helped
fuel the climate of distrust. It took the actual experience of arbitrary government by Parliament during the course of the war, and the rise of radical
religious and political groups during the same period, to produce a significant reaction in favor of Charles I. But second, it must be recognized that
Royalists failed to use the media as effectively as they might have done.
Their appeal to the middle ground was never totally committed. Much
Royalist propaganda continued to be highly authoritarian and elitist, refusing to make any compromises and stressing the need for unconditional
obedience to the monarch. The Royalists' attitude towards popery was am-
bivalent, because many English Catholics loyally supported the Crown. So
while attacking Jesuits and be-Jesuited papists, their propaganda often
showed sympathy toward other Catholics; we can even find examples of
anti-Parliamentarian tracts in 1641 maintaining that since English Catholics
were loyal to king and country, they should be tolerated.[61] Nor is it clear
how many defenders of the Crown really understood the need to exploit
the full potential of the media. Significant in this regard is Charles I's terrible blunder in deciding to issue his commission of array in Latin, which
enabled the Parliamentarians to misrepresent its intentions by translating it
into "what English they pleased."[62] And although we can see manifestations of public support for the Crown and church in the form of petitions in
defense of episcopacy in late 1641 and early 1642, Charles I abandoned
both London and the crown to the Parliamentarians. He thus allowed it to
appear that the political nerve center of the nation and the ordinary men
and women whose only means of political expression was taking to the
streets in protest were overwhelmingly against him. No attempt was made
to use the crowd as a form of propaganda, to show that the masses were
not predominantly for Parliament. Such mistakes Charles II and his Tory
allies were determined not to repeat in the early 1680s.

Let us turn then, to an examination of the strategy adopted by Tory propagandists during the Exclusion Crisis and subsequent Tory reaction to
counter the challenge of the Whigs. As Jonathan Scott has suggested, the
crisis over the succession between 1678 and 1683 witnessed what was in
many respects a rerun of the crisis of popery and arbitrary government of
1637-42.[63] The Whig concern was that a Catholic successor would not only
threaten the security of the Protestant religion but would also be compelled to rule in an arbitrary and tyrannical manner; he would show little
concern for the liberties of his Protestant people and would be forced to
abandon Parliament and rule through a standing army. The Whigs, how-

ever, also had criticisms of the style of rule of Charles II and of the religious intolerance of the high-Anglical establishment in the church.[64]

Historians usually stress that the way the Tories responded to the Whig challenge was by exalting the powers of the Crown and championing the cause of divine-right, absolute monarchy.[65] There is, of course, much truth in this. We do find examples of Tory pamphleteers and especially the high-Anglican clergy in their sermons adopting such positions. But if the Tories had only taken that line, their propaganda would not have been effective. What has not been sufficiently emphasized by historians is that the Tories also set themselves up as the defenders of the rule of law and of the people's liberties and interests against the threat of popery and arbitrary government. Rather than denying totally the validity of the Whigs' premise—and asserting that England was ruled by an absolute and arbitrary monarch and there was nothing anyone could do about it, even if threatened with the prospect of a Catholic king (a tactic which would have been counterproductive—the Tories deliberately sought to recapture the middle ground from the Whigs, stressing that if people were really concerned for the rule of law and the security of the Protestant religion, then they should abandon the Whigs and rally in defense of the succession. As the literary scholar Steven Zwicker has pointed out, the need to persuade forced protagonists in the debate, Tory loyalists as well as Whig exclusionists, to use themes that had a "wide ideological appeal": they had to cover themselves "with the garb of moderation" and employ "the accepted language of political discourse," such as the defense of liberty, property, and the true religion.[66]

It is certainly true that Tories would have agreed that monarchs did rule by divine right and would have been quick to deny that subjects had any right to resist their kings. Nevertheless, most writers made important qualifications to their absolutist statements, stressing that kings were not to "reign without control" and that even the most absolute princes were "tied and circumscribed in the exercise of their power by laws." The king could not be held accountable by his subjects if he broke the laws, but this did not mean that he had no obligation to observe them, and he would certainly be held accountable by God.[67]

Supporters of the Crown deliberately sought to represent themselves as concerned to uphold the law and the legally constituted government of England.[68] Charles II was styled as a monarch who was scrupulously determined to observe the rule of law. As John Dryden put it in his famous and influential poem *Absalom and Achitophel,* the king was "Good, gracious, just, [and] observant of the laws." As the character of David (that is, Charles II) later proclaims in the same poem, "The law shall still direct my peaceful sway, and the same law teach rebels to obey."[69] Charles II himself played up to this image. In a declaration issued in April 1681, explaining why he had dissolved the last two Parliaments, he proclaimed his resolution "in all things to govern according to the laws of the kingdom."[70] The legalist argument was also used to defend the succession: England was a hereditary monarchy, and the Duke of York was the legal heir; exclusion was therefore both "unjust and unlawful."[71] Indeed, one opponent of exclusion maintained that "the present monarchy is so founded, that neither the king nor the parliament can possibly alter the true and essential form of it," and therefore the Duke of York could not be debarred from the succession. At the same time, Tories were at pains to point out that the law would protect English subjects under a popish successor, since the Protestant religion was "sufficiently guarded by several Acts of Parliament, which he can never repeal."[72]

This last point invokes another area where Tories sought to garb themselves with the language of moderation and a political discourse with wide ideological appeal: namely, in their discussion of Parliament. Tories undoubtedly had a very different view of the constitutional position of Parliament from that of the Whigs. They challenged the Whig view that Parliament was sovereign, denied the theory of co-ordination, and upheld the king's right to determine the calling, sitting, and dissolution of Parliament.[73] One of the doctrines condemned by the Oxford Decree of 1683, during the height of the Tory reaction, as "destructive to the kingly government" was the view that England was a mixed government with sovereignty vested in king, Lords, and Commons.[74] And defenders of the succession were quick to deny that the Whig Parliaments, in pressing for exclusion, were expressing the desires of the people, since the electoral system as it then operated in England was so "unequal" and "unjust" that the House of Commons was "not at all the representative of the people."[75] As one author pointed out, the House of Commons could not "be esteemed the representative body of the commons of England" because "mean peasants, servants, women and children, who are undoubtedly the major part of the nation . . . were not allowed to have any vote or suffrage in the election" of its members.[76] Yet Tories in their propaganda repeatedly claimed that they believed in the mixed constitution and the importance of Parliament. One writer, for example, maintained that "the government of England is a rare and admirable mixture of monarchy, aristocracy, and democracy." He was adamant that the king of England was absolute and held supreme executive power, but he also stressed that "the laws by which he is to govern cannot be made but by consent of the House of Peers, and by the Commons duly chosen," that the Commons were entrusted with the responsibility of voting taxes and impeaching ministers who had violated the law, and that the Lords held a judicative power that protected both king and people "against the encroachments of the other."[77] Tories even claimed that they too welcomed frequent meetings of Parliament; what they did not like were the tactics pursued by the Whig-dominated Parliaments of the Exclusion Crisis, which seemed very similar to those pursued by Charles I's Long Parliament in the early 1640s.[78]

In many other areas we see the attempt by Tory polemicists to recapture the middle ground. In response to the Whig accusation that those who supported the Catholic succession were complicitous in a design to establish popery and arbitrary government in England, Tories sought to represent themselves as the true defenders of English liberties and the Protestant religion, even suggesting that the Whigs were the real promoters of popery and arbitrary government. For the Whigs, they asserted, were Nonconformists and republicans who, like their counterparts in the 1640s, were bent on destroying the church and state as by law established. From here it was an easy step to accuse the Whigs of popery, since what else did the pope want but the destruction of the Church of England and the Protestant monarchy? In short, the Whigs would not only achieve what the papists wanted—namely, to "destroy our church and state"—but in advocating the dethroning of kings and resistance to monarchs they were also acting on jesuitical principles.[79] The comparison with the Civil War years also enabled the Tories to represent the Whigs as a threat to the rule of law. During the 1640s and 1650s, they repeatedly alleged, Dissenters and republicans had governed in the most arbitrary way: "We had lost our religion, laws, and liberties; and were reduced to a perfect condition of slavery," ruled over by "a mercenary army."[80] Should the Whigs succeed, arbitrary government and rule by a standing army were bound to follow.

What sort of popular purchase did Tory propaganda possess? It is often assumed that the Tory position was antipopulist, and in certain respects this is true. The Tories denied that the people were sovereign or had any right to call their rulers to account for misgovernment; they alleged that popular government would mean tyranny and anarchy; they accused the Whigs of wanting to level all social hierarchies.[81] One Royalist tract of 1685 asserted that "great harm has often been done by small contemptible creatures: no less hurt likewise does the contemptible multitude in a state, because there is a disparity in their understandings."[82] Or as a Tory cleric put it, in a sermon delivered on the anniversary of Charles I's "martyrdom " in 1681, "'tis not for every clownish peasant . . . [or] every pragmatical mechanic, rudely to censure his prince's actions."[83] Having said this, Tory propagandists did nevertheless try to appeal to popular sensibilities, primarily by emphasizing how badly the lower classes had fared under the Commonwealth, when trade was disrupted, the economy was depressed, and the common people were hit by heavy taxation (the excise and monthly assessments).[84] "We challenge all you, that are of the republican faction," one author wrote, "to shape us a form of government, wherein the people shall be exempt from payments, . . . [for] we never paid greater taxes, than when this monarchy was reduced to a commonwealth"; he went on to conclude that the people are "most oppressed under a republic." The Whig claim to be standing for the "good of the subject," therefore, was nothing else but "delusion."[85] The Tories further sought to appeal to the lower orders by representing the Whigs as enemies of traditional popular culture; they would seek to suppress "all sorts of public sports, exercises, and recreations that have long been in use"—such as wrestling, football, May games, Whitsun ales, morris dances, and bear baitings—"as having their original from times of paganism, or popery."[86]

Rhetoric by itself, however, could never have been enough. The Tories could not just claim they had a great respect for the rule of law, the Protestant religion, and the interests and well-being of the people; they also had to show it. In this regard it becomes important to consider the impact of the Tory reaction after 1681, sometimes considered a period that saw a drift toward royal absolutism. Parliament was not called again for the rest of the reign; a vigorous campaign was conducted against the enemies of the Crown; Whigs and their Nonconformist allies were persecuted in the courts; and those suspected of disloyalty were driven from local office. Yet for most of the period of the Tory reaction, strict care was taken to stick closely to the law. Indeed, Lord Chief Justice North advised the king to let the laws be "his offensive weapons."[87] The offensive weapons that the law provided were admittedly very powerful, as the ferocious crackdown on dissent after 1681 proves, but all that was happening was that the penal laws were being enforced very effectively. And although the attack on borough corporations may seem to be evidence of arbitrary interference by the center in the political complextion of local town governments, it has to be recognized that in many corporations Dissenters had intruded into local office (often in significant numbers) in direct violation of the Corporation Act of 1661. Moreover, the main aim of the purges carried out during Charles's last years was apparently to ensure that those responsible for law enforcement in the localities would be prepared to take legal action against the Whigs and Dissenters. In short, the government could justify its actions by claiming that all it was doing was using the full rigor of the law to protect the established Church of England from the threat of fanaticism.[88]

The government even made moves to try to protect the economic welfare of the lower orders. During the harsh winters of the early 1680s the king took care to arrange for the collection of special benevolences for the poor. But relief often worked in a discriminatory way. Nonconformists were denied parish poor relief, while fines levied on conventiclers were designated for the use of the poor who did come to church. By such means the government helped make come true their argument that if the lower orders remained loyal to the establishment in both church and state, they would be better off.[89]

It was not just what the government did but also the actions of the Whigs that made the Tory position seem so plausible. The tactics of the Whigs were indeed very similar to those used by the Parliamentarians in the early 1640s. The arguments were similar—exploiting fears about popery and arbitrary government, and of a popish plot—and the Whigs attempted, as had been done in 1640-42, to mobilize mass opposition to the government by encouraging petitions and demonstrations. It was the case, as the Tories alleged, that there was a close association between Whiggery and dissent. Many leading Whig politicians and propagandists were either Nonconformists themselves or sympathetic to dissent, as were many of their supporters in the streets, and the Whigs were very critical of the intolerance of the high-Anglican establishment and particularly of the bishops. The implication of the Whig position seemed to be that the people had the right to resist their rulers, and some radical Whigs did contemplate rebellion after the failure of the parliamentary Exclusion movement with the dissolution of the Oxford Parliament on 28 March 1681. There were various rumors of Whig plots, culminating in 1682 with Shaftesbury's Association (to resist the Duke of York should he become king) and the Rye House Plot in 1683. And, of course, there was a rebellion in the west in 1685 led by the Duke of Monmouth. Again, we can see that there was a sense in which the Tory arguments were true: the Whigs, or at least some of them, did represent a genuine threat to the existing government in church and state as by law established.

There is little doubt that Tory propaganda was effective in swinging public opinion back behind the Crown. Historians normally stress the Whigs' success in mobilizing the masses at this time, pointing to their monster petitions in favor of Parliament and the famous pope-burning processions of 17 November, held in the years from 1679 to 1681. But as the Exclusion Crisis progressed we see a definite rise in public support for the

Tories—as evidenced by loyal addresses and demonstrations. Much of this loyalist activity, I would argue, should be seen as a genuine reflection of Anglican-Royalist and anti-Nonconformist sentiment. Nevertheless, initially at least, it was the case that supporters of the Crown did much to encourage such manifestations of loyalist opinion. For example, if we look at the addresses in "abhorrence" of Whig petitions in 1680, we find that many of these were encouraged by a few energetic courtiers. In the spring of 1680 the Tory apprentices from the Strand planned to stage a Rump-burning procession for 29 May—the king's birthday and anniversary of his Restoration—in order to demonstrate their loyalty to the king and the established church, and it seems that the Tory propagandist Nathaniel Thompson might have had some role in encouraging this design. When the Duke of York returned to London from Scotland in the spring of 1682, there were a number of demonstrations on his behalf. Although some of the bonfires and festivities appear to have been encouraged by York's servants and captains of the guards, once the ball had started rolling, there were more and more public demonstrations of loyalty. Numerous loyal addresses were presented to the Crown in the years 1681-83, from all sorts of groups or political bodies (justices of the peace, grand juries, militia officers, borough corporations, and even apprentices), and though we have to be cautious about making generalizations, many appear to have been the product of local initiative. In 1681-82 we have evidence of a large number of loyalist demonstrations—pro-Charles II and the Duke of York, anti-Whig and Dissenter—in London and various other parts of the country, and most of these appear to have been organized "from below."[90]

It would be wrong to suggest that public opinion swung unanimously to the Tories; in fact, England became a bitterly divided society. Nevertheless, enough people rallied behind the Crown to discredit the Whig claim that they represented the voice of the people. In this sense, these public manifestations of loyalty served an important propaganda purpose for the Tories. Roger North, discussing the Whig petitioning campaign of 1680, observed, "It was noted that the confederacy of a few busy men makes a show of great numbers; because all join in one noise whilst honest men are silent." But "the little or no opposition, at first, to this handgathering trade did not conclude, as seemed, that the generality approved," and the fact that the most "conformable" people in England "detested it" was soon shown by the presentation of the abhorrences.[91] John Northleigh, writing in 1685, was able to claim that the bill of exclusion was not widely supported by the people: "The generality have for the most part protested against it in addresses declaring more the sense of the people, than a prevailing party in an House of Commons."[92] Nathaniel Thompson gave wide publicity in his newspaper, the *Loyal Protestant Intelligence*, to these loyal addresses. In May 1681 he was able to boast, "It does now appear that those petitions and addresses published in the names of several counties and corporations [i.e., Whig petitions] were mis-representatives, and not *Vox Populi*; for we now abound with addresses, letters and congratulations of a different nature."[93]

The question of the role played by the media in the revolutionary crises of the seventeenth century in England is a big one. I have only skimmed the surface here, leaving a number of areas untouched and no doubt begging many questions along the way. Any conclusions must necessarily be somewhat speculative. I have attempted to explore how propaganda worked by comparing the parliamentary effort to mobilize public opinion against the Crown on the eve of the Civil War with the successful counterpropaganda campaign launched by the Tories in the early 1680s. I have shown that it was important for propagandists to appeal to the middle ground, to commonly held values, yet at the same time to seek to redirect the middle ground, to make people believe that the holding of such values should lead them to support the propagandists' particular cause. This means that despite conservative posturing, propaganda could have radical implications. But overt radicalism might be counterproductive; the emergence of separatist religious groups that seemed to threaten the traditional order in church and society gave Royalist propagandists a certain leverage and enabled them to rally some support behind the Crown on the eve of the Civil War, and the increasingly explicit radicalism that emerged after the outbreak of war in 1642 (especially from the mid-1640s on) certainly caused a reaction in favor of the monarchy.

I have also stressed the need to look at the relationship between the arguments developed in propaganda and the course of events and to consider the plausibility of the positions developed by the protagonists in the debate. The actions of Charles I prior to 1642 were such as to convince people that the king could not be trusted; no matter how skillful Royalist propagandists might have been, the political ineptitude of the king was a serious disadvantage to their cause. In the early 1680s, however, there were enough factors working against the Whigs to enable the Tories to craft a successful counterattack. The memory of the experiences of the 1640s and 1650s, and the fact that the Whigs did seem to represent a radical challenge to church and state and to be encouraging popular resistance to the government which might result in another civil war, all helped forge a conservative reaction.

Another theme that has emerged from this study is the importance not only of winning over public opinion but also of being able to demonstrate that backing. This was an area where the royalist slipped down badly in 1641-42. It is true that there was a petitioning campaign in defense of episcopacy, but the actions of crowds—especially in London—conveyed the impression that the Crown had lost the support of the masses. Indeed, Charles I himself was convinced of this, and that was a major reason why he fled the capital. In the early 1680s the Tories were determined to show that the masses were not overwhelmingly on the side of the Whigs, and did their best to encourage manifestations of loyalty. Perhaps, therefore, it is worth expanding our definition of the media to include such things as petitions, addresses, public rituals, and demonstrations; during the Exclusion Crisis the actions "out-of-doors" of both Whig and Tory groupings served an important propaganda purpose in the sense that they helped propagate the particular political viewpoints of their respective sides.

Finally, we should reflect on the significance of the media revolution of the mid-seventeenth century, whether it had any lasting implications. There were attempts to reimpose censorship, first in the 1650s and then more successfully after the Restoration with the Licensing Act of 1662. The lapsing of this act in 1679, however, led to a renewed flurry of publishing activity, and even though the government still sought to control the media through the use of the common law of seditious libel, the experience of the 1640s had taught members of the governing elite the value of using the media in aid of their own cause. Although censorship was reimposed in 1685, the Licensing Act finally lapsed in 1695. As a result, political rivalries came to be fought out in the media during the great rage of parties at the end of the Stuart period. One of the most important lessons of England's century of revolution was surely the realization that one of the most important battles to be won was the struggle for the hearts and minds of the people.

NOTES

1. I am very grateful to my research assistant, Ethan Shagan of Brown University, for his help on the Civil War section of this essay. Many of the references and leads I owe to him. In addition, I have drawn on the work of a former student of mine from Cambridge University, Alice Donald, and her undergraduate thesis, "Religion in the Popular Prints, 1640-1649" (1987). I am also deeply thankful to the National Endowment for the Humanities for the award of a summer stipend, which helped fund the research I undertook for this study.

2. The best attempt to date is Anthony Fletcher, *The Outbreak of the English Civil War* (London, 1981), though its treatment of the media and propaganda is still rather limited.

3. Christopher Hill, *The World Turned Upside Down* (London, 1972); Brian Manning, *The English People and the English Revolution* (London, 1976). For criticisms, see John Morrill, *The Nature of the English Revolution* (London, 1993), chaps. 10, 18; J.C. Davis, *Fear, Myth, and History: The Ranters and the Historians* (Cambridge, 1985).

4. For attempts to assess the impact of the media and propaganda during the 1620s, see Richard Cust, "News and Politics in Early Seventeenth-Century England," *Past and Present* 112 (1986): 60-90; Thomas Cogswell, "The Politics of Propaganda: Charles I and the People in the 1620s," *Journal of British Studies* 29 (1990): 187-215.

5. See, e.g., David Underdown, *Revel, Riot, and Rebellion: Popular Politics and Culture in England, 1603-1660* (Oxford, 1985); Anthony Fletcher, *A County Community in Peace and War: Sussex 1600-1660* (London, 1975), chap. 4.

6. Eunice Cooper and Marie Jahoda, "The Evasion of Propaganda: How Prejudiced People Respond to Anti-Prejudice Propaganda," *Journal of Psychology* 23 (1947): 15-25.

7. Tim Harris, *London Crowds in the Reign of Charles II* (Cambridge, 1987).

8. David Cressy, *Literacy and the Social Order: Reading and Writing in Tudor and Stuart England* (Cambridge, 1980).

9. Keith Thomas, "The Meaning of Literacy in Early Modern England," in Gerd Bauman, ed., *The Written Word: Literacy in Transition* (Oxford, 1986), 101-3; Barry Reay, "The Context and Meaning of Popular Literacy: Some Evidence from Nineteenth-Century Rural England," *Past and Present* 131 (1991): 111-15.

10. Tessa Watt, *Cheap Print and Popular Piety, 1550-1640* (Cambridge, 1991); Tamsyn Mary Williams, "Polemical Prints of the English Revolution 1640-1660" (Ph.D. diss., Courtauld Institute, University of London, 1987), chaps. 3, 4; Harris, *London Crowds*, 28-29, 107-8; Cust, "News and Politics," 62-69; Steven Pincus, "'Coffee Politicians Does Create': Coffee Houses and Restoration Political Culture," *Journal of Modern History* (forthcoming).

11. [John Nalson], *The Complaint of Liberty and Property against Arbitrary Government* (London, 1681), 6.

12. *A Preamble with the Protestation made by the whole House of Commons the 3. of May 1641* (London, 1641).

13. *A Plea for the Parliament; or, XIV Considerations* (London, 1642), 7-8.

14. M. Dorothy George, *English Political Caricature to 1792* (Oxford, 1959), 18.

15. *A Description of the Passage of Thomas Late Earle of Strafford, over the River of Styx* (London, 1641), sig. A3.

16. George, *English Political Caricature*, 21 and pl. 4. Cf. A.H., *An Exact Legendary Compendiously Containing the Whole Life of Alderman Abel, the Maine Protector and Patentee for the Raising of Wines* (London, 1641); *The Projectors Down-Fall; or, Times Changeling* (London, 1642).

17. *Four Wonderful, Bloudy, and Dangerous Plots Discovered* (London, 1642).

18. Francis Mussell, *Good Newes For All True Hearted Subjects: Videlicet, The Parliament Goes On* (London, 1641).

19. *Great was Surnam'd Gregorie of Rome* (London, 1641); Williams, "Polemical Prints," 79; George, *English Political Caricature*, 21.

20. *A New Play Called Canterburie His Change of Diot* (London, 1641), sig. A2.

21. George, *English Political Caricature*, pl. 8; John Miller, *Religion in the Popular Prints, 1600-1832* (Cambridge, 1986), no. 7.

22. *The Arminian Nunnery* (London, 1641), 10.

23. Thomas Stirry, *A Rot Amongst the Bishops* (London, 1641), 9.

24. Benjamin Rudyerd, *The Speeches of Sir Benjamin Rudyerd in the High Court of Parliament* (London, 1641), 15, 17, 18.

25. Ibid., 6-8.

26. *Canterburies Dream* (London, 1641), sig. A3.

27. Rudyerd, *Speeches*, 16.

28. John Bastwick, *The Confession of the Faithfull Witnesse of Christ Mr John Bastwick* (London, 1641), sig. A3v.

29. *The True Character of an Untrue Bishop* (London, 1641), 2.

30. John Morrill, "The Religious Context of the English Civil War," in his *Nature of the English Revolution*, chap. 3 (esp. 58, 61).

31. [Robert Baillie], *Prelacie is Miserie* (London, 1641), 1.

32. *The Bishops Manifest; or, A Comparative Relation of Conformitie of the English Prelates to those treacherous and deceitful ones in the Reign of King Hen. the Eighth* (London, 1641), 7-8.

33. I owe this point to Alice Donald; see her "Religion in the Popular Prints," 27.

34. *Newes, True Newes, Laudable Newes, Court News, Country Newes* (London, 1642), 2, 7.

35. [Henry Parker], *Observations Upon Some of His Majesties late Answers and Expresses* (London, 1642), 41; Margaret Atwood Judson, "Henry Parker and the Theory of Parliamentary Sovereignty," in Carl Wittke, ed., *Essays in History and Political Theory in Honor of Charles Howard McIlwain* (Cambridge, Mass., 1936), 138-67; Michael Mendle, "The Ship Money Case, *The Case of Shipmony*, and the Development of Henry Parker's Parliamentary Absolutism," *Historical Journal* 32 (1989): 537-60.

36. Thomas Jordan, *Rules to Know a Royall King from a Disloyall Subject* (London, 1642); *A Declaration or Remonstrance of the Office of a Prince, and his Counsellors* (London, 1642).

37. William Ball, *A Caveat for Subjects, Moderating the Observator* (London, 1642), 16.

38. E[dward] B[rowne], *Rules for Kings, and Good Counsel for Subjects* (London, 1642), 2.

39. Conrad Russell, *The Causes of the English Civil War* (Oxford, 1990), chap. 6.

40. Charles I, *His Majesties Answer to the XIX Propositions of Both Houses of*

Parliament (London, 1642); C.C. Weston and J.R. Greenberg, *Subjects and Sovereigns: The Grand Controversy over Legal Sovereignty in Stuart England* (Cambridge, 1981), chap. 3; Michael Mendle, *Dangerous Positions: Mixed Government, the Estates of the Realm, and the Answer to the XIX Propositions* (University, Alabama, 1985).

41. *England's Absolute Monarchy . . . Composed out of these Kindes, Monarchy, Aristocracie, and Democracie* (London, 1642).

42. *Animadversions upon those Notes which the Late Observator Hath Published* (London, 1642), 2, 5.

43. Charles I, *His Majesties Declaration, To all His loving Subjects, Published with the Advice of His Privie Councell* (London, 1641), 5.

44. [John Taylor], *The Brownists Synagogue* (London, 1641), 2.

45. [John Taylor], *The Anatomy of the Separatists* (London, 1642), 4.

46. Ibid., 2.

47. [Henry Peachum], *Square-Caps turned into Roundheads* (London, 1642).

48. [John Taylor], *Religion's Lotterie; or, the Churches Amazement* (London, 1642).

49. George Carleton, *Bishop Carleton's Testimonie Concerning the Presbyterian Discipline in the Low-Countries, and Episcopall Government Here in England* (London, 1642), 4.

50. *Animadversions upon those Notes*, p. 4.

51. G.E. Aylmer, "Collective Mentalities in Mid Seventeenth-Century England: II. Royalist Attitudes," *Transactions of the Royal Historical Society*, 5th ser. 37 (1987): 12.

52. John Taylor, *Mad Fashions, Od Fashions, All Out of Fashions; or, the Emblem of these Distracted Times* (London, 1642), sig. A4.

53. [John Taylor], *The Hellish Parliament, Being a Counter-Parliament to this in England* (London, 1641), title page.

54. [Taylor], *The Brownists Synagogue*, 1.

55. William Stampe, *A Sermon Preached Before His Majestie at Christ-Church in Oxford, on the 18. of April 1643* (Oxford, 1643), 9.

56. Joyce Malcolm, *Caesar's Due: Loyalty and King Charles, 1642-1646* (London, 1983).

57. Fletcher, *Outbreak*, chap. 9; Russell, *Causes*, esp. chap. 6.

58. Underdown, *Revel, Riot and Rebellion*.

59. *Plea for the Parliament; or, XIV Considerations* (London, 1642), 3.

60. Russell, *Causes*, 209-11.

61. *A Dialogue or Discourse between a Parliament-Man and a Roman Catholic* (London, 1641).

62. John Morrill, *The Revolt of the Provinces* (1976; London, 1980), 40.

63. Jonathan Scott, *Algernon Sidney and the Restoration Crisis, 1677-83* (Cambridge, 1991), chaps. 1, 2.

64. Tim Harris, *Politics under the Later Stuarts* (London, 1993), chap. 4.

65. Mark Goldie, "The Political Thought of the Anglican Revolution," in Robert Beddard, ed., *The Revolutions of 1688* (Oxford, 1991), 106; H.T. Dickinson, *Liberty and Property: Political Ideology in Eighteenth-Century Britain* (London, 1977), 14, 26.

66. Steven N. Zwicker, *Politics and Language in Dryden's Poetry: The Arts of Disguise* (Princeton, N.J., 1984), 10, 88.

67. T.L., *True Notion* (London, 1681), 26-27 (misnumbered pp. 18-19). This argument is developed in greater length in Tim Harris, "Tories and the Rule of Law in the Reign of Charles II," *Seventeenth Century* 8 (1993): 9-27.

68. See Alan Craig Houston, *Algernon Sidney and the Republican Heritage in England and America* (Princeton, N.J., 1991), chap. 4.

69. [John Dryden], *Absalom and Achitophel* (London, 1681), in *Poems on Affairs of State*, ed. G.F. de Forest Lord et al., 7 vols. (New Haven, Conn., 1963-75), 2:468, 491-92. Cf. Steven N. Zwicker, *Lines of Authority: Politics and English Literary Culture, 1649-1689* (Ithaca, N.J., 1993), 135-37, 142.

70. Charles II, *His Majesties Declaration To All His Loving Subjects, Touching the Causes and Reasons that Moved Him to Dissolve the Two Last Parliaments* (London, 1681), 9.

71. *A Letter on the Subject of the Succession* (London, 1679), 3, 8.

72. B. T[horogood], *Captain Thorogood His Opinion of the Point of Succession* [London, 1680], 7, 9. Cf. *Fiat Justitia* (London, 1679), 2; [Matthew Rider], *The Power of Parliaments in the Case of Succession* (London, 1680), 42; Edmund Bohun, *The Third and Last Part of the Address to the Free-Men and Free-Holders of the Nation* (London, 1683), 66.

73. *Advice to the Men of Shaftesbury* (London, 1681), 2.

74. J.P. Kenyon, *The Stuart Constitution, 1603-1688* (Cambridge, 1966), 471-74 (doc. 135).

75. T[horogood], *Captain Thorogood His Opinion*, 3, 6. Cf. W.W., *Antidotum Britannicum* (London, 1681), 66.

76. [Rider], *Power of Parliaments*, 3-4.

77. W.W., *Antidotum Britannicum*, 6-7, 34.

78. L.S., *A Letter to a Noble Peer of the Realm* (London, 1681), 2.

79. *Advice to the Men of Shaftesbury*, 1-2; *Fiat Justitia*, 2. This is a theme I have discussed at length elsewhere: see Harris, *London Crowds*, 140-44; Harris, *Politics under the Later Stuarts*, 98-99, 122.

80. *The Way of Peace* (London 1680), 9. Cf. [Sir Roger L'Estrange], *Tyranny and Popery Lording it over the Consciences, Lives, Liberties, and Estates of Both King and People* (London, 1678); Sir Roger L'Estrange, *The Character of a Papist in Masquerade* (London, 1681); [John Nalson], *The Character of a Rebellion* (London, 1681); [Nalson], *Complaint of Liberty*.

81. Harris, *London Crowds*, 136-38.

82. *The Misleading of the Common People by False Notions* (London, 1685), 3.

83. Samuel Crossman, *Two Sermons* (London, 1681), 25-26.

84. [L'Estrange], *Tyranny and Popery*, 69, 83.

85. *Misleading of the Common People*, 15, 20.

86. [L'Estrange], *Tyranny and Popery*, 93.

87. Roger North, *Lives of the Norths*, 3 vols. (London, 1826), 2:80.

88. Ibid., 2:14-15; Roger North, *Examen* (London, 1740), 624-25; John Miller, "Britain," in John Miller, ed., *Absolutism in Seventeenth-Century Europe* (New York, 1990), 211; R.G. Pickavance, "The English Boroughs and the King's Gov-

ernment: A Study of the Tory Reaction of 1681-1685" (Ph.D. diss., Oxford University, 1976).

89. Harris, *London Crowds*, 209-11.

90. Ibid., chap. 7; Harris, *Politics under the Later Stuarts*, chap. 4; Tim Harris, "Party Turns? or, Whigs and Tories Get Off Scott Free," *Albion* 25 (1993): 581-90.

91. North, *Examen*, 544.

92. John Northleigh, *The Triumph of our Monarchy* (London, 1685), 393, Cf. *Misleading of the Common People*, 7, 25.

93. *Loyal Protestant Intelligence*, no. 19, 10 May 1681.

5

The Enticements of Change and America's Enlightenment Journalism

JEFFERY A. SMITH

The revolutions of eighteenth-century America and France were fostered by real grievances and persuasive political theories. Yet discontent and philosophy, even if combined in convincing rhetoric, do not necessarily produce radical political change. Populations can endure considerable hardship and humiliation without revolting. In the years between 1765 and 1800 Americans did not endure a costly and precarious movement from British monarchy to Jeffersonian democracy only to alleviate consitutional anxieties or to oppose the threat of despotism.[1] Rebellion becomes a dynamic force as it acquires—however gradually—moral and emotive dimensions that propel people beyond considerations of their own immediate security. Such sentiments may not represent righteous anger or a psychological state[2] so much as they involve positive obligations and aspirations regarded as sacred or at least highly meaningful.[3]

Popular upheavals may be difficult to comprehend with any particularized set of facts, but the facts of imagination, assessments of what is possible, must weigh heavily.[4] Breaking with the past becomes a more inviting prospect if something alluring beckons. Revolutionary communication creates not simply frustrating or frightening images but also eloquent, enticing ones. In the eighteenth century the American press not only performed the repetitive task of spreading indignation but also knowingly carried out the more affirmative functions of reassurance and inspiration.

Newspapers in particular forged perceptions that the imagined new order was both attractive and attainable.

For early Americans, the primary printed sources of education in civic zeal included the Bible and the classics of Rome and Greece. The country's foremost Enlightenment moralists, Thomas Jefferson and Benjamin Franklin, attested to the impact of reading religious and philosophical texts, particularly those of Christ and Socrates.[5] Such writings sought both to excite elevated thoughts in readers and to infuse a spirit of action. Americans also read works of Enlightenment philosophy, collections of republican political theory such as *Cato's Letters*, and the kind of nationalistic poetry written by Philip Freneau and Joel Barlow. Yet although books and other writings of a more timeless nature may have helped shape fundamental beliefs, the journalism of the day had the potential to operate more directly in the volatile realm of immediate feelings about public affairs. Timely news and opinion kept the political movements of the revolutionary period alive on a day-to-day basis.

The presence of a largely unfettered press was still a fairly new and unusual phenomenon in the eighteenth century, and respectful attention was paid to its perceived ability to mobilize public opinion by involving readers emotionally. News reports and commentaries on British rule of the colonies were capable of assigning responsibility for problems to individual leaders and of gaining the attention of the politically inert with stories that might sensationalize and oversimplify but also raised the stakes in the handling of issues.[6] Thomas Jefferson often penned exuberant statements about the role of the press in animating the citizenry, making one well-known remark that he would prefer newspapers without government to government without newspapers.[7] Even the staid George Washington acknowledged having "an high idea of the utility of periodical Publications." In a letter written to printer Mathew Carey, Washington declared, "I consider such easy vehicles of knowledge, more happily calculated than any other, to preserve the liberty, stimulate the industry and meliorate the morals of an enlightened and free People."[8] Discussing the role of journalism in achieving independence, Franklin was able to observe:

> The ancient Roman and Greek orators could only speak to the number of citizens capable of being assembled within the reach of their voice. Their *writings* had little effect, because the bulk of people could not read. Now by the press we can speak to nations; and good books and well written

pamphlets have great and general influence. The facility, with which the same truths may be repeatedly enforced by placing them daily in different lights in *newspapers*, which are everywhere read, gives a great chance of establishing them. And we now find, that it is not only right to strike while the iron is hot, but that it may be very practicable to heat it by continually striking.[9]

If intended for a particular moment, an impassioned pamphlet like *Common Sense* might attract sudden, widespread attention,[10] but in general it was the publishing of newspapers that regularly kindled the fires of politics. Pamphlets might be lengthier than newspaper writings but were not as well suited to immediate interchange on public issues or the repetition and reinforcement of messages intended to evoke popular emotion. During the Revolutionary War the patriot press sought to involve readers in the military effort by amplifying calls for sacrifice and stressing the need for unity. Some newspapers adopted nationalistic emblems for their nameplates, and most gave encouraging accounts of the fighting when possible. Outrage was engendered with atrocity stories that accused the British of mistreatment of the dead and crimes against the living, such as poisoning medicine left behind at the evacuation of Boston.[11] Sarcastic humor was also not unknown, as one patriot paper demonstrated when it reported that James Rivington, a loyalist editor and bookseller driven from New York by a mob in 1775, had been appointed "Cob-Web Sweeper of his Majesty's Library."[12]

Loyalists meanwhile attempted to undermine patriot hopes. Upon his return to British-occupied New York in 1777, Rivington, an editor determined to deflate his opponents, used his *Royal Gazette* to deny "a thousand tales concerning the cruelty of the British army"[13] and to spread some tales himself. One was to report that the French populace—facing economic problems because of the war—had turned on Franklin and forced him to take refuge in Versailles.[14] Another was to publish a series of forged letters purportedly by George Washington, which indicated that the general loved his king and was deciding, like other Americans, that the cause had been misguided from the start.[15] In a number of stories Rivington also used the loyalist theme that the colonies, formerly safe and happy in the British empire, were headed for government by Franklin and other Americans who would give up Protestant religion and rule the country for the French and the pope. According to one *Royal Gazette* account in 1778, the capture of a French vessel had revealed dispatches to Comte d'Estaing with instructions to proclaim Louis XVI in every province and to take possession of New England as security for debt to France. The cargo, the report said, consisted of 50,000 mass books, 200 racks and wheels, 3,000,000 consecrated wafers, 15,000 crucifixes, 70,000 rosaries, 200,000 wooden shoes, five chests of paint for women's faces, and 10,000 boxes of pills for venereal disease.[16]

Recognizing that doubts about the alliance with France and various wartime controversies had the potential to undermine morale, American and French leaders orchestrated favorable press treatment on both sides of the Atlantic. In some cases, works of revolutionary fervor were considered essential enough to be secured with subsidies. The most prominent propagandist was Thomas Paine, who sought and obtained payments from both the French and American governments for his newspaper and pamphlet writings, some of which were submitted for advance approval by officials.[17] Paine, of course, was exceptionally gifted as a writer of soaring prose. For the most part, the boosting of public morale was left to printers and their contributors, who portrayed the revolution as an epochal struggle and the future prospects of the nation as glorious. Announcing publication of his *Freeman's Journal* in 1781, for instance, Philadelphia editor Francis Bailey said that liberty "fairly promises to resume its pristine majesty here" after sickening under the trammels of despotism in the Old World. He, like contemporary patriot historians of the period,[18] projected an image of the states being "exalted into empire" and achieving a political system "where every freeman is himself a ruler."[19]

Revolutionary optimism waned after the war, however, as the former colonies encountered considerable difficulties in governing themselves, particularly in matters of monetary and fiscal policy. In 1787 delegates from the states met in Philadelphia to ponder remedies. When it was presented to the public, the Constitution proposed as the answer to the national ills appeared to have a roughly equal number of supporters and detractors, and the two sides moved quickly to praise and denounce the document in the newspapers. Within two months of the convention's adjournment, "Brutus, Junior," a critic of what he regarded as the "artful and ambitious men, who are determined to cram this government down the throats of the people," summarized for readers of the *New York Journal*, not too inaccurately, the two emotionally powerful arguments that were being exploited by the Federalists in arguing for the plan in the press:

1st. That the men who formed it, were wise and experienced; that they were an illustrious band of patriots, and had the happiness of their country at heart; that they were four months deliberating on the subject, and therefore, it must be a perfect system.

2d. That if the system be not received, this country will be without any government, and of consequence, will be reduced to a state of anarchy and confusion, and involved in bloodshed and carnage; and in the end, a government will be imposed upon us, not the result of reason and reflection, but of force and usurpation.[20]

Following the anti-Federalist tack of predicting oligarchy and a loss of freedoms if ratification did occur, "Brutus, Junior," warned the public that many of the delegates were aristocrats maneuvering for personal gain. Such ambitious individuals represented the true danger for the republic, he said, adding that the country was at peace, property was protected, and problems of the economy could be addressed without a rash adoption of a new government. One of the harsher opponents of the Constitution, "Centinel," similarly wrote in Philadelphia's *Independent Gazetteer* that such an audacious conspiracy against liberty as the political structure being suggested was folly "in this enlightened age." The country, in fact, was exhibiting "a lively picture of emulation, industry and happiness" to the world.[21]

For a nation that had already witnessed Shays's Rebellion and contended ineffectually with postwar depression, neither the scare-tactic suggestion that leaders like Washington were the threat nor a pleasant portrait of the present may have been realistic. Unlike the anti-Federalists, supporters of ratification were offering a specific solution for the future, which they made every effort to defend in the press.[22] The thrust of the *Federalist* and other newspaper arguments in favor of the Constitution was that the new system would work.[23] Independence and ratification of the Constitution were steps into the unknown, and to a generally receptive public journalists offered reasons to transform their political existence.

Although they took pride in their agitation against Britain, American editors of the late eighteenth century insisted that it was part of their professional mission to go beyond finding fault with the past and to participate in the process of finding the revolutionary future. As they introduced their publications to readers, editors frequently maintained that they were intending to work for the "public good"[24] and, in signing their inaugural pieces, referred to themselves as the public's "humble" or "obedient" servants.[25] Starting his *New York Journal* after the war, Francis Childs stated that he wanted to print essays "tending to promote the good of society, and independence of our new republic, just recovering itself from the stabs and wounds of its merciless enemies." Much of the paper, he said, would be devoted to "inspiring the people with a high and commanding sense of their importance and invaluable birth-rights."[26]

Printer-publishers may have been laboring entrepreneurs, but many said they were performing a public service by making their newspapers instruments of egalitarian enlightenment.[27] If their rhetoric can be any measure, journalists believed they were involved in a business of transcendent importance, a business that had a larger purpose than merely providing prompt accounts of unseen and often distant events. In the first issue of his *New Bedford Medley* in 1792, for example, John Spooner said he would attempt "to scatter the rays of Knowledge, of Morality, and of Refinement, among the People."[28] Those who were moved by the revolutionary ardor of the time also spoke of keeping autocracy at bay in the United States and hoping for its downfall elsewhere.[29] Philip Freneau told the readers of his *Jersey Chronicle* in 1795 that he hoped to be contributing to public knowledge at a time "when the great family of mankind are evidently making their egress from the dark shadows of despotism which have so long enveloped them." He wrote: "NEVER was there a more interesting period than the present, nor ever was there a time within the reach of history when mankind have been so generally united in attending to the cultivation of the mind, examining into the natural and political rights of nations, and emancipating themselves from those shackles of despotism which have so long impeded the happiness of the human species, and rendered the rights of the many subservient to the interests of the few."[30]

Such rebellious sentiments were particularly strong among the eighteen British and Irish radical journalists who, facing repression of the democratic ferment inspired by the American and French revolutions, emigrated to the United States and eventually formed the backbone of the Jeffersonian Republican press.[31] The first to arrive, John Miller, declared as he began his *South-Carolina Gazette* that the people of his state had achieved fame in Europe for their defense of freedom and that America would be a kind refuge for the persecuted of the Old World. The editor expressed a hope that the country could act with "one mind and one heart" and that "the only contention will be who shall most zealously promote the interest and glory of the Commonwealth." He would be truly dedicated, he said, to advancing "in every way, the liberty and the happiness of the people."[32]

Editors of the 1790s often pledged themselves to invigorating the minds of readers with useful information and with essays on a multitude of topics. They touted the freshness of their news, the quality of their paper and type, and the availability of their job printing, but many introduced their newspapers by expressing a sense of wonder at the ability of the press to diffuse knowledge affordably to the general public. "Politicians, divines, farmers, mechanics, philosophers, civilians, moralists, speculators, poets, newsmongers and loungers," promised Charles Holt in his *New London Bee*, "shall all have their inclinations studied, [that is, if they take the paper] and at least in some degree gratified." Holt, a Republican editor in a mostly Federalist state, gave typical assurances that his paper would have news from distant parts of the world and information on manufacturing and agriculture in the United States, all of which could be "read by your quiet fireside" and would "furnish your children with a vehicle of instruction that is sought after and read with greater avidity than all the schoolbooks in the universe."[33] If journalism could arouse the people to fight for a new form of politics, it seemed, then the press could surely accomplish the relatively mundane task of securing the revolution by educating citizens for self-government.

At a time when the amount of reading material was quite limited for most people, newspapers did provide much of the intellectual stimulus available in eighteenth-century America. "In no Country on earth, not even in Great-Britain," said a *Philadelphia Gazette* essay in 1794, "are Newspapers so generally circulated among the body of the people, as in America."[34] Space in newspapers was severely limited by income and technology, however, and, although not as costly as magazines, they were not inexpensive.[35] Frequently plagued by unpaid bills,[36] newspapers resorted to discounts of various kinds and allowed barter payments. The *New London Bee*, for instance, offered to accept anything *"eatable, drinkable, wearable, burnable,* or *saleable"* from those who had difficulty paying for a subscription.[37]

The reality was that often newspapers could publish only about two pages of editorial matter per issue, usually weekly or daily, and that they had to be highly selective about what they actually printed. As a rural Massachusetts paper acknowledged, it was difficult "to provide a dish for every different palate."[38] Encouraged by his grandfather Benjamin Franklin to establish a newspaper that would give special attention to the arts and sciences, Benjamin Franklin Bache asked the readers of his *Philadelphia General Advertiser, and Political, Commercial, Agricultural and Literary Journal* to be patient if they did not like everything he published. "What will interest one person may be useless or unintelligible to another," he wrote. All he could do, Bache said, was to try "to offer to the public whatever he imagines may prove of greatest and most general utility, and unite the greatest number of interests."[39]

Despite their aspirations of providing what the editors of the *Hartford Gazette* called "a variety of useful and entertaining Essays" in an "enlightened period,"[40] newspaper publishers in practice gave most of their attention to politics, a topic of general interest. Political writings, of course, could be divisive and defamatory in a way that might prove troubling to those who were envisioning for the future a glorious, unified republic. Early American editors routinely made statements professing their impartiality and abhorrence of attacks on private character, policies that were consistent with the emphasis on political independence in republican theory and logical in view of the threat of personal libel suits. But such professional niceties were often ignored in the heat of battle.[41] During the last years of his life, in his memoirs, his letters, and the press, Benjamin Franklin decried partisan invective in the nation's journalism.[42] In the part of his autobiography written in 1788, he stated that he had attempted to make his *Poor Richard's Almanack* and *Pennsylvania Gazette* vehicles of "Instruction" for the common people. "In the Conduct of my Newspaper I carefully excluded all Libelling and Personal Abuse, which of late Years [has] become so disgraceful to our Country," he said.[43] Libertarians such as Franklin, Jefferson, and Madison took the position that individuals should be able to sue for damage to reputation, but they opposed prosecutions for criticism of government.[44]

Most of the revolutionary-era state constitutions as well as the First Amendment to the federal Constitution, ratified in 1791, gave fundamental protection for printing freely on public affairs.[45] Nevertheless, journalists involved in the political debates of the final decades of the eighteenth century were sometimes threatened, boycotted, and mobbed for their aggressiveness in public controversy.[46] Still, there were incentives to be partisan; one was the patronage which could come in such forms as government printing or postmasterships if a printer made a political commitment.[47] A second, however, was personal conviction about what was right for the country. The level of militancy that printer-publishers acquired by the end of the century—as they took sides in the ideological conflicts of the Federalists and Jeffersonian Republicans—was evident in newspapers such as Benjamin Franklin Bache's *General Advertiser.* Bache admitted that his Republican diatribes and vilifications of Washington were making enemies: "The editor, however, never will shrink from what he conceives his duty," he wrote of himself. "Public men are all amenable to the tribunal of the press in a free state; the greater, indeed, their trust, the more responsible are they."[48] The editor of the *New York Register of the Times* also spoke of a free press as bringing "public men and public measures" before the "tribunal" of the people. "Much good has already been produced, and much more may be expected, from periodical and newspaper publications," the paper said. "Tyrants and Princes, after banquetting for ages on the grave of public happiness, tremble at the light that is bursting around them."[49]

Accepting arguments about the importance of diffusing information—particularly that of a political nature—in a self-governing nation, Congress in 1792 set low postal rates for newspapers and allowed editors to continue exchanging their publications among themselves free of charge, a traditional practice that made it easier to gather news from distant points. Yet even the low postal rates—one cent for the first mile and a half-cent more thereafter—were regarded as too high by a number of prominent officials, including President Washington, who in 1796 wrote his Farewell Address for the newspapers rather than for oral delivery. Federalists saw the cheap circulation of newspapers across the country as promoting nationalism, party unity, and a strong central government. Republicans such as James Madison argued that any postal charge amounted to a "tax" that would keep the public ignorant of misconduct in politics. Magazines (which were considered less important in public affairs) and pamphlets cost as much to mail as letters until the 1794 postal act allowed both to receive preferential rates. Magazines, however, were still charged somewhat more than newspapers and, as bulkier items, did not have to be accepted into the mail at all if they were inconvenient for a local postmaster.[50]

By the 1790s, then, newspaper editors could see themselves as occupying positions of extraordinary influence in society and their publications as especially valuable in the task of informing the public. "Newspapers, from their cheapness, and the frequency and rapidity of their circulation, may, in America, assume an eminent rank in the catalogue of *useful* publications," said an essay in the *Philadelphia Gazette*, "They, in a great degree, supersede the use of Magazines and Pamphlets."[51] The medium's strengths, however, could also be viewed as related to its shortcomings. A contributor to the *Philadelphia General Advertiser*, "A French Citizen of the United States," remarked that short, seemingly unimportant newspaper paragraphs "work much more surely and effectually upon the public opinion, than the most elaborate essays or pamphlets, because they are much better suited to the indolent disposition of the greatest part of mankind, who hate the trouble of thinking." The correspondent explained that readers weren't inclined to follow a "chain of arguments, observations and deductions" and warned that they could be manipulated by a small number of individuals whose repeated and varied writings could "appear to be the echoes of the popular voice."[52]

The *General Advertiser*'s proprietor did not see the same potential for the public to be deluded. Responding to another contributor who complained that too much attention was being given to newspapers and too little to books, Benjamin Franklin Bache articulated a defense for the editor's role. Few people had time to read and analyze lengthy works, he contended, but newspapers amply and conveniently took their place. A "free and original discussion of political subjects in newspapers," he said, was "as likely to hit upon the TRUTH" since it would be conducted without "a previous bias from the opinions of others" including ancient authors whose works were "replete with erroneous ideas" about political science and the happiness of humanity. The American Revolution, Bache said, was brought about by people *"thinking for themselves"* rather than analyzing books. In an editorial published in 1792 Bache said that the world had several examples of enlightened nations—America, France, and England—and that experience would show which of the three forms of government would prove to be the best means of promoting public liberty and happiness.[53]

If newspapers had the capacity to allow a fresh public interplay of ideas on societal problems, then journalistic integrity was a matter of some significance. "To conduct a Newspaper properly in a country where they have so great an effect, is certainly no trifling task," said an address to readers of the Newport (Rhode Island) *Companion.* "A suppression, or partial detail of important facts; an exaggeration, or even false colouring of them, may give a wrong bias to the public mind, and involve pernicious consequences."[54] In fact, despite its many claims of impartiality and serious purpose, the newspaper press of the revolutionary era displayed partisanship and accelerated thought in ways that altered the relationships and rhythms of public deliberation. Large numbers of citizens simultaneously encountered politics and, as never before, were invited to evaluate present realities and form their expectations for the future.[55] In articulating their positions on the revolution, the Constitution, and the Federalist and Republican programs of the 1790s, journalists broke through practical constraints and professional norms to advance powerful ideals and help leaders organize support. Between 1765 and 1800, not only did ideas of what was possible for the country gradually come into focus but choices could be made with what appeared to be a legitimate foundation in public opinion, even if the newspapers revealed the divisions that existed.

Accordingly, visionary fervor flared up less intensely than in France, where a free press burst into being with bewildering force and was soon suppressed.[56] With the collapse of the *ancien régime* and the forced attempts to fabricate liberty, equality, and fraternity, the French Revolution employed mass ritual, mass execution, and mass communication to obliterate the past, but it struggled fitfully with the future.[57] With little experience in legislative deliberation and an inadequate level of consensus on the value of fundamental liberties, the nation soon reverted to autocracy.

In contrast, though American leaders such as Franklin and Madison sought change, they were seasoned politicians who had few illusions about trusting either the people or their rulers.[58] During the late eighteenth century, as they worked out the course the nation would take, the public[59] and the political elite supported a conception of freedom of the press which the Continental Congress described as allowing the "diffusion of liberal sentiments" and the "ready communication of thoughts" among citizens.[60] The revolutionary generation used newspapers and other means of communication to carry on a relatively long, free, and individualistic tradition of open political debate. Knowledge of the limits of human reason and cooperation, much of it obtained through battles in the press, brought a degree of caution and compromise to the formation of the United States Constitution; but a nation of readers and writers, aspiring to make a better world, learned enough about what they wanted and how to get it to bring about lasting change.

NOTES

1. For the view that the American Revolution was "above all else an ideological, constitutional, political struggle" and that at its heart was a "fear of a comprehensive conspiracy against liberty," see Bernard Bailyn, *The Ideological Origins of the American Revolution* (Cambridge, Mass., 1967), vi, ix.

2. Taking the position that the American revolutionaries were driven by concepts such as "virtue," "corruption," "liberty," and "equality," Gordon Wood has insisted on a need for "working through the ideas." He has argued that American rhetoric was always "psychologically true" even if it was not "for the most part factually true" ("Rhetoric and Reality in the American Revolution," *William and Mary Quarterly*, 3d ser., 23 [January 1966]: 31).

3. See James H. Billington, *Fire in the Minds of Men: Origins of the Revolutionary Faith* (New York, 1980).

4. A top consultant in the Nixon, Reagan, and Bush presidential campaigns has maintained that facts provide the information while emotion provides the interpretation and that when "emotion is positive and genuine, there is no more constructive and powerful force of persuasion." See Roger Ailes, *You Are the Message: Secrets of the Master Communicators* (Homewood, Ill., 1988), 76, 79. Studies have indicated that information gained through communication often does not affect attitudes and that opinion change is more likely when explicit conclusions are drawn for the audience in persuasive messages. Fear ap-

peals seem to be most effective when coupled with specific recommendations for action. See Herbert H. Hyman and Paul B. Sheatsley, "Some Reasons Why Information Campaigns Fail," *Public Opinion Quarterly* 11 (Fall 1947): 412-23; Harold Mendelsohn, "Some Reasons Why Information Campaigns Can Succeed," *Public Opinion Quarterly* 37 (Spring 1973): 50-61; Marvin Karlins and Herbert I. Abelson, *Persuasion: How Opinions and Attitudes Are Changed*, 2d ed. (New York, 1970), 9-14, 33-34.

5. Charles B. Sanford, *Thomas Jefferson and His Library* (Hamden, Conn., 1977), 115-43; *The Autobiography of Benjamin Franklin: A Genetic Text*, ed. J.A. Leo Lemay and P.M. Zall (Knoxville; 1981), 10-17, 35-36, 80. Although having "some Doubts" about Christ's divinity, Franklin thought "the System of Morals and his Religion, as he left them to us, the best the World ever saw or is likely to see" (Benjamin Franklin to Ezra Stiles, 9 March 1790, in *The Writings of Benjamin Franklin*, ed. Albert H. Smyth [New York, 1905-7], 10:84).

6. A case for the importance of detailed and dramatic newspaper allegations of British corruption is made in Thomas C. Leonard, *The Power of the Press: The Birth of American Political Reporting* (New York, 1986), 33-53. See also Arthur M. Schlesinger, *Prelude to Independence: The Newspaper War on Britain, 1764-1776* (New York, 1958). For assessments of how the modern press can operate in such ways, see Doris A. Graber, *Processing the News: How People Tame the Information Tide*, 2d ed. (New York, 1988); Shanto Iyengar and Donald R. Kinder, *News That Matters* (Chicago, 1987).

7. Thomas Jefferson to Edward Carrington, 16 Jan. 1787, in *The Papers of Thomas Jefferson*, ed. Julian P. Boyd et al. (Princeton, N.J., 1950-). See Frank L. Mott, *Jefferson and the Press* (Baton Rouge, La., 1943).

8. George Washington to Mathew Carey, 25 June 1788, in *The Writings of George Washington*, ed. John C. Fitzpatrick (Washington, D.C., 1931-44), 30:7-8. This letter was quoted in the *Providence Journal*, 2 Jan. 1799.

9. Benjamin Franklin to Richard Price, 13 June 1782, in *The Writings of Benjamin Franklin*, 8:457.

10. Within three months of its publication, Paine was able to estimate that his pamphlet had sold 120,000 copies; see Richard Gimbel, *Thomas Paine: A Bibliographical Check List of Common Sense with an Account of Its Publication* (New Haven, Conn., 1956), 57. See also Thomas R. Adams, *American Independence, the Growth of an Idea: A Bibliographical Study of the American Political Pamphlets Printed between 1764 and 1776 Dealing with the Dispute between Britain and Her Colonies* (Austin, Tex., and New Haven, Conn., 1980).

11. See, e.g., *New York Constitutional Gazette*, 23 Sept. 1775, 24 April 1776.

12. Ibid., 4 May 1776. See Dwight L. Teeter, Jr., "'King' Sears, the Mob, and Freedom of the Press in New York, 1765-76," *Journalism Quarterly* 41 (Autumn 1964): 539-44.

13. *New York Royal Gazette*, 21 Oct. 1778.

14. Ibid., 23 Dec. 1778.

15. *The Spurious Letters Attributed to Washington*, ed. Worthington C. Ford (Brooklyn, N.Y., 1889).

16. *New York Royal Gazette*, 17 Oct. 1778; see also 31 Oct. 1778, and 6 Jan. 1779.

17. William C. Stinchcombe, *The American and the French Alliance* (Syracuse; N.Y., 1969), 118-32; Eric Foner, *Tom Paine and Revolutionary America* (New York, 1976), 139, 189, 192, 197. For the influence exerted on one international newspaper by the French and Americans, see Jeremy D. Popkin, *News and Politics in the Age of Revolution: Jean Luzac's* "Gazette de Leyde" (Ithaca, N.Y., 1989). For examples of ridicule aimed at the American-French alliance, see Michael Wynn Jones, *The Cartoon History of the American Revolution* (London, 1977), 32, 72, 94, 134, 158, 180, 183.

18. For the views of patriot historians on the emergence of the new nation, see Lester H. Cohen, *The Revolutionary Histories: Contemporary Narratives of the American Revolution* (Ithaca, N.Y., 1980).

19. *Philadelphia Freeman's Journal*, 25 April 1781.

20. *New-York Journal and Weekly Register*, 8 Nov. 1787. On the role of the press, see Robert Allen Rutland, "The First Great Newspaper Debate: The Constitutional Crisis of 1787-88," *Proceedings of the American Antiquarian Society* 97 (1987): 43-58. On the range of opinion and the narrow margins that secured ratification in key states, see Alfred F. Young, "The Framers of the Constitution and the 'Genius' of the People," *Radical History Review* 42 (Sept. 1988): 8-18.

21. *New York Journal and Weekly Register*, 8 Nov. 1787; *Philadelphia Independent Gazetteer*, 2 Jan. 1788.

22. On the Anti-Federalists having a philosophy that was primarily one of the limitations on power and lacked a vision of national government, see Cecelia M. Kenyon, "Men of Little Faith: The Anti-Federalists on the Nature of Representative Government," in Jack P. Greene, ed., *The Reinterpretation of the American Revolution, 1763-1789* (New York, 1968), 526-66.

23. On the efforts to promote the results of the convention before they were even known to the public, see John K. Alexander, *The Selling of the Constitutional Convention: A History of News Coverage* (Madison, Wis., 1990).

24. See, e.g., *Salem Mercury*, 4 Oct. 1786; *Philadelphia General Advertiser*, 1 Oct. 1790; *Baltimore Evening Post*, 13 July 1792; *Stonington (Conn.) Journal of the Times*, 10 Oct. 1798. Statements here and in following paragraphs are based on an examination of eighty introductory essays from eighteenth-century newspapers.

25. See, e.g., *Providence American Journal*, 18 March 1779; *[Charleston] South-Carolina Gazette*, 22 March 1783; *[New York] Independent Journal*, 17 Nov. 1783; *[Charlestown, Mass.] American Recorder*, 9 Dec. 1785; *[Rutland] Herald of Vermont*, 25 June 1792; *Baltimore Evening Post*, 13 July 1792; *Hartford Gazette*, 13 Jan. 1794; *[Newport] Rhode-Island Museum*, 7 July 1794; *Mott and Hurtin's New-York Weekly Chronicle*, 1 Jan. 1795; *Providence Journal*, 2 Jan. 1799.

26. *New-York Journal and State Gazette*, 18 March 1784.

27. For the view that printers made their papers bland and impartial to avoid losing friends and customers, see Stephen Botein, "'Meer Mechanics' and an Open Press: The Busines and Political Strategies of Colonial Printers," *Perspectives in American History* 9 (1975): 127-225; Stephen Botein, "Printers and the American Revolution," in Bernard Bailyn and John B. Hench, eds., *The Press and the American Revolution* (Worcester, Mass., 1980), 11-57.

28. *New Bedford (Mass.) Medley,* 27 Nov. 1792.

29. See Jeffery A. Smith, *Franklin and Bache: Envisioning the Enlightened Republic* (New York, 1990), 102-71.

30. *Mount Pleasant Jersey Chronicle,* 2 May 1795. For similar statements on the press as a means of diffusing knowledge, see e.g., *Philadelphia Gazette,* 1 Jan. 1794; *New-York Evening Post,* 17 Nov. 1794; *Keene (N.H.) Rising Sun,* 11 Aug. 1795; *New York Register of the Times,* 3 June 1796; *Washington Gazette,* 15 June 1796.

31. See Michael Durey, "Thomas Paine's Apostles: Radical Emigrés and the Triumph of Jeffersonian Republicanism," *William and Mary Quarterly,* 3d ser., 44 (Oct. 1987): 661-88.

32. *Charleston South-Carolina Gazette,* 22 March 1783.

33. *New London (Conn.) Bee,* 14 June 1797. For other examples of apparent delight at the prospect of reaching a large readership, see *Burlington (N.J.) Advertiser,* 13 April 1790; *Baltimore Evening Post,* 13 July 1792; *Providence State Gazette,* 4 Jan. 1796.

34. *Philadelphia Gazette,* 1 Jan. 1794.

35. The costs of publications did not necessarily mean that readership was confined to higher social classes. See David Paul Nord, "A Republican Literature: A Study of Magazine Reading and Readers in Late Eighteenth-Century New York," *American Quarterly* 40 (March 1988): 42-64.

36. See, e.g., Smith, *Franklin and Bache,* 105, 159.

37. *New London (Conn.) Bee,* 14 June 1797. For an example of barter items being accepted and discounts being offered for group subscriptions as well as for advertisements by subscribers, see *Stonington (Conn.) Journal of the Times,* 10 Oct. 1798.

38. *Leominster (Mass.) Rural Repository,* 22 Oct. 1795.

39. *Philadelphia General Advertiser,* 1 Oct. 1790.

40. *Hartford Gazette,* 13 Jan. 1794.

41. Jeffery A. Smith, *Printers and Press Freedom: The Ideology of Early American Journalism* (New York, 1988); Maryann Yodelis Smith and Gerald J. Baldasty, "Criticism of Public Officials and Government in the New Nation," *Journal of Communication Inquiry* 4 (Winter 1979): 53-74; Gerald J. Baldasty, "Toward an Understanding of the First Amendement: Boston Newspapers, 1782-1791," *Journalism History* 3 (Spring 1976): 25-30, 32. For examples of statements rejecting partisanship and personal libel, see *Salem (Mass.) Essex Gazette,* 2 Aug. 1768; *Burlington New-Jersey Gazette,* 5 Dec. 1777; *Federal Gazette and Philadelphia Evening Post,* 1 Oct. 1788; *Keene (N.H.) Rising Sun,* 11 Aug. 1795; *Washington Gazette,* 15 June 1796.

42. Smith, *Printers and Press Freedom,* 151-54.

43. *The Autobiography of Benjamin Franklin,* 93, 94.

44. See Smith, *Printers and Press Freedom,* 11, 57-92, 151-56, 162-67.

45. See David A. Anderson, "The Origins of the Press Clause," *U.C.L.A. Law Review* 30 (Feb. 1983): 455-541.

46. See, e.g., Jackson Turner Main, *The Antifederalists: Critics of the Constitution* (Chapel Hill, N.C., 1961), 249-51. Fear of revolutionary France and of its Jeffersonian supporters induced the Federalist Party to pass the Sedition Act of

1798 for use against the opposition press, but the law was clearly unconstitutional and helped sweep the Federalists from power in 1800. James M. Smith, *Freedom's Fetters: The Alien and Sedition Laws and American Civil Liberties* (Ithaca, N.Y., 1956).

47. Culver H. Smith, *The Press, Politics, and Patronage: The American Government's Use of Newspapers, 1789-1875* (Athens, Ga., 1977), 1-55; Carl E. Prince, "The Federalist Party and Creation of a Court Press, 1789-1801," *Journalism Quarterly* 53 (Summer 1976): 238-41.

48. *Philadelphia General Advertiser,* 1 Jan. 1794.

49. *New York Register of the Times,* 3 June 1796.

50. Richard B. Kielbowicz, "The Press, Post Office, and Flow of News in the Early Republic," *Journal of the Early Republic* 3 (Fall 1983): 255-80. In 1815 Kielbowicz notes (269), the postmaster general determined that magazines (except for religious publications) and pamphlets were an interference with the mail and would be excluded. On the press and post office prior to the
√ revolution, see Jerald E. Brown, "'It Facilitated the Correspondence': The Post, Postmasters, and Newspaper Publishing in Colonial America," *Retrospection* 2 (1989): 1-15. For examples of a Republican newspaper's portrayal of the postal charges as a threat to liberty, see *Philadelphia General Advertiser,* 12 Feb., 14 Nov., 1 and 24 Dec. 1791; 2 and 6 Jan., 10 Feb., 16 July, 8 Nov. 1792. For the strategies behind the first president's valedictory, see Victor H. Paltsits, ed., *Washington's Farewell Address* (New York, 1935).

51. *Philadelphia Gazette,* 1 Jan. 1794.

52. *Philadelphia General Advertiser,* 24 May 1791.

53. Ibid., 6 Aug. 1791; 12 April 1792.

54. *Newport (R.I.) Companion,* 2 May 1798.

55. For a discussion of this role of the press, see Popkin, *News and Politics,* 2-71, 129-36, 249-64.

56. See Jeremy D. Popkin, *Revolutionary News: The Press in France, 1789-1799* (Durham, N.C., 1990); Robert Darnton and Daniel Roche, eds., *Revolution in Print: The Press in France, 1775-1800* (Berkeley, Calif., 1989); Hugh Gough, *The Newspaper Press in the French Revolution* (London, 1988); Jeremy D. Popkin, *The Right-Wing Press in France, 1792-1800* (Chapel Hill, N.C., 1980).

57. See esp. Robert Darnton, *The Kiss of Lamourette: Reflections in Cultural History* (New York, 1990), 3-20; Simon Schama, *Citizens: A Chronicle of the French Revolution* (New York, 1989).

58. On Franklin's experience and caution, see Jeffery A. Smith, "'Infamous Practices': Risk-Taking in Franklin's Early Journalism," in J.A. Leo Lemay, ed., *Reappraising Benjamin Franklin: A Bicentennial Perspective* (Newark, Del. 1993), 40-51; and Barbara B. Oberg, "'Plain, Insinuating, Persuasive': Benjamin Franklin's Final Speech to the Constitutional Convention of 1787," in Lemay, *Reappraising Benjamin Franklin,* 175-92. On the "puzzling and chilly world which Madison depicted," see Kenneth A. Lockridge, *Settlement and Unsettlement in Early America* (Cambridge, 1981), 112-19. For discussions of the early American distrust of both the public and politicians, see Smith, *Franklin and Bache,* 3-24; Douglass G. Adair, "Experience Must Be Our Only Guide: History,

Democratic Theory, and the United States Constitution," in Greene, *Reinterpretation of the American Revolution*, 397-416.

59. For examples of public support for press freedom, see Jeffery A. Smith, "Public Opinion and the Press Clause," *Journalism History* 14 (Spring 1987): 8-17.

60. "To the Inhabitants of the Province of Quebec," 26 Oct. 1774, in Worthington C. Ford et al., eds., *Journals of the Continental Congress, 1774-1789* (Washington, D.C., 1904-37), 1:108.

6

The Revolutionary Word in
the Newspaper in 1789

PIERRE RÉTAT
Translated by François Le Roy, University of Kentucky

The revolutionary commotion in the France of 1789 produced several effects that profoundly modified the informational content of periodicals. A progressive liberation, then a nearly total freedom brought about a quantitative explosion and permitted a real and direct commitment in the news and in domestic political struggles. The new relationship that developed between journalists and their audience thus inspired in the former ambitions of which their predecessors could barely have dreamed and in the latter an enhanced impatience, a need for information, and sometimes a will to respond actively to this information.

The intervention of the journalist, together with the employment of all the stylistic and rhetorical effects that such intervention implies, constitutes one of the remarkable aspects of this relationship. The reality of the journalist's interaction with the public is not the issue here. That Camille Desmoulins actually climbed on a chair at the Palais-Royal to harangue the Parisians, that testimonies clearly prove that bulletins and newspapers were read in public or in political clubs—such things are evidence that helps recreate an atmosphere and explain the possibility of the journalistic phenomenon.[1] But the phenomenon itself must be understood in its discursive particularity as one of the forms that the emotional heat and violence of the revolutionary event take in the written press.

Here I want to describe briefly this new form of journalistic speech as it appeared in the press of 1789 and, above all, to explain its significance, without forgetting that the French Revolution in 1789 must be placed in its proper ideological context. A true revolution of the Enlightenment, born in the euphoria of an endless confidence in the progress of reason, it mainly produced newspapers that aspired to enlighten the nation, to declare true principles, to cooperate in the work of constitution-making.[2] It was from this mission that so many of these newspapers got their legitimacy. Therefore, we touch here on only one aspect of the revolutionary function that the newspaper exercises, an aspect not in contradiction with the general project of a press that claims to be didactic, even catechetical, in any case creating and unifying an enlightened "public opinion."[3]

The newspaper cannot be isolated from the ensemble of rhetorical interventions that mark the beginning of the revolution. The genre of the "address," massively practiced in the first months of 1789, penetrates the pamphlet and the periodical series that remain very close to it, such as Nicholas Bonneville's *Tribun du Peuple* in May and June. The call to action that rings in it (against the privileged, against all those who resist the just claims of the "commoners") and the impassioned exhortation mark the tone of the critical moment preceding the victory of the Third Estate. Written eloquence thus is probably already an important political actor.

With the revolutionary week of July appears one of the most successful newspapers, one whose example and style profoundly mark the press of the following years: the *Révolutions de Paris*, a vibrant account of the events, animated by the immediate presence and the voice of a patriot who encourages the citizens, curses the aristocrats, and addresses all the actors of the drama.[4]

The word rings out again, and with violence, in the pamphlet-newspapers that appear outside the fringes of the new legal sphere of publicity (for instance, the *Furet Parisien* before the days of October and until January of 1790), in the articles that Louis-Sébastien Mercier and above all Jean-Louis Carra write for the *Annales patriotiques et littéraires*, and, with a much greater continuity and strength, in the "speeches to the people" and the similar texts of which the numbers of Jean-Paul Marat's *Ami du Peuple* are composed.

In less striking forms, the urgent need to speak also manifests itself in the numerous readers' letters that newspapers publish, especially the sensationalist sheets such as the *Observateur*: vehement and accusatory letters that respond to the journalists' own ardor, second it, and give it new energy. Many small, ephemeral newspapers are characterized by the presence of an authorial persona who accords himself the authority of delivering the most diverse and sometimes the most eccentric ideas to his readers.

The subjective word is a fundamental cause of the effect of energy that the revolutionary newspaper produces and wants to produce. Those who practice this subjective rhetoric most consciously and with the greatest vigor—Bonneville in the *Tribun du Peuple*, Antoine Tournon in the *Révolutions de Paris*—present themselves as modern tribunes invested with the mission to direct the people, to defend it against its enemies by the lucidity of their views and the purity of their intentions. Even if Marat does not label himself as "tribune," he exercises, with a very particular pathos, a similar function. The tribune-journalists acquire by their unshakable devotion, by their identification with the people, an absolute authority; their newspapers become sacred objects, which they place under the safeguard of the nation. This mechanism of self-legitimization, perfectly perceptible in Marat, gives the newspaper an extraordinary meaning and importance, quasi-religious in nature.

This tribunician journalism mobilizes all the resources of eloquence to achieve its object of conveying and exciting the full range of passions. Bonneville exalts the powers of the "prophet's tongue," which alone is capable of communicating the "sacred fire," and that is what he himself practices. The apostrophe, the interpellation, the imperative exhortation punctuate the accounts or the commentaries of the *Révolutions de Paris*. The "speeches" of Marat, finally, progress and sound like great political sermons successively aimed at making the people feel ashamed, at instilling anxiety and despair into them, and at awakening and exhorting them to the redemptory uprising.

Marat, Carra, Desmoulins, in significant comparisons, assimilate the journalist, the orator, and the soldier.[5] These functions become interchangeable in the service of the cause. The journal, vehicle of the living word of the revolution, becomes a weapon.

How can we understand and interpret the revolutionary recreation of the newspaper? The revolution is also an uprising of the word. Its liberation is celebrated like a conquest but is described as an irresistible explosion. Autoine-Louis Gorsas compares "the voice of the freeborn man" to the compressed saltpeter that subsequently explodes with even more violence: "When it is released, it is no longer a voice, but the piercing cry that stuns the tyrants and breaks the idols of despotism."[6] In 1789 the way in which events carry language away is often celebrated: the mimetic impulse easily reverses itself, and the conviction imposes itself because of the power of the word. The liberated word now can create the event, particularly the word of "patriot writers," since they are believed to be able to govern "public opinion" and to modify the evolution of events. A reader writes to the author of the *Révolutions de Paris*: "Try, by the influence of your written words, to remedy the ills that threaten the fatherland."[7] Even more than its content, the tone of the press then becomes a primordial issue to contemporaries, who evoke what they label as the most dangerous newspapers, the "inflammatory sheets," either because of the news they spread or because of the passion they attempt to stir up by their speech. This is why one must pay the greatest attention to the newspapers that combine the effect of the periodical press with that of the word and produce a politically explosive compound.

Indeed, the journalistic word possesses a virtue of its own: its periodicity and its circulation, one favoring the other (and this is why Jacques-Pierre Brissot so ardently desired to create a "political gazette"), make of it a continual functioning tribune from which it is possible to talk to the crowds, and this capability resurrects an antique *agora*, place of direct democracy, and the direct relationship of the orator to the assembled people. The newspaper presents a model of active citizenship, but in two very different ways whose opposition reveals a characteristic specific to the tribunician newspaper. One can, like Brissot, insist on the pedagogic and philosophical value of the newspaper, make of it an instrument of reflection and mediation, capable of establishing a regular exchange between the people and its representative assemblies. On the contrary, one can, like Tournon and Marat, make of it an organ of incitement and direct appeal to the people, meant to short-circuit the established authorities. On the one hand is a citizenship that can be called cold, of which the newspaper keeps up the reasonable zeal; on the other hand, a "hot" citizenship whose fervor ignites and renews itself in the fictive orality of the harangue. In the most openly committed "patriot" press of 1789, these two models reveal political choices, radically different conceptions of the development of the revolution and of the role that the "sovereign" (in the Rousseauist sense) must play in it.

Not only is the committed newspaper a powerful means of political expression (and to that extent a lever of power); it becomes the figurehead and the symbol of the revolution itself, and it derives an absolute legitimacy from it. The heroic and epic account of the *Révolutions de Paris* is in some ways the spontaneous creation of the July days: it owes its extraordinary success to its concordance with the lived intensity of the event. Much of the effect that it produces comes from the intervention of a spectator who is simultaneously a reporter, from the presence of a central consciousness—both vocal and visible in the text—whose intervention gives the event its passionate strength and its exemplarity. The revolution instigates a type of journalism destined to perpetuate it, a text that becomes the consciousness of the revolution, at once representation of and reflection on what a revolution is, what it will become, what it must be. One understands that in these conditions the newspaper itself becomes a myth, a fantastic object, impassioned, sacralized—or, on the contrary, cursed and feared.

This new and extraordinary value given to the newspaper leads easily to an overvaluation of the press in general and to a mythification of it. So it seems that the French Revolution produces one important characteristic of the modern press: its overconfidence in itself and its sometimes monstrous ambition and claims. Perhaps we should say that a revolutionary situation is well suited to making people believe in the impact of the medium that represents and expresses it. The revolutionary crisis thus fixes its imaginary place, its status, and the value attributed to it.

The tribunician style communicates to the newspaper traits that profoundly contrast with those of the earlier press. The institutional press of the Old Regime, political or literary, is a complex cultural object elaborated during the seventeeth century, characterized, in the form of the "journal," by the erudite code of the critic (*l'extrait*) and, in the "gazette," by a multiplicity of messages that must be seized and interpreted according to the "political" context, that of the European balance of power. Journals appearing in the late 1770s, such as S.H.N. Linguet's *Annales Politiques,* new in form as in tone, while sharply contrasting with the other newspapers by the exhibition of an exceptional and agitated journalistic personality and by the vigor of their language, make themselves even more conspicuous by their discursive subtlety and their consummate art of argument, brilliant and deliberately paradoxical.[8] In 1789 the most politically engaged revolutionary newspapers break with these codes: to the distance that cultural and political constraints impose, they oppose an intense and emotional participation; to the discursive and controlled written word, the miming of the spoken word, of the interpellation, of the injunction; to the perspective imposed by the critic or by the dispersion, the uncertainty, the distance from the "news," the incitement to action, the proliferation of a word that is also a political and insurrectional project.

Of course, one must always be aware of the radical difference in nature between written speech and genuine oral discourse. Rhetorical traditions have always governed a specifically scriptural field that one must not

confuse with spoken eloquence. The tribune-journalists are, before everything else, writers (they claim to be "patriot writers") and sometimes experts in the art of speech, like Marat. But the revolutionary urgency of the
word they convey and stage-manage imposes in the newspaper what one
might call a regression (or the simulation of a regression), a regression that
is also, however, a revivification in which the revolutionary regeneration
authenticates itself in the dimension of the written word. It is regression
toward orality and public reading, against the long and slow movement
that has been leading since the sixteenth century toward individual and
silent reading; regression toward the repetitive forms of a strictly performa-
tive speech; regression toward a summary form of interlocution that ig-
nores all the mediations to which the news has been submitted since the
birth of the press; finally, regression toward a sustained and passion-
dominated account in which history makes a return to the simple form of
the chronicle and to the immersion of the individual in the event. In the
revolutionary situation the newspaper thus comes back to primitive forms
of communication and narration, and in this regard the analysis of the text
leads to the same conclusions as the analysis of the forms of publication,
which are marked by the return to the isolated sheet, by the close relationship between the new periodicals and the pamphlet.

This is why the study of revolutionary media must be conducted both in
continuity with and in opposition to the study of the media in a regime of
normal functioning. The rupture of 1789 is not only that of the freedom of
speech and of the accompanying quantitative explosion. The transformation of the press in 1789 is above all qualitative. It does not affect so much
the material form of the newspaper as the types of speech, the mission that
journalists assign to themselves, the personas they adopt and the position
they occupy in the political struggle that has just begun. Therefore, the historian must take the measure of all the innovations of which the newspaper is the place and object: they attest to its close participation in the
revolutionary event in a civilization of the written word. It must be understood by this that the newspaper is an indissoluble part of the revolutionary process, a driving element, an actor, and not only a reflection, a means
of expression among others. For too long the press has been treated like a
document; it must be reinvested with its truly strategic function of historical
actor. The revolutionary movement provides the best opportunity to do
this.

    If one studies the tribunician newspaper, the specific focus of this pre-
sentation, one notices the intimate involvement of journalistic style with

political struggle. The reprobation, the sarcasm, the fear it inspires in 1789 attest to the significance and the effectiveness attributed to it, and the willingness to oppose to it other forms of journalism. The patriots themselves perceived the danger, both political and cultural, of a regression that some contemporaries felt as evidence of the decadence of taste, the effect of a juvenile "enthusiasm" or an unworthy lack of constraint on the part of reasonable citizens. In the reactions of writers such as Jacques Beffroy de Reigny, Louis Fontanes, and Brissot one can read, as early as the first months of the revolution, very diverse sensitivities and political choices but all equally opposed to those that the newspaper of tribunician agitation suggests.[9] In Brissot this opposition takes its most theoretical and most meaningful form: it proves once again that the newspaper is an essential means of expression, one of the vectors of the effervescent division of opinions, inseparable from liberty and from the revolutionary drama.

When we reflect upon the relationship between media and revolution, we should also distinguish clearly between different types of revolution and different meanings of the word. When we are concerned, as in the case of 1789, with an upheaval, a violent rupture that proclaims itself as total, we need to ask how and by what means the media express and create the *emotional force* that accompanies the event. The newspaper of the French Revolution had to compensate for the absence, the slowness, or the poverty of pictorial propaganda. Through representations in words and passionate rhetoric, it succeeded in stimulating and exalting the emotion of the "patriots." As we see how it fulfilled this function, we can also see that the revolutionary event strove to represent itself before the largest possible public. Its intensity particularly required mediatization, and derived new strength from it. When the newspapers of 1789 claimed that "all of Europe has its eyes on" Paris or on France, they created in the public imagination the equivalent of modern-day "direct" or "real-time" reporting. The words and passion-filled narratives that some of them carried were, to the extent that the technical means of the time allowed, the expression of a radical new effort to extend the audience and the spectacle of the revolution as far as they could go.

NOTES

1. See Claude Labrosse and Pierre Rétat, *Naissance du journal révolutionnaire* (Lyon, 1989), 80-82. To complete and thoroughly study this presentation, one can consult the whole of this work and Jeremy D. Popkin, *Revolutionary News: The Press in France, 1789-1799,* (Durham, N.C.), 124-68.

2. For a detailed inventory of the French press in 1789, see Pierre Rétat, *Les journaux de 1789: Bibliographie critique* (Paris, 1988).

3. For instance, Jean Marat always presents himself as a "wise man" who meditates in the "silence of the study" and recalls "principles." See the prospectus for *Ami du Peuple*, or no. 2, Sept. 1789, 19.

4. For a fuller interpretation of the journalism of the *Révolutions de Paris*, see Pierre Rétat, *Forme et discours d'un journal révolutionnaire* (Lyon, 1985), 139-78.

5. E.g., Carra, *Annales Patriotiques*, no. 80, 21 Dec. 1789: "The revolution advances; it will be carried through to completion, for such is the determination of the men of good will, the generous writers, the orators, and patriot soldiers."

6. *Courrier de Versailles à Paris*, vol. III, no. 64, 138.

7. *Révolutions de Paris*, no. 16, 24-31 Oct. 1789, 4.

8. There is as yet no thorough study of Linguet's journalistic style. Jeremy Popkin showed in a convincing way how some of its traits announce the revolutionary newspaper; see "The Prerevolutionary Origins of Political Journalism," in Keith Baker, ed., *The Political Culture of the Old Regime* (Oxford, 1987), 216-20.

9. See, e.g., Brissot's *Patriote Français*, no. 33, 8 Sept. 1789, 4: "Minute details or rhetorical phrases do not form Patriots."

7

"The Persecutor of Evil"
in the German Revolution of 1848-1849

JONATHAN SPERBER

One of the first acts of the provisional governments and liberal ministries created after the victories of the insurgents on the barricades in February-March 1848 was to proclaim freedom of the press. Doing so meant revolutionizing newspaper production. Even in the relatively liberal constitutional regimes of pre-1848 Europe, such as the July Monarchy, the press had been constrained by strict libel laws and requirements for large sums in caution money. In the states of central Europe, ruled in absolutist, or, at best, partially constitutional fashion, prior censorship was compulsory, and periodical publishing required a license. Without official approval, which was seldom granted, a newspaper could not appear.[1]

The end of this authoritarian regime meant that journalists in the German states and the Austrian empire were not just free to print what they wished but free simply to print, to start newspapers without government consent. This new freedom, combined with a greatly increased interest in political affairs as a result of the revolution, expanded and transformed the journalistic universe. In terms of the percentage of increase in the number of newspapers, the results of this new state of affairs emerged most clearly among the Slavic nationalities of the Habsburg empire: 1848-49 saw the publication of the first Ukrainian-language newspaper ever; during the midcentury revolution the number of Czech-language papers increased fourfold, from thirteen to fifty-two; the Slovenian press grew sixfold, albeit from only one to six.[2]

German-speakers of central Europe were numerous and more literate.[3] They had many more newspapers to begin with, so that although the
percentage of increase in the German language press was smaller, the
growth in absolute numbers was much greater, from some 940 newspapers in 1847 to an estimated 1,700 two years later.[4] Developments followed the same general trend in the region under discussion here, the
Prussian Rhine Province at the far western end of central Europe, where
the number of newspapers approximately doubled during 1848.[5]

This expansion of the press among a predominantly literate population changed the relationship between newspaper writers and readers. As
journalists quickly discovered, their audience had come to include craftsmen, peasants, and laborers who were able to read and write but lacked
the secondary school education needed to follow the language of the
press, with its sophisticated vocabulary and allusions to literary high culture. This disparity was of particular concern to left-wing journalists, since
it meant that they, as supporters of universal manhood suffrage and forth-
right adherents of the notion of popular sovereignty, would have difficulty
communicating with their own potential supporters.

During the revolution, leftists sought ways to deal with this problem.
One solution, frequently practiced, was to turn newspaper reading into a
collective oral experience. At meetings of democratic political clubs a
better-educated member would read articles out loud, explaining and elu-
cidating them as he went along. This could be an enlightening procedure,
but if poorly done, it ran the risk of creating excruciating boredom, which is
apparently why the statutes of the democratic club in Saarbrücken prohib-
ited the practice.[6] In addition, club meetings were not an ideal setting for
communication between democratic journalists and their readers. A contemporary noted that nonattenders obviously could not be reached and
"even those present might like to have repeated or consider at their leisure
that which they missed or did not understand."[7] For this, a newspaper
would be appropriate, but a popular one, written in simple and easily understood language, designed to appeal to a plebeian audience. The quotation is from the founding issue of just such a journal, the *Volksblatt* of Trier,
one of several existing in the Rhineland during the 1848 revolution; others
were published in Kaiserslautern, Speyer, and Cologne. Such newspapers,
though for the people, were not by the people: their editors —the law graduate Nikolaus Schmitt, for instance, and the feminist socialist, freelance
journalist Mathilde Franziska Anneke came from the educated classes, often with prior journalistic experience.

In Cologne, the metropolis of western Germany, the gap between

journalists and their readers was bridged in the other direction, by someone stepping out of the popular audience to start his own newspaper: the
master baker Mathias Wessel. In February 1849 he began bringing out a
weekly entitled *Der Verfolger der Bosheit,* "The Persecutor of Evil." Considering this newspaper as a typical example of revolutionary journalism is a
lost cause. It was a one-man affair, published, edited, and almost entirely
written by Wessel, an unusual (by definition, since bakers were not newspapermen) and eccentric individual. His product, to boot, has been only
very partially preserved.[9]

Wessel was an uneducated man. However, he was not politically inex-
perienced. He had been an active member of Cologne's Workers' Association, where we find him in the fall of 1848 promoting his bakery by offering to sell bread to association members at a discount and deliver it to their
houses, speaking in debates, and serving on a committee to audit the
group's finances.[10] It is precisely this combination of a lack of formal education and a strong involvement in organized politics, that makes Wessel
and his newspaper—in spite of their extremely exceptional character—a
good point of entry for consideration of journalists and their reading public
during the revolution of 1848. His newspaper displayed both unmediated
popular experience and the influence of left-wing intellectuals. A discussion of its themes, in comparison with the more conventional journalistic
products of Cologne's left, will help sort out different influences and suggest something of the nature of journalism and its relation to popular political participation during the mid-nineteenth-century European revolution.

We might begin with the newspaper's strange name and realize that its
editor and publisher meant for it to be taken literally. As he explained in a
statement of purpose, his newspaper would expose suffering and oppression. "First of all, in our persecutor we wish to show the proletariat (the
class of poor people) how it has been enslaved up to now, by the rule of
the saber; by the damned priests [*vom Pfaffenthume*], under the veil of
illusion; by the evil of the great merchants."[11] Wessel did just that. Alternat-
ing between generalizing broadsides and offering one constant and concrete example after another, he denounced the people's oppressors.

"You court bailiffs stand around like the hangman's servants at the
scaffold, with bloodthirsty glances, as you sell off [the things of] some poor
devil," began one article. In the next issue Wessel described to his readers
how the Bailiff Kniffer, bearing a "false judgment" auctioned off the grain
and cattle of a married couple, tenant farmers in Bedburg, near Cologne,
and so ruined them and their farm. The magistrate, he continued, in ca-
hoots with the bailiff, prevented an investigation of the illegality of these

actions. Wessel had equally sharp words for the justices of the peace who issued such judgments in the first place.[12] The Prussian District Government in Cologne, which did nothing to help impoverished beggars and refused to offer contracts to small bakers to furnish bread to the city's garrison, came in for its share of opprobrium, as did the magistrate in Merheim who would not let the villagers gather wood in the state-owned forest, and his opposite number in Pfaffendorf who sent the gendarmes after a poor begging couple.[13]

Wessel flayed the capitalists no less than the government officials. He exposed "the number one swindler of Cologne . . . Franz Pallenberg, square footer, rentier, Ursulaplatz," a landlord who ruthlessly evicted sick and unemployed tenants who fell behind in the rent, flouting the last wish of a proletarian to die in his own bed. Peter Kerp, dealer in coal slack, bought large quantities at low prices during the summer, and then, refusing the poor "the fraternal hand" in the winter, charged them a premium for small purchases. After being denounced in Wessel's newspaper, Kerp changed his policies and prices.[14] Rural property owners who jacked up their tenants' rents or offered meager wages to day laborers also came under fire. More general denunciations of capitalists as "money wolves," "money chasers," or "bloodhounds" who bathed in champagne and lived in drunken revelry (*Saus und Braus*), while refusing to think of their human brothers, filled the newspaper's pages.[15]

Yet of the trio capitalist, bureaucrat, and priest, none aroused Wessel's ire as did the clergy. Virtually every issue of the newspaper contained at least one and often several anticlerical broadsides, in which two major themes stood out. One was clerical greed, priests' insistence on their lucrative privileges and their refusal to help the poor. Pastor Steiger in Mülheim kept the chain on his door when answering callers until he found out whether they had brought money. If they had not, even if they were elderly or pregnant women, he sent them away. Vicar Heuter of the Cologne cathedral beat the poor away from his door with a stick; Johann Filz, canon of the cathedral chapter and a favorite target of Wessel's, had his cook do the same for him. Pastor Overrath in Merheim, with an income of three *Taler* per day (more than a day laborer could make in a week) was "stone rich," had become "thick and fat," and wore silk shirts, while two to three hundred of his parishioners went barefoot. From Palm Sunday until Easter the parishioners did nothing but bring him eggs, yet he would not let them take water from his well. He had more meat at one dinner meal than the twelve apostles together in a week. He lived in a palace yet collected tithes. Did Christ collect tithes, Wessel wondered?[16]

This last remark contains the key to much of Wessel's anticlericalism. The clergy had renounced its Christian vocation: clerics had "gone on so long in the footsteps of Christ, that there is scarcely a single successor to Christ left." Rather than comforting the poor and visiting the sick, Catholic priests and Protestant pastors spent their time drinking champagne with estate stewards or doing favors for owners of sugar refineries; they charged such exorbitant fees for performing marriages or officiating at funerals that their services were reserved exclusively for the rich. The one favorable mention of a priest confirms this idea: the newspaper praised the vicar in Wiesdorf as "a genuine apostle of Jesus, [who] goes daily into the huts of the poor and visits the sick, and shares with them his bread."[17]

The second main failing of the clergy in Wessel's eyes was that they were not just greedy but bigoted and reactionary as well. Protestant Pastor Engels, who rebuked a radical, unemployed tailer for telling his daughter that she need not pray for the king, was, according to Wessel, really from "Satan." When the vicar in the village of Worringen, on the first anniversary of the barricade fighting in Berlin, celebrated a mass for the souls of the Catholics who fell there, leaving out the Protestants and Jews, he was rebuked for forgetting that "all men are our brothers." Wessel combined both themes of his anticlericalism in condemning Cologne's Archbishop Johannes von Geissel, who spoke "very darkly" about the "rule of the people [*Volksherrschaft*]" in his pastoral letter but allowed those who paid five *Thaler* to eat meat on Good Friday, and "you all know that Judas sold himself to the devil for money."[18]

Wessel's anticlericalism and his anticapitalism were combined in his anti-Semitism. He condemned the Jews as the worst sort of capitalists, whose hearts were "stubborn and closed" against their "brothers." Jews swindled poor widows; they beat a cow's udders with nettles until they were swollen, and would then sell the beast to an unsuspecting peasant who thought he was getting a good milk producer. They ran outworking establishments in the garment trade (*Kleidermagazine*) that pushed down prices and prevented master tailors from supporting their families. Just as bad, though, were Christians who did the same, "Christian Jews, who daily place the crown of thorns on Christ and suck the blood and sweat from their brothers."[19]

The notion Jew = capitalist is a familiar topos of anti-Semitism; Wessel added a rather different twist when he asserted that Jew = bigoted priest. In condemning the leaders of Cologne's Jewish community for appealing for alms for the Jewish poor, he noted that "religion, understood in true and pure form . . . treats everyone in this, as in many other respects, completely alike. . . . Those who believe that each man is only called upon to help his brothers in faith, have been led astray by the teachings of those damned priests. That priesterly scum [*Pfaffengeschmeiß*], be it a Jewish, Catholic, Protestant, or Turkish damned priest (Mufti), all have conspired against humanity and in that way have made men into the enemy of other men." Jews should give up their medieval "caste system" and help the poor of all confessions. Pointing out that Christian charitable efforts were confessionally limited was no excuse: "one should never take a bad example." Wessel continued, "May they (the Israelites) also show that they are thankful to the poor people, the proletarians, through whose shed blood they were redeemed from servitude and granted political equality. May the year 1848 . . . always remain in their memory and so change their views." [20]

In discussing nineteenth-century German anti-Semitism, it is common to understand it as a precursor to Nazism, a temptation that ought to be resisted in Wessel's case. The master baker made no secret of his hatred of Jews, but he saw them as just one example of the broader social evils that he attacked with much greater frequency in his newspaper. "The Persecutor of Evil" did not identify the Jews as the single source of all evil, a characteristic of late nineteenth- and twentieth-century German anti-Semitism. If anything, the newspaper opposed such an identification, printing an article denouncing the charges of ritual murder that had been raised in the Rhineland, with support of some of the well-educated population, as late as 1834. [21]

In the long list of evils castigated by the crusading master baker, there is a curious omission: namely, any of the evils of industrial capitalism. Factories and factory labor made no appearance in the newspaper; even the protoindustrial and outworking precursors of mechanized industrial capitalism received just an occasional mention. [22] In contrast, conflicts of rural society—forest use, farm rent, day laborers' wages, debt and forced sales, tithes and seigneurial dues—were among Wessel's main themes. When he thundered against conditions in "the second England" (England being then, as today, the model of unbridled, laissez-faire capitalism), he was referring not to a German version of Manchester but to the lands around the Erft River, a region of intensive agricultural production with its population of large landowners, tenant farmers, and day laborers. [23]

Now Wessel did intend to attract rural readers, and he sold his newspaper door to door and in the taverns of villages in the vicinity of Cologne. [24] His was far from being only a rural newspaper, however; he found plenty of evil to denounce in urban areas. In all these denunciations, whether directed against the state authorities, the clergy, or the rich of city and country, one cannot help but be struck by the fixation on, almost obsession with, begging and charity. The refusal of the powerful to help the "poor"—defined as the begging unemployed, elderly, widowed, and sick—runs like a red thread through the columns of the newspaper. Cologne was notoriously a city of beggars, a dubious reputation it had retained since the seventeenth century. By 1848, there had been almost a hundred years of effort to stamp out mendicancy.[25] "The Persecutor of Evil" gives us the other side of the picture, the anger of the lower classes—who were not yet the classical industrial proletariat of the later nineteenth century but were still scrounging an uncertain living in city and country, in casual labor or small business, frequently under- or unemployed, deeply resentful of those in power and authority for repressing their pleas for help when all else failed.

Another and equally strange omission of Wessel's editorial policy is the lack of national political news. The late winter and spring of 1849 was an extraordinary event-filled period for the mid-century German revolution. It included the completion of a constitution for a united German state by the Frankfurt National Assembly, that assembly's offering the imperial crown to the king of Prussia, the latter's refusal, and the nationwide mass movement in favor of the assembly, culminating in uprisings and insurgent governments in several parts of the country which were suppressed by Prussian troops in a minor civil war. The Rhineland was a major center of these events, and in May 1849 insurrections were taking place just a few miles away from Cologne, in Elberfeld, Düsseldorf, and the lower Rhine silkweaving districts.[26] There were allusions in "The Persecutor of Evil" to some of these momentous occurences, or little snippets of poetry about them, but Wessel offered no editorial comments or direct reports.[27] His interests remained firmly fixed on small-scale local matters, rather in the manner of late twentieth-century social historians, seeking out instances of exploitation and oppression in everyday life.

The lack of direct references to national politics, however, does cause one to wonder about Wessel's own political ideals, about the positive vision he opposed to the evil he saw around him. The master baker was a self-proclaimed communist calling for the abolition of the right of inheritance in private property, a democrat, a "red republican." At the same time, he was a Christian, identifying his radical goals with a true Christianity that he saw as abandoned by the representatives of organized religion and the powers-that-be in state and society. His statement of purpose concluded, "We write in the name of God and in the cause of the people."[28]

In his condemnation of the justices of the peace, Wessel called on them to cease being black-white (that is, reactionary, an allusion to the Prussian colors) judges and to become of another color altogether, "of the rosy-colored heart blood of Jesus Christ, of the red republic." In a slashing attack on a priest who had condemned radicals as those who had "no religion, they believe neither in God nor the commandments," Wessel replied: "The hour is come when avarice, gluttony, drunkenness, champagne swilling, when arrogance, proud ostentation shall cease its drunkenness, so that the poor man as well can enjoy his life. Christ wanted that; yet, we want that too; that is what the democrats want."[29] This citation, repeated in many variations in "The Persecutor of Evil," suggests the fundamental outlines of its editor's world: on one side were the seven deadly sins and those who protected and promoted them, including the hypocritical representatives of organized religion; on the other stood the impoverished proletariat, the democrats, the true disciples of Christ.

For Wessel's own role in this conflict, we need to come back to the title of his newspaper. Wessel referred to himself personally as the persecutor of evil, and he was known publicly by that name.[30] He took this role seriously, and his declarations had a prophetic, even apocalyptic tone. It could be mild and humorous, as it was in a little vignette recounting how several democrats had bought fourth-class railroad tickets because the fourth-class cars were where the workers rode; the piece concluded, "We remark to the management of the Bonn-Cologne railroad the words of Christ: (very soon) the last will be first and the first last."[31] That tone also came in a stronger vein, as in this passage written in May 1849, at the height of insurgent movements in Germany: "The bullets are forged, the sabers sharpened; the people wish only to have their long drawn-up bill paid in the coin of justice, from the day it was due. The people will no longer allow themselves to be paid by the hypocritical paters with the words, praised be Jesus Christ. No, no hand could be laid on Jesus Christ; reeking of powder and lead, the people will call out with Christ: away with all scoundrels [*Schurken*] in all eternity, amen."[32]

As befits a prophet, Wessel's attacks on the perpetrators of evil included an appeal to them to change their ways. He called on the magistrate of Merheim to take up his role as "first citizen of the community" and to protect its inhabitants from government forest policy, quartering of soldiers, high farm rents, low wages for day labor, and clerical exaction of tithes, rather than enforcing all these oppressions. If Jews did not abandon their capitalist and exclusive ways and give the workers their due for the Jews' emancipation, then the poor "would make a revolution . . . [out of which the Jews] will fall into the chaos of the Middle Ages and of perdition." "Israelites!" he concluded, "you have been warned, so repent and improve yourselves." [33]

This demand for improvement, coupled with the apocalyptic threat of red revolution, appeared in its most characteristic form in Wessel's denunciation of the clergy. The parish priest Overrath in Merheim, whom Wessel condemned for his greed, hostility to the poor, and exaction of tithes, received in that same article a warning from the persecutor of evil: The priest was to burn all his un-Christian practices at the stake or face the consequences. "Don't let it come to the point that the men with the red caps, with the red scarves around their blouses (around their smocks) are forced by hunger and called upon by the revenge of justice to put an end to the old swinishness, where the damned priests eat up everything and produce nothing, in regard to the tithes. For these men gladly sing the words of Freiligrath—'The new rebellion, the total rebellion / March, march, march, march / March be it to the death, and our flag is red.' Herr Pastor Overrath, you would then think, had I only followed [the advice of] the Persecutor of Evil." [34] These were the words of a communist John the Baptist, calling out in the wastes of Cologne and its vicinity to repent or be destroyed by the workers' revolution. [35]

Where does such a journalist and political activist belong in the context of the 1848 revolution, as it occurred both in his immediate vicinity and, more broadly, across Europe? One answer is that Wessel's newspaper was a product of his membership in the Cologne Workers' Association, the extreme left-wing group in the city's politics during the midcentury revolution. Throughout its existence the group was torn by bitter factional struggles between the followers of the charity physician Andreas Gottschalk, a "true socialist," and those of Karl Marx, who during the 1848 revolution was editor of the radical newspaper (albeit one written in a highly educated language) *Die Neue Rheinische Zeitung* and active member of the city's Democratic Society and the Rhineland's federation of democratic political clubs. Like everyone else in the association, Wessel was involved in these quarrels; he was an ardent supporter of Gottschalk, a self-proclaimed disciple of the charity physician. [36]

Gottschalk had founded the group in April 1848 and was its dominant figure during the subsequent months. [37] Under his leadership the association's meetings and the pages of its newspaper were devoted to exposing the exploitation of the workers by the capitalists and publicizing the complaints of the proletariat. Although not completely neglecting the larger issues of national politics, the group maintained a certain distance from them, refusing to participate in left-wing political campaigns and following

Gottschalk's appeal to boycott the German National Assembly elections of May 1848. On the day of those elections Gottschalk gave a major speech proclaiming in great detail the identity of communism with Christianity. All three of these aspects of the Workers' Association in its early months—the focus on exposing social evil, the neglect of national politics, and the relationship of communism to Christianity—were also main characteristics of Wessel's newspaper and suggest some of the sources for his ideas.

In July 1848 Gottschalk was arrested, and control over the Workers' Association quicky passed into the hands of Karl Marx and his political associates. They completely changed the orientation of the organization and the newspaper, replacing the accounts of capitalist exploitation with lectures on political economy and emphasizing issues of national politics, including cooperation between the labor and democratic movements. Denunciations of instances of social evil did not completely vanish from Cologne's left-wing politics. They were found in the popular newspaper *Die Neue Kölnische Zeitung*, started in August 1848 and edited by the socialist feminist Mathilde Franziska Anneke, who was loosely allied with Marx in the leftist factional confrontations in Cologne.

All the while, Gottschalk sat in jail until his trial and acquittal in December 1848. Then he and his followers attempted to regain control of the association. Marx and his friends beat off their challenge, but the two groups, each possessing its own newspapers, hurled insults at each other through the spring of 1849. The leaders of these factions of the extreme left, Marx and Gottschalk, were both converted Jews, and both factions employed anti-Semitic accusations in their polemics. Here as well, Wessel's ideas may be seen as part of a broader, if not particularly admirable, political culture.

Yet if Wessel was Gottschalk's pupil, and if the founding of "The Persecutor of Evil" occurred in the context of radical Cologne politics, whose leaders were well-educated intellectuals, the master baker gave his own distinct twist to the ideas he had learned. One evident example is the central place of charity in Wessel's denunciations of social evil and his identification of almsgiving with revolutionary fraternity and communism. This was in marked contrast to Gottschalk, who sharply denounced appeals for charity and called on the workers to aid one another fraternally. On this point, Wessel's attitude almost certainly represented popular opinion, as suggested by the testimony of Hermann Becker, in 1848-49 a radical activist and, decades later, Cologne's mayor. Becker recalled in his memoirs that the members of the Workers' Association had understood socialism as "help from philanthropic means."[38]

In refusing to discuss national politics and concentrating on exposing social evils, Wessel's newspaper represented a diametric opposite to Marx's version of left-wing politics. Although the newspaper edited by Gottschalk and his other followers, as well as Anneke's popular journal, devoted noticeably more space to individual, local accounts of oppression than did Marx, they all offered explicit discussions of the broader political world of the midcentury revolution. The lack of such discussion in "The Persecutor of Evil" suggests that its editor understood the red revolution he propounded as a sudden, apocalyptic outburst. Typical of this attitude was one of Wessel's responses to the revolutionary uprisings of May 1849, a commentary on various religious prophecies concerning Germany's glorious future. Following lengthy revolutionary struggles, for example, a peasant emperor would be crowned who would bring peace to the world and found colonies in America; a church council would create a new religion, excluding everything not corresponding "to the laws of nature and reason"; and a plague would strike those guilty of gluttony.[39]

What was the place of religion in Wessel's view of the world? His extreme anticlericalism was unique on the Cologne left. Once again, the contrast with Marx is most extreme, as the latter went out of his way to accommodate Catholic sentiment, hoping to exploit the religious hostility of the predominantly Roman Catholic Rhinelanders to the Protestant Prussian monarchy for revolutionary purposes. Although other radical Cologne newspapers; particularly Anneke's, occasionally attacked reactionary priests, none shared Wessel's obsession with the clergy. But if none of these other newspapers were equally anticlerical neither were they equally religious. Wessel's constant and reiterated identification of socialism with a "true" Christianity, one purged of clerical distortion and centered on the performance of charitable good works, was a unique feature of the master baker's political outlook.

Political radicalism during the 1848 revolution in Germany was, to be sure, associated with anticlerical, rationalist, religious sects who frequently identified democracy or socialism with a true Christianity. Both educated members of the middle class and ordinary craftsmen and peasants were involved in them. Sectarian congregations, however, existed almost exclusively in Protestant areas, not in a heavily Catholic city such as Cologne.[40] Though perhaps showing certain parallels, Wessel's opinions nonetheless seem distinct from those of the sectarian groups, reflecting in a personally distinct way the milieu of the Catholic lower classes of the Rhineland's metropolis.

The place of this remarkable newspaper and its editor and publisher in the revolution of 1848 is best understood in terms of a dialectic of typicality and uniqueness. Wessel's experiences as a member of the Workers' Association and a reader of the radical press were characteristic of many members of the lower classes, a result of the expansion of the journalistic universe during the mid-nineteenth-century revolution. But his decision to go from being part of the journalists' audience to becoming a voice from that audience, to start his own newspaper, was a unique one, reflecting the master baker's profound involvement in the political and social movement of the day and his sense of his own importance to it. Wessel *was* the persecutor of evil, not just the paper's editor and publisher. As such, he was frankly peculiar, an eccentric and a crank.

For all his eccentricity, the pages of his newspaper, with their popular reinterpretations of the doctrines of socialist leaders and their direct expressions of the misery of the lives of the lower classes, gave a detailed and immediate voice to popular experience in a way that other democratic and socialist papers—even those specifically aimed at a lower-class audience—could not. In one respect, such a newspaper was most likely to arise in Germany during the 1848 revolution. In mid-nineteenth-century Eastern Europe, popular literacy was still too limited for a figure like Wessel to emerge. In France, on the other hand, workers' journalism was already a well-established and increasingly intellectual genre before the outbreak of the revolution, a reflection of the more liberal press laws of the July Monarchy and the greater political experience and sophistication of the lower classes.[41]

In another sense, Wessel's newspaper seems characteristic of the 1848 revolution. This was the moment—in Europe at least—in which popular culture, with all its traditional and archaizing elements, emerged most directly and immediately into radical politics, unlike the classicist and educated Jacobinism of the great French Revolution, or the theoretically schooled labor movement of the late nineteenth and early twentieth centuries. Pierre Rétat's contribution to this volume discusses the "tribunician newspapers" of 1789, written by the "tribune journalists." Characteristic of these for Rétat are the strongly personalized and individual tone of the journalists and their newspapers; the orality of the writing, which both imitates speech and is designed to be read aloud; and the attempt to recreate via the newspaper the direct, immediate, and personal connection between spokesperson and populace that was typical of the direct democracy of the forum and the agora in classical antiquity.

These three charateristics also typify "The Persecutor of Evil." Wessel clearly put his personal stamp on the newspaper. It was written in simple everyday language, and we know that Wessel himself read it aloud to peasants in taverns in the vicinity of Cologne. Nor can there be any doubt of Wessel's powerful commitment to creating a direct link between himself and his readers, and we have his explicit statement that he wrote "in the cause of the people." Yet Wessel was no tribune, and "tribunician" hardly describes the rhetoric of his newspaper. Unlike his educated fellow journalists—and Karl Marx is a good example here—Wessel had not been exposed to the rhetorical tropes of the classics; the models he followed came from the popular Roman Catholic culture of the Rhineland. The public persona displayed in his newspaper was a John the Baptist, not a Tribune of the People.

It is precisely a mark of the 1848 revolution that a popular journalist would appear as a John the Baptist. Another way to put this is to follow Maurice Agulhon's formulation that the mid-nineteenth century was the time when "the life of folklore and leftist ideas existed side by side," the age of a "red folklore."[42] In "The Persecutor of Evil" we may see a journalistic version in which the print medium and the newspaper format were used to express an unschooled political radicalism, deeply influenced by a frankly backward-looking popular experience and popular prejudice, a religious milieu, and a moralizing world view.

NOTES

1. Irene Collins, *The Government and the Newspaper Press in France, 1814-1881* (Oxford, 1959), 82-83; Hans-Ulrich Wehler, *Deutsche Gesellschaftsgeschichte*, 4 vols. (Munich, 1987-) 2:340-41, 506-29, 541-45.

2. John-Paul Himka, *Ukrainian Villagers and the Ukrainian National Movement in the Nineteenth Century* (London, 1988), 31; Stanley Z. Pech, "The Nationalist Movements of the Austrian Slavs in 1848: A Comparative Sociological Profile," *Histoire Sociale/Social History* 9 (1976): 336-56.

3. In 1847, 100 percent of school-age children attended school in the German-speaking provinces of the Austrian half of the Habsburg monarchy, 39 percent in the predominantly Slovenian provinces, and only 16 percent in predominantly Polish- and Ukrainian-speaking Galicia-Bukovina. Peter Burian, *Die Nationalitäten in "Cisleithanien" und das Wahlrecht der Märzrevolution 1848/49* (Graz and Cologne, 1962), 202 n. 117.

4. Wolfram Siemann, *Die deutsche Revolution von 1848/49* (Frankfurt, 1985), 116-17 (see also 114-24 for a good overview of the press during the German revolution). There were similar increases in the periodical press during the 1848 revolution in Hungary, Italy, and France. Domokos G. Kosáry, *The Hungarian Press during the Revolution of 1848-1849* (Boulder, Colo., 1986), 44-45; Simonetta Soldani, "Contadini, Operai e 'Popolo' nella rivoluzione del

1848-49 in Italia," *Studi Storici* 14 (1973): 557-613, esp. 611-12; John Merriman, *The Agony of the Republic: The Repression of the Left in Revolutionary France 1848-1851* (New Haven, Conn., 1978), 26.

5. Jonathan Sperber, *Rhineland Radicals: The Democratic Movement and the Revolution of 1848-1849* (Princeton, N.J., 1991), 210; Martin Henkle and Rolf Taubert, *Die deutsche Presse 1848-1850: Eine Bibliographie* (Munich, 1978), 13; see also 9-44 for an idiosyncratic but stimulating discussion of the German press before and during the 1848 revolution.

6. On reading of newspapers in club meetings, see Sperber, *Rhineland Radicals*, 209. Saarbrücken statutes in Landesarchiv Koblenz 442 no. 6497, 169.

7. *(Trier) Volksblatt*, 23 April 1848. This and all other translations are the author's, unless otherwise indicated.

8. On popular newspapers in the Rhineland, see Sperber, *Rhineland Radicals*, 212-13. Such newspapers were published elsewhere in Germany, in France, and in Hungary. See Henkel and Taubert, *Die deutsche Presse*, 31-33 (which exaggerates, somewhat, the popular character of the journalists); Edward Berenson, *Populist Religion and Left-Wing Politics in France, 1830-1852* (Princeton, N.J., 1984), 138-39; Kosáry, *The Hungarian Press*, 157-95.

9. On this newspaper, see Landesarchiv Koblenz 403 no. 7153, 211-13. The most complete set, in the Municipal and University Library in Cologne, contains only the issues for February-June 1849 and January-February 1850.

10. See *Zeitung des Arbeitervereins zu Köln* (hereafter *ZAVK*), no. 31, 14 Sept. 1848; *Freiheit, Brüderlichkeit Arbeit*, no. 6, 12 Nov. 1848, and no. 13, 7 Dec. 1848. Wessel's own newspaper has some brief mentions of the Workers' Association: see "Hölterhoff und Heuer Stadträthe," in *Verfolger der Bosheit* (hereafter *VdB*), no. 5, 17 March 1849; "Mehreren Stadträthen," no. 6, 24 March 1849.

11. Lead article, *VdB*, no. 1, 17 Feb. 1849. Similarly, "Geehrte Abonnenten und Leser!" no. 14, 19 May 1849.

12. "Sämtliche Gerichts-Vollzierher," *VdB*, no. 3, 3 March 1849; "Dem General-Prokurator Nicolovius," no. 4, 10 March 1849; "Sämtliche Friedensrichter," no. 5, 17 March 1849, and similarly, "Man erzählt aus Sechten," no. 11, 28 April 1849.

13. Note from Cologne, in *VdB*, no. 2, 24 Feb. 1849; "Fraget die Bäcker-Gesellen!" no. 5, 17 March 1849; report from Merheim, in no. 10, 21 April 1849, and from Paffendorf in no. 12, 5 May 1849. Similarly, see the general denunciation of state officials in the lead article, no. 8, 7 April 1849; "Volk die Augen auf!" no. 9, 14 April 1849.

14. "Der erste Preller von Köln," *VdB*, no. 2, 24 Feb. 1849; "Peter Kerp, Gerißhändler," no. 7, 31 March 1849; "Über einen Sünder der Buße thut, is mehr Freude als über 90 Gerechte," no. 10, 21 April 1849, and similarly, the report from Hittorf in no. 13, 12 May 1849.

15. Statement of purpose and "Im zweiten England," in *VdB*, no. 1, 17 Feb. 1849; "Den Geldjägern in Heumar Kr. Mülheim," no. 3, 3 March 1849; report from Ranzel, no. 4, 10 March 1849; "Sämtliche Friedensrichter," no. 5, 17 March 1849; report from Merheim, no. 9, 14 April 1849; "Geehrte Abonnenten und Leser!" and letter from Mülheim, no. 14, 19 May 1849; report from Lechenich,

no. 18, 16 June 1849. Wessel had no love for the aristocracy, either, admittedly a social group of less importance in the bourgeois society of the Rhineland. See the report from Bedburg in no. 2, 24 Feb. 1849; "Das aristokratische Fräulein," no. 6, 24 March 1849; denunciation of *Privat-Geistliche* Süß in Kalk, no. 35, 5 Jan. 1850.

16. Report from Mülheim, in *VdB*, no. 3, 3 March 1849; "Sämtliche; Domherren," no. 2, 24 Feb. 1849; report from Merheim, no. 9, 14 April 1849. Similarly, see "Dem Erzbischof Johannes von Geissel," no. 4, 10 March 1849; article on Protestant pastor Küppers, no. 6, 24 March 1849; "Volk die Augen auf!" no. 11, 28 April 1849; denunciation of cathedral pastor Filz, no. 12, 5 May 1849; note from Deutz, no. 15, 26 May 1849; denunciation of Pastor Hoch in Lanck, no. 19, 23 June 1849; article on Filz, no. 37, 19 Jan. 1850. Wessel's contribution to the debate in the Cologne Workers' Association on how to combat the influence of the Catholic clergy, in which he described how he heckled a priest during his sermon, suggests that his active anticlericalism predated his decision to start a newspaper. See *Freiheit, Brüderlichkeit Arbeit*, no. 6, 12 Nov. 1848.

17. Report from Hamersbach, *VdB*, no. 13, 12 May 1849; "So ernährt man das Alter," no. 3, 3 March 1849; "Dem Erzbischof Johannes von Geißel" and report from Ranzel, no. 4, 10 March 1849; note on inequality in cemeteries, and report on Protestant Pastor Küpprs, no. 6, 24 March 1849; "Man soll nichts über die Herren Geistlichen sagen," no. 7, 31 March 1849; "Pf. Franz Peter Berg," no. 16, 2 June 1849; "Ehre dem Ehre gebührt!" no. 5, 17 March 1849.

18. "Das ist auch wahr," in *VdB*, no. 1, 17 Feb. 1849; "Nicht nur in Januarias und Februarius," no. 6, 24 March 1849; "Sämtliche Domherren," no. 2, 23 Feb. 1849. Similarly, see "Dem Pastor in Rheindorf," no. 11, 28 April 1849; "Allen Priestern und Leviten," no. 14, 19 May 1849; "Pf. Franz Peter Berg," no. 16, 2 June 1849; report from Niehl, no. 39, 2 Feb. 1850. The incident in Worringen apparently caused something of a stir and was reported elsewhere in the left-wing press. See *Neue Rheinische Zeitung*, 23 March 1849, Beilage.

19. "Sämtlichen Juden, sowie allen Christen-Juden!" *VdB*, no. 16, 2 June 1849.

20. "Israelitischer Sonderbund," *VdB*, no. 39, 2 Feb. 1850.

21. The article is in *VdB*, no. 14, 19 May 1849, although to judge by its style it was one of the few not written by Wessel personally. On the charges of ritual murder, see Sperber, *Rhineland Radicals*, 214-15.

22. Besides attacking the Jewish garment merchants, as mentioned above, the newspaper did publish a letter (*VdB*, no. 14, 19 May 1849) condemning the merchant contractors of Mülheim across the river from Cologne, for not paying that city's outworking silk weavers the agreed wage.

23. "Im Zweiten England," *VdB*, no. 1, 17 Feb. 1849. Other uses of this phrase appear in the note from Bedburg, no. 2, 24 Feb. 1849; report from Hamersbach, no. 13, 12 May 1849; "Pf. Franz Peter Berg," no. 16, 2 June 1849.

24. In his statement of purpose (*VdB*, no. 1, 17 Feb. 1849) Wessel noted that he would write so "the simple countryman" (*der schlichte Landmann*) could understand him. On the marketing of the newspaper, see "Dem Bürgermeister von Frechen," no. 2, 24 Feb. 1849; report from Frechen, no. 20, 30 June 1849.

25. Norbert Finzsch, *Obrigkeit und Unterschichten: Zur Geschichte der rhe-*

inischen Unterschichten gegen Ende des 18. und zu Beginn des 19. Jahrhunderts (Stuttgart, 1990); Pierre Ayçobery, *Cologne entre Napoléon et Bismarck: La croissance d'une ville rhénane* (Paris, 1981), 96-98, 102-4, 184-87.

26. On the events of the spring of 1849, see Sperber, *Rhineland Radicals,* chaps. 9-11.

27. Poem on the Elberfeld uprising, *VdB,* no. 13, 12 May 1849; report from *Kreis* Bergheim, No. 15, 26 May 1849; poem on the Palatine uprising, no. 17, 9 June 1849.

28. Statement of purpose in *VdB,* no. 1, 17 Feb. 1849; opposition to inheritance of property, lead article in no. 35, 5 Jan. 1850.

29. "Sämtliche Friedensrichter," *VdB,* no. 5, 17 March 1849; "Pf. Franz Peter Berg," no. 16, 2 June 1849. Similar identification of democracy and socialism with the true teachings of Christ appears in the lead article and "So ernährt man das Alter," no. 3, 3 March 1849; "Das Esel ist vom Volk," no. 5, 17 March 1849; "Nicht nur im Januarius und Februarius," no. 6, 24 March 1849; "Volk die Augen auf!" no. 12, 5 May 1849; report from Hamersbach, no. 13, 12 May 1849; "Allen Priestern und Leviten," no. 14, 19 May 1849; "Zu seiner Zeit hielten Einige den göttlichen Heiland für einen Volksverführer," no. 20, 30 June 1849; report from Niehl, no. 39, 2 Feb. 1850.

30. See attack on the "Jew Oppenheim," *VdB,* no. 17, 9 June 1849; report from Frechen, no. 20, 30 June 1849; report from Niehl, no. 39, 2, Feb. 1850.

31. *VdB,* no. 18, 16 June 1849.

32. "Volk die Augen auf!" *VdB,* no. 12, 5 May 1849. Similarly, see "Zu seiner Zeit heilten Einige den göttlichen Heiland für einen Volksverführer," no. 20, 30 June 1849.

33. Report from Merheim, *VdB,* no. 9, 14 April 1849; "Israelitischer Sonderbund," no. 39, 2 Feb. 1850. Similarly, see "Dem Bürgermeister von Frechen," no. 3, 3 March 1849; "Sämtliche Friedensrichter," no. 5, 17 March 1849; "Aufforderung an alle Herrschaften," no. 6, 24 March 1849; report on the "Kranken-Kasse St. Johann-Baptist," no. 12, 5 May 1849; correspondent from Mülheim, no. 14, 19 May 1849; report on the *Landrat* of *Kreis* Bergheim, no. 15, 26 May 1849; "Sämmtliche Juden sowie allen Christen-Juden!" no. 16, 2 June 1849.

34. Report from Merheim, *VdB,* no. 9, 14 April 1849. Similarly, see report from Hamersbach, no. 13, 12 May 1849; note from Deutz, no. 15, 26 May 1849; "Pf. Franz Peter Berg," no. 16, 2 June 1849; note from Niehl, no. 39, 2 Feb. 1850. The song is a version of the Marseillaise, written by the revolutionary poet Ferdinand Freiligrath and premiered at the festivity in honor of the first anniversary of the barricade fighting in March 1848, sponsored by Cologne's Democratic Society and its Workers' Association. See *Neue Rheinische Zeitung,* 21 March 1849.

35. In one of his anti-Semitic and anticlerical tirades, Wessel compared himself to St. Peter, a name ostensibly painful to the Jews, since "the Jews . . . crucified [him], because he condemned the Jews for their injustice, their swindles, just as the persecutor of evil looks beneath the cloaks of those gentlemen in black robes, who also cannot bear the name 'Wessel'" (from denunciation of the "Jew Oppenheim," *VdB,* no. 17, 9 June 1849).

36. Given the involvement in it of the founder of modern communism, the history of the Cologne Workers' Association has been frequently written. A dis-

cussion of the group and its leaders, as well as a consideration of the extensive literature on it, is in Sperber, *Rhineland Radicals*, 223-31, 297-304, 351-54 (which is also the source for all otherwise unreferenced discussions of politics on the Cologne left and its publications). On Wessel's position in the factional conflict, see *Freiheit, Arbeit*, no. 32, 17 June 1849; two articles on the split in the Workers' Association signed "W." and "F." in *VdB*, no. 13, 12 May 1849; denunciation of *Privat-Geistliche* Süß, no. 35, 5 Jan. 1850.

37. No membership lists have been preserved, so it is impossible to prove that Wessel was actually a member then, but he mentioned in an article on the smaller bakers of Cologne and Deutz (*VdB*, no. 5, 17, March 1849) a speech Gottschalk made concerning bakers at the 21 April 1848 meeting of the Workers' Association (*ZAVK*, no. 2, 30 April 1848).

38. *ZAVK*, no. 5, 21 May 1848; Walter Kühn, *Der junge Hermann Becker: Ein Quellenbeitrag zur Geschichte der Arbeiterbewegung in Rheinpreußen* (Dortmund, 1934), 106-10.

39. "Trostgedanken für Deutsche," *VdB*, no. 15, 26 May 1849, and no. 17, 9 June 1849.

40. On these rationalist sects, see Sylvia Paletschek, *Frauen und Dissens: Frauen im Deutschkatholizismus und in den freien Gemeinden 1841-1852* (Göttingen, 1990). Cf. Sperber, *Rhineland Radicals*, 126-29, 285-86. The contrast raised by Edward Berenson in his interesting *Populist Religion and Left-Wing Politics in France, 1830-1852* (Princeton, N.J., 1984), 237-38, between a French socialist movement based on a radicalized, rationalist Christianity and a "scientific," Marxist German radicalism, suffers from the author's lack of awareness of the importance of precisely these semi-religious ideas in early radicalism and the labor movement of central Europe.

41. On French working-class journalists and writers, see William H. Sewell, Jr., *Work and Revolution in France: The Language of Labor from the Old Regime to 1848* (Cambridge, 1980), 197-218, 236-42; or, from a very different point of view, Jacques Rancière, *The Nights of Labor: The Workers' Dreams in Nineteenth Century France*, trans. John Drury (Philadelphia, 1989).

42. Maurice Agulhon, *The Republic in the Village: The People of the Var from the French Revolution to the Second Republic*, trans. Janet Lloyd (Cambridge, 1982), 164. Like all students of the revolution of 1848, I have been strongly influenced by this great work.

8

Antislavery, Civil Rights, and Incendiary Material

THOMAS C. LEONARD

Once in the nineteenth century and once in our century, many Americans believed that new media were sounding the call for a racial revolution. In the 1830s, antislavery activists used print in new ways while their enemies, north and south, tried to stop this media revolution. In the civil rights era of the 1950s and 1960s, innovative national media put the white South on trial and again provoked outrage among conservatives. The reach of the media helps to explain the depth of feelings in these crises. Incendiary media illuminate the complex ways that texts are read when social relationships are renegotiated. When media play a role in revolution, the reason is often that leaders manage to force new readings of news and draw legitimacy from these interpretations. When talk of revolution is serious, coverage meant to buttress one side may end up as the chief prop of the enemy. Words and pictures that once seemed safe become infuriating in a new context. I suggest that we look at this process of subversion to understand the power of the press, beginning with the media revolution for antislavery in the nineteenth century.

Attacks on slavery had small circulation before the 1830s. New organizations arose early in this decade that were determined to dramatize for a much larger audience the injustice of bondage. The American Anti-Slavery Society, formed at the end of 1833, united protesters from the West and from New England and found the money for a publicity drive in New York.

The campaign was modest at first: in 1834 some 122,000 newspapers and tracts carried the news of antislavery. But in 1835 more than a million anti-slavery publications went out from New York to a nation of fifteen million. No issue of fundamental political change had ever generated such a flow of paper in the United States. In this volume, Jeffery Smith has drawn our attention to the fears of revolution and the suppression of a dissenting press by the Adams administration; in Jacksonian America this wish to cud-gel the press reached just as high into the government and attracted a broader public.[1]

President Andrew Jackson denounced these "incendiary publications" in his message to Congress in December 1835. The phrase was more than a metaphor: many towns burned antislavery publications. In Charleston, South Carolina, for example, the hated papers had been seized at the post office in July and provided a communal bonfire, and southern legislatures specified that this news be put to the flame. It is axiomatic to conclude that southerners who burned the antislavery argument acted in fear. But fear may open debates rather than close them. Virginia, the state with the most slaves, had openly debated abolition only a few months after Nat Turner's insurrection in 1831 had massacred more than fifty whites in the state. Fear-ful Virginians circulated arguments for abolition in the press in 1832— arguments so plausible that the Virginia House of Delegates declared slav-ery to be "evil." A southern editor said then that he knew of no Virginia paper opposed to the eventual emancipation of slaves. Only three years later, in calmer times, white fears could not be contained. This antislavery literature carried arguments that southern whites dismissed out of hand. Why, then, the obsession to burn this news?[2]

The key to understanding the southern fear of antislavery publications is to be found in the response of the North to this literature. All across the free states in the summer and fall of 1835, meetings were held to take stock of the new antislavery press and its angry readers. Philadelphians in "an immense assemblage" resolved "that we regard the dissemination of in-cendiary publications throughout the slave-holding states with indignation and horror." Feelings ran just as high in many smaller towns. A Rochester paper said that the meeting that damned the antislavery crusade was one of the largest in the history of that city. In Portland, Maine, the meeting to condemn the "incendiary machinations of Northern fanatics" was the larg-est gathering the town had ever seen.[3]

Everywhere, leading citizens took charge of these mass meetings. New Haven, Connecticut, was swayed against the "incendiary documents" by the words of Noah Webster, the lexicographer. Harrison Gray Otis, a commanding figure in Massachusetts politics since the 1790s, gave a celebrated speech in Boston's Faneuil Hall. In New York City and Boston the mayor chaired the meeting that drafted the censure; in Albany and in New Haven it was the state governor.

Resolutions were judged insufficient by many northern critics of the antislavery press. Mobs formed to turn back the surge of abolitionist meetings and tracts. The leading antislavery papers reported 209 hostile mobs in the North in the 1830s and 1840s. A Philadelphia mob tore abolitionist literature into pieces and dumped the paper into the Delaware in August 1835. There was more shredding of antislavery papers in Utica in October, and a local publisher who defended the right of abolitionists to assemble had his type thrown into the street. In Boston the same day, a mob that grew to four or five thousand threw antislavery papers into the gutter and led editor William Lloyd Garrison on a walk with a noose around his neck. In July 1836 a Cincinnati mob broke into the printshop of the town's antislavery newspaper, scattered the type set for the next issue, and dismantled the press. When abolitionists quickly repaired the damage, a second mob (which included the mayor) repeated the sacking. Elijah Lovejoy's press was destroyed as it arrived in Alton, Illinois, that same month. In 1837 Lovejoy's press was wrecked by mobs two more times, and it was in defense of his fourth press in November that editor Lovejoy was shot and killed. The mob did not scatter but stayed calmly to dismantle the new press. The terror continued in scores of communities until the early 1840s.[4]

What did northerners fear and hate in the antislavery press? It was not simply the idea of a larger measure of justice for blacks; a minority of Americans had been left in peace to argue this unpopular cause until the middle 1830s, and the North had no slaves to lose. Yet the suppression of this news was high on the agenda of the mobs. A city that sat astride a river of southern trade, such as Cincinnati, had a good reason to rally for its customers, the planters. But what economic motive could drive the citizens of Rochester, Utica, and even Cooperstown, New York, to fill sweltering meeting halls? In any case, citizens took to the streets to damn the antislavery press before the South had threatened economic retaliation.

Obviously, racism is a tempting explanation of what led northerners to rally around the white South. Many northerners were sickened by the "amalgamation" that they saw in the association of blacks and whites in antislavery. But the communities that hated the antislavery press were not hotbeds of racism. Philadelphia with its Quaker heritage was not well schooled in

racial hate. Cincinnati had been home to the organization of antislavery in
the West through the Lane Seminary. Alton, Illinois, had the novelty of inte-
grated schools, and just four months before Elijah Lovejoy was killed by a
mob, his enemies assembled to insist that "we abhor and deprecate the evil
of Slavery." Men like Harrison Gray Otis did not deal in racial epithets. Noah
Webster had denounced slavery as a young man and worked his sentiments
into one of his school texts.[5]

In his classic study of antiabolition mobs, Leonard L. Richards has argued that the issues between the North and the South—indeed, the contents of the antislavery publications—were incidental to the feeling of crisis
that gripped so many communities in the mid-1830s. Rather, both North and
the South reacted so sharply because they sensed that political communication was changing. The "gentlemen of property and standing" who chaired
meetings and often led others in the streets saw in antislavery a challenge to
what they stood for. Politicians and editors had carried the name and reputation of their community to the nation; now the masthead of a dissident sheet
would stain the town's reputation as it circulated and as upstart contributors
to this press dared to assume leadership. Antislavery linked to mass circulation proceeded with a blind eye—or a nod of defiance—to local political
leadership. Local communities rose up against antislavery because it threatened to turn their world upside down.[6]

News in print, for the first time in the United States, was an invitation to
citizens assigned no political role in the normal course of Whig or Democratic campaigns. Addressing blacks was bad enough, but in the patriarchy
of American democracy, antislavery literature was also diabolical because
it reached white women and children. This notorious feature of abolitionism was highlighted by papers with special sections for the young and for
women. "[Woman] is to be converted into a fiend," John Tyler, the future
president, warned his fellow Virginians after he read the incendiary publications.[7]

The defenders of slavery were in awe of this new way of conducting
political disputes. They denounced the pictures that made points even the
illiterate could grasp. The cheapness of this news seemed as alarming as its
content. Tyler stood before his townsfolk and read them the subscription
prices of the leading antislavery papers. Presses capable of this could do
boundless evil. "Such are not harmless weapons," a Georgian wrote from
the North's publishing center. "THEY ARE ALL-SUFFICIENT TO DO DESTRUCTION
UPON THE SOUTH." A Charleston editor saw abolitionists "hurling their moral
firebrands of desolation and death, from their catapult in New York, into
the very bosom and vitals of the South." "Some poisonous missile may yet

pass the barrier," the *Richmond Enquirer* said. Mobs and their bonfires could not stop a press with this range.[8]

Why didn't the South at least dream of its own powerful presses, especially as it learned that the northern public was turning out to express sympathy? Proslavery had powerful themes: race prejudice, fears for the union, nativist sentiment against British influence among the abolitionists. Why didn't the South flood the northern post with *these* incendiary appeals? In a celebrated pamphlet of 1836 a northern statesman invited the South to fill the mails of the free states with their most candid and abusive observations. No one in the South took the dare.[9]

The South, of course, was handicapped technologically. It was not a publishing center, and presses like those that "thundered" so ominously in southern ears would have been difficult to establish. On the eve of the Civil War the fifteen slave states and the District of Columbia produced just 25 percent of the quantity of printing turned out in the state of New York. Slave states might have spent more to develop their own presses, but no such visionary scheme was necessary to compete with antislavery: the North stood ready to print the proslavery argument. This was a part of the publishing business that some southern editors kept from their readers. *DeBow's Review*, the South's leading periodical and most militant defender of slavery in the 1840s and 1850s, was the product of northern printshops. Proslavery publicists, backed by government and business, were in a better position to arrange mass circulation than the abolitionists, a despised minority in the North. But for all these opportunities, the white South did not put its heart into a battle for public opinion. Like the northern gentlemen of property and standing, defenders of slavery feared a broad public brought into politics by mass circulation.[10]

This was the hard lesson learned by the southern journalist who was in the best position to answer the incendiary publications, the redoubtable Duff Green. His *United States Telegraph* in Washington championed the slave cause. This Kentuckian was living proof of the restless energy of the American democrat. Green had studied medicine, law, and land values. He fought Indians and had a hand in every form of speculation that the West offered. Green had run the first stagecoach line west of the Mississippi, founded a town in Missouri, and prospered as an editor and merchant in St. Louis. At first he was a bulldog for Andrew Jackson, but he had gone over to John C. Calhoun of South Carolina by the time abolitionists picked a fight. The editor had defended slavery since the debates over the admission of Missouri to the Union in 1820, so his loyalty to the South was above question. His daughter had married Calhoun's son, if blood lines were to count as well as conviction. In 1835, when abolitionist news filled the mails, Green used his paper to defend the white South. He dreamed of more work with powerful rotary presses and had a scheme to cut the cost of setting type by running a printing school for boys. But Green's enterprise went unrewarded. The editor was repudiated by spokesmen for the slaveholders. They feared he was spreading abolitionism by refuting its doctrines. Southern editors argued that only silence could stop the heresy. The *Telegraph* soon died.[11]

Antislavery publications, however, continued to appear. In 1838 Theodore Dwight Weld, a tireless lecturer for emancipation, began work on a book to "thrill the land with horror" about slavery. He purchased the discarded southern newspapers from the New York Commercial Reading Room, hauled at least 20,000 issues out to his home in New Jersey, and set his household to work reading the news. Weld was married to Angelina Grimké of Charleston, and her sister Sarah lived with the couple. The three abolitionists settled down with southern newspapers in the fall of 1838 and were hard at the reading throughout the winter.[12] "Heart sickening as the details are," Sarah Grimké wrote, "I am thankful that God in his providence has put into our hands these weapons prepared by the South herself, to destory the fell monster."

American Slavery as it Is: Testimony of a Thousand Witnesses (1839) was a subversive scrapbook. Almost all of the more than four hundred items taken from southern papers—notices of runaway slaves and accounts of slave catching and punishment—had been originally published for the purpose of keeping blacks in bondage. For example, the *Montgomery Advertiser* of 29 September 1837 had printed: "$20 REWARD.—Ranaway from the subscriber, a negro man named Moses. He is of common size, about 28 years old. He formerly belonged to Judge Benson, of Montgomery, and it is said, had a wife in that county." Such newspaper items had been common in the South for a century. The white community needed such news in order to police its labor system. Everyone knew how to read these notices, and not one had thought that they undermined slavery. *American Slavery as It Is* changed the context so that the news could be read another way. The South had long argued that the conscience of slaveholders protected black families, yet this master thought nothing of separating Moses from his wife. Scores of items exposed the same callousness. The author of the notice for Moses was John Gayle, governor of Alabama when the incendiary publications first came South, a man who read the circulation figures of these papers aloud as the strongest evidence of northern malevolence. In the hands of antislavery editors, his own words had become incendiary.[13]

American Slavery as It Is showed the talent for mass circulation that was the white South's nightmare. The 224-page collection appeared just a few months after the last news item had been clipped. It sold for 25 cents in bulk orders, and local antislavery committees presented free copies of the work to opinion leaders. The southern newspapers used in the volume were each sent a copy gratis, with its unwitting contributions marked. Sales topped 100,000 the first year and the book proved to be the most popular item on antislavery lists until *Uncle Tom's Cabin* appeared in 1852. Further, these press runs, however impressive, understate the new life it gave to obscure news items. Borrowing from the Weld-Grimké collection of southern news became a literary industry. In his *American Notes* (1842) Charles Dickens lifted forty-four items on runaways. Harriet Beecher Stowe said that she slept with *American Slavery as It Is* under her pillow while writing *Uncle Tom's Cabin* and in *A Key to Uncle Tom's Cabin* (1853) she recycled Weld-Grimké clippings and added her own from more than 200 southern papers to support her novel. Southern critics of *Uncle Tom's Cabin* were told to spend more time reading their own newspapers.[14]

In the quarter-century between the rise of incendiary publications in the North and the Civil War, no southerner made systematic use of American news items to support the status quo. The white South was shy of the news because it lacked confidence in the whole enterprise of using print to rally a national public. Southern efforts to use the printing press against abolitionists were haunted by fear and defeatism. Consider that assembly of South Carolina citizens gathered in the Barnwell District to mark the first bonfire of news in Charleston. Edmund Bellinger, Jr., a twenty-eight-year-old lawyer, gave his neighbors as belligerent a defense of slavery as any audience heard before the Civil War. But Bellinger was timid about printing the speech: "Although published, I have used proper precautions to prevent its being circulated among any but those who are Southern in sentiment, and Southern in conduct—*to none other is it addressed.*" Several proslavery writers said that they wrote with no thought to publication, and one even apologized for the "trouble" of publication. William Gilmore Simms, for instance, was a novelist and newspaper editor and certainly not the most timid of the proslavery spokesmen about breaking into print. But Simms apologized about agreeing to "extended circulation" of his defense of the morality of slavery. Proslavery arguments were bound to the world of the regional review: journals in which fine arguments were spun for the South's better citizens. Circulation was minuscule. The panic of the white

South in the 1830s did not drive many southerners into print. In this decade, in fact, northerners actually wrote twice as many books and pamphlets *defending* slavery as southern authors did.[15]

Although the South lost the Civil War, it seemed to win the argument over the attention to be paid to the argument for racial equality. By the end of Reconstruction in 1876, all mainstream publications had given up on stories that might bring the political aspirations of blacks into focus. African Americans refused to ride public transportation in more than twenty-five cities in the South half a century before the celebrated bus boycott in Montgomery, Alabama, but this early protest was ignored by national media.[16] Popular magazines rarely went near the subject of race until well after World War II.

The change occurred in the mid-1950s. The Supreme Court's decision in *Brown v. Board of Education* (1954) became an ongoing story as the forces of resistance took their stand. In August 1955 the lynching of Emmett Till brought more than fifty reporters from across the nation into a courthouse in the Mississippi Delta. In December the bus boycott and Martin Luther King, Jr., brought Montgomery into focus. These stories marshaled a national press corps that would stay in attendance on the race issue for a decade. For the first time since the nineteenth century, the mail from the North brought an abundance of incendiary material: "Approved Killing in Mississippi," William Bradford Huie wrote for *Look*, 24 January 1955. "A Bold Boycott Goes On—" said *Life*, 5 March 1956, as it introduced its readers to the Reverend Mr. King. *Life* did a five-part series on segregation the following year, beginning by putting a slave auction on the cover.

This attention came in the dizzying final years of growth in general circulation magazines. The publishers were in a race with television for the mass public, and subscription drives were relentless. *Life* alone estimated that it reached more than a third of all American families: nearly 60 million Americans held a copy in the six weeks following the publication date. Never again would print be such a common denominator of American homes, for eventually this reach for readers put most of these magazines out of business. But no one foresaw such an outcome in 1955. Slick magazines lay on the coffee table, near the television set that would soon bring racial conflict into focus when the civil rights movement was a bit older.[17]

In telling the story of civil rights, the new media earned as excited a welcome as did the publicists of antislavery. Antiabolitionist crowds had seized the papers they hated, but in the nineteenth-century South the mobs could only dream of catching the authors. At virtually every step in the civil rights struggle, angry white southerners looked into the faces of journalists. The white South fought the press in courts and business offices by filing suits, pulling ads, and canceling subscriptions.[18] Segregationists also fought the press in the streets. Each of the reporters who covered the civil rights movement has a crowd story: they were engulfed and insulted, and the unlucky were physically assaulted. There were major confrontations in Arkansas, Alabama, and Mississippi; briefer skirmishes in Tennessee, Maryland, Georgia, and Florida. More than fifty members of the press were beaten.[19] At Little Rock in 1957 a correspondent for the Hearst chain who had covered World War II and Korea said that the campus of Central High scared him as few battlefields had. Covering this story, he said, was like standing next to an open gas jet, waiting for a flame to be struck. The beatings of four black journalists at Little Rock showed the murderous potential. Five years later, at the University of Mississippi, Paul Guihard of Agence France Presse was taken behind a tree, made to kneel, and executed.[20]

Frequently the assaults and harassment took on a life of their own, independent of the crowd's hunt for blacks who dared to integrate. "We ought to wipe up the street with Yankee reporters," citizens yelled repeatedly at Central High in Little Rock. "Let's kill every reporter we can find," was the call at Ole Miss. On the May morning in 1961 when freedom riders reached Montgomery on a Greyhound bus, a mob delayed its attack on the passengers in order to finish off the press. John Lewis, the black civil rights leader, saw white men rush forward and smash the press corps, leaving his own group alone for the moment. The fury at journalists exploded before the whites turned their clubs on the freedom riders.[21]

In the tradition of mobs that stretches back to the American Revolution, these activities seemed an extension of legitimate authority in the minds of many in the crowd. "We've got permission to kick the —— out of them," an activist shouted in Alabama. In many cities, this man was right. In Little Rock, Birmingham, Oxford, and Marion there was coordination between southern police forces and the mob. Law officers condoned and even encouraged the attacks.[22]

Many of the citizens who formed mobs sized up the press with some care. This may be a hard idea to accept. The mobs that are best known today from the PBS television series *Eyes on the Prize* do not look like students of media techniques; still less do they seem fortified by research. But many were. On several occasions there was method in the madness of press haters. White reporters with a southern accent often had a shield; if that failed, they were more likely than others to win an apology from the southerners who had beaten them. But mastheads mattered as much as regional loyalty, according to reporters at the scene. The *Arkansas Gazette* had staff beaten for the sins of its editorial page in defying Governor Orval Faubus. Mobs settled scores with southern news organizations that had crossed them on racial matters.

There was no surer way to become a press martyr than to work for the Yankee with the largest circulation and gall, Henry Luce. In the judgment of a southern reporter who talked with a mob at Little Rock, Time-Life was made to pay for its early discovery of black America and its weekly criticism of segregationist heroes. *U.S. News and World Report* devoted as much attention to integration as did *Time*, but this conservative weekly deplored the civil rights movement and told the story the way the white South saw it. Employees of *U.S. News and World Report* were conspicious by their absence in casualty reports. In the opinion of a Justice Department official, this was more than luck: finding that segregationists cooled down when one mentioned that publication, in Birmingham this federal lawman used the magazine as his cover.[23]

At Little Rock the hotheads wanted to edit, not just destroy. On assignment at Central High, Benjamin Fine of the *New York Times* accused a heckler of not having read the stories he filed. This segregationist sent away for a subscription and passed the paper on to friends. "Within a day, some twenty of the segregationists, who had been ready to tear me apart, and had given me a hard time, apologized," Fine said. This reporter noticed that his new readers now protected him at rallies.[24]

Crowds did their own reporting and were outraged by the prospect that what they saw and felt would not be what they would find in print. In Little Rock, shouts from the streets through the day told the story: "Oh, my, God, they're going in. . . . The niggers are in. . . . The niggers got in. . . . They tricked us. The niggers got in. . . . Look at that. They arrest a white girl and let the niggers in our school." This narrative was supplemented by segregationists' sheets, circulating through the crowd. "That's what we're fighting, you see," one man said as he pointed to a headline on the Communist conspiracy. In calling out their story, segregationists challenged the press to see the world as they saw it. In Little Rock, the moment after blood was shed, reporters heard calls to write stories that would confirm Governor Faubus's claim that violence was inevitable if integration went forward. They would accept no other story.[25]

Antebellum mobs wanted to smash presses and see the news in flames. Segregationists did not return to this ritual of impersonal bonfires and sackings. The newsstands and offices were safe; it was the embodiment of the press, the witnesses with their recording devices, that drove mobs to fury.

Segregationist mobs were smashers of the instruments that threatened the widest distribution of their activities: cameras and broadcasting gear. Cameras and all types of electronic equipment such as lights and tape recorders were invitations to mayhem in the South. This hardware, a reporter for *Newsday* said, is "often more dangerous than guns in the midst of race-baiting mobs." In the eight years of street violence against the press, cameras were often the first things a mob grabbed (and the only things they sprayed with paint). Blinding the press was the first priority of a southern mob.[26]

Why, of all people, should friends of Jim Crow have feared the camera? They assembled to show the South that blacks could be turned back and that federal forces were tyrants; they carried signs and placards. Photography could help. "Evidence of the naked force of the Federal Government is here apparent in the unsheathed bayonet in the backs of school girls," Governor Faubus said in a television address as he held up a news photo. He also showed his audience a news photo of a bleeding leader of the mob, introduced as a martyr. Coverage of Little Rock, especially in pictures, helped to build resistance in the deep South, according to correspondents. George Wallace's stand at the door to bar a black student from the University of Alabama made no sense without cameras to record it. This may have been a reason that Col. Al Lingo, leading the Alabama state police in the preservation of segregation forever, gave cameramen a ringside seat for the protest on the Edmund Pettus Bridge at Selma in 1965. Standing up to defy integration and blinding the witnesses would seem to be self-canceling politics.[27]

For people who were acting outside the law, of course, there was a logic in destroying the evidence that could lead to arrest or retaliation. But that is not how racist vigilantes had conducted themselves before the civil rights movement. Posing for a photograph had been a venerable tradition of lynchers in the South. The posing stopped in the 1930s, but dependence on the camera remained. In 1959 whites of Poplarville, Mississippi, pasted a news photo of the town's jail on their auto windshields, marking the cell of a black prisoner who had just been lynched. The purpose was to scare blacks and whites who questioned the American apartheid. Was this purpose less pressing when integrationists had come out in the open that it had been when they lay hidden?[28]

At issue here was the reach of the stories told by still cameras and broadcasting gear. Like antislavery agitation in the 1830s, pictures of racial conflict were circulating too widely in the 1950s to be lived with in peace. Photojournalism for a mass market was only two decades old. Television was an infant (especially in Little Rock, whose residents waited until the

Korean War ended for the broadcasts to begin). But the number of television stations increased five times between 1953 and 1957. Little Rock's troubles reached a viewing public that dwarfed the television audience when the decade began: 85 percent of all homes were watching for five hours a day. Television had come of age ignorant of black America, especially in the South, where local stations would often drop network programs that featured black entertainers. As late as 1960 the television networks cut away from black speakers at the national party conventions to spare the feelings of segregationists. As we've seen, print journalism had never incorporated black Americans into routine coverage. In breaking this taboo with civil rights demonstrations, the mass media told stories that held talismanic power.[29]

When a phalanx of white men in bib overalls rushed John Chancellor in a small Mississippi town, the broadcaster held up his microphone and shouted, "All right, come on, the whole world is going to know what you're doing to me." The mob backed off.[30] A sure sense that the whole world was watching raised the stakes for everyone following the civil rights story. The white South was aware that it was being humiliated abroad. Southerners noted that there were more than ten foreign reporters at King's trial during the Montgomery bus boycott. The mobbing of freedom riders in Birmingham was a picture on the front pages of papers in Tokyo and an embarrassment to a touring Alabama business delegation.[31]

The civil rights movement itself believed that the right media outlets had magical power. John Lewis of the Student Nonviolent Coordinating Committee, saw that television was transforming the protests that he had begun without regard to press coverage. During the Birmingham demonstrations Lewis and his friends at Fisk University pinned the stories from the press on trees so that students would mobilize. In the early 1960s the Congress of Racial Equality issued handbills that were reprints from the national press, prominently displaying the source. Rather than tell their own stories of the mobs and demonstrations, CORE members sought the imprimatur of prestigious media. This was precisely what segregationist mobs seemed to know instinctively, that images let loose by the national media were deeply wounding.[32]

Mobs were not simply guardians of their community's image; they had been protectors of its means of intimidation. Isolation and a sense of impotence were required if blacks were to remain second-class citizens. Too many witnesses complicated the abridgment of rights. Lynch photographs were meant to be private, memory pieces for a small audience who shared assumptions (and sometimes were reminded of the racist rationale in notes written on the back of the photos). Press photographers of the crowd were therefore not welcomed. The creation of a vast audience for beatings spoiled everything.[33]

Meanwhile, the victims learned they had allies. The number of marches, sit-ins, and freedom rides grew in tandem with the national coverage. Always before, these tactics had played out without being carried by the mainstream media. Now photojournalism and broadcasting, especially, kept issues alive. Segregationists themselves could visualize an audience conscious of its strength and willing to persist in these protests. As a worried planter told Theodore H. White, "Every one of those Negroes on my land has a television set in his shack, and he sits there in the evening and watches." "Bloody Sunday" in Selma, as filmed by the television cameras that Alabama authorities had welcomed, turned out to be a public relations disaster for segregationists. The Wallace administration's explanation was that there had been "too much film," too graphic a record for too large an audience. This supply of images was the new and fearful breach in the defense of the segregated South.

The mobs' attempts to terminate photojournalism and broadcasting were astute.[34] "A great body of opinion here is against the printing of race news," Hodding Carter of Mississippi observed in 1961. "The mob is just an extreme form of this view." Thus, the white South was true to its fears about the media of 1835. Again, the media of the region were not able to produce a counterpoint news weekly or network, but this time there were strong voices who took on the northern press, capitalizing on the resentments felt against it and subverting its reporting.[35]

The southern editor most successful in taking the fight to the northern press, a cordial antagonist of Martin Luter King, Jr., was Grover Cleveland Hall, Jr. This stylish bachelor made the editorial offices of the *Montgomery Advertiser* into a club for northern reporters during the bus boycott of 1956. "King is a souped-up Swami," Hall said. The editor was a segregationist committed to peaceful resistance. Hall's tactics against the civil rights movement caused more disarray in the ranks than any mob achieved.[36]

Hall dared the northern press to explore racial feelings at home. He goaded the *New York Post* to send reporters to see how black and white New Yorkers were getting along. When an open exchange of letters with the *Post's* liberal publisher James Wechsler did not yield these stories, the Alabama editor produced his own. Hall turned to the Bible for his running title "Tell it not in Gath, publish it not in the streets of Askelon," which headed a mischievous encyclopedia of northern failures to report on race unless that story lay conveniently in the South. The *Montgomery Adver-tiser*, one of the papers the Weld household had clipped to expose the South, now picked apart the northern press to vindicate the South. The *Advertiser* asked Yankee editors when they had last published the picture of a black bride on their society pages. A box score, printed under the famous mastheads of these papers, showed that black citizens were invisible to society editors of urban America; the *New York Times* could point to only one black bride in its whole history. Detroit papers that featured series such as "Thunder over Dixie" were caught hiding the news of a white mob that demanded segregation in the motor city. The Montgomery paper found the National Association for the Advancement of Colored People (NAACP) eager to talk about a story that northern editors wouldn't touch, of systematic discrimination in their towns.[37]

The series was sydicated in the South to great praise and summarized in national magazines with pained admiration. The Alabama legislature commended the Askelon stories and challenged the northern press to report on its own communities. Hall had charted a safe course for the editors of Dixie. Memphis papers, for example, followed Hall in featuring reports of street crime in which northerners had had their way in the race question. Harry S. Ashmore, fighting a lonely struggle for integration on the *Arkansas Gazette*, saw that Hall had built "a moral escape hatch" for southerners who could not face their own sins.[38]

The mobilization of the press of the white South to embarrass the North would be of limited interest if Hall's indictment had gone no further. But Hall was the voice of a paper that John Lewis, Ralph Abernathy, and Martin Luther King, Jr., read. Indeed, blacks of this region followed the *Advertiser* (and praised that paper) because it was more likely to give respectful attention to black life than most other white papers. King's own account of the Montgomery bus boycott shows that the movement followed the *Advertiser* closely. African American leaders did not need Hall to tell them that racism was a national curse and that the northern press was selective in its attention, but the *Montgomery Advertiser's* emphasis on the point cannot have escaped their notice. The NAACP actually commended the Askelon series at the same time that segregationists cheered it.[39]

Hall had a friend who took this story north and waged a counter-revolution to the civil rights movement. This friend called Hall nearly every day to ask for help on some of his most important speeches. His name was George Wallace. "You and I together will be able to make this nation see that it's not just the South that's so terrible," the Alabama governor told the editor.[40] Wallace had learned early in life of the power of national magazines. During the Great Depression he had traveled through the upper South and the Midwest as a magazine salesman and found that even the illiterate and the blind wanted their homes furnished with these publications. Television fascinated Wallace, and he was quick to use it in his rise in Alabama. When the King marched on Montgomery in 1965, the governor sat and watched sets tuned to every channel. Wallace was obsessed about what the press, especially the national press, thought of him. A third to a half of Wallace campaign speeches were a gloss on news coverage, according to a reporter who sat through this hunt for demons. "We got the *Newsweek* and the *Time* travelin' with us today," he would say at the beginning of a rally. "They're lookin' us over. Smile and look pretty today, because you may wind up on national television." The governor had a stock vocabulary for the people who provided this coverage: "intellectual morons" and "sissy britches editors" and "slick haired boys" and "TV dudes."[41]

Wallace used these terms even as he seized every chance for coverage in the media controlled by these creatures. At rallies he bragged of appearances on the networks and proudly held up national magazines that had written about him. Indeed, when his wife ran for governor in his place in 1966, her chief function at rallies, after introducing him, was to hold the archive of clippings that he wanted to have within easy reach. "See here, they got a picture of yo guvnuh in this magazine that goes all over this nation," Wallace said. "The national press now, anything's that bad about yo guvnah, oh yes, they gonna run that." National correspondents were granted access to the governor that local journalists could not hope for. When Colonel Lingo, head of the state troopers, barred national journalists from the confrontation at the University of Alabama, Wallace made sure that the reporters most likely to hate him could see him send the blacks away. Wallace newsletters prompted followers to look for him on national programs and in famous magazines, giving him occasions to claim misrepresentation and to scorn these media. It was as if a gambler who knew the dice were loaded should insist the game continue and the stakes be raised. Wallace was clear about why: the crooked media conferred honor. "I took 'em all on . . . and they are more respectful now," the governor would remind his audience. "They say MISTER Wallace. And when they say that, they're sayin' MISTER Alabamian, and MRS. Alabamian, and MISS Alabamian." By putting stories in his own context before his own audience, Wallace was as bold and as successful as the Welds with their scrapbook. He, too, subverted an enemy press.[42]

Wallace was not the first southern leader to court a national press while he let loose on them; Huey Long had done it. But Wallace was the first southerner to take his argument north and play on the lapses in northern reporting and the hypocrisy that Grover Hall had helped to place at the center of segregationist argument. The conservative white South never had a more effective salesman. In 1968 his presidential campaign won nearly ten million votes. Wallace did what the slave South had never dared to do: he laid out a program to the widest possible audience by embracing the media—on his own terms.[43]

The debris of a press in Alton, Illinois, and the smashed cameras in Little Rock, Arkansas, were separated by twelve decades, and the fury arose in different political contexts. Yet there are common features to these violent receptions of journalism. The media have no more powerful function than the sense they give that the whole nation, indeed the whole world is watching. The comfortable world of local elites is shattered. The meanings of words and pictures seem up for grabs. When the audience expands, locals not only lose the power to silence the press; they lose the power to attach a meaning securely to a text. Leaders who make their own selections from the enemy media help to change the meaning of texts they have appropriated. What happens, whether a Weld or a Wallace collects the clippings, is that stories become cues to social action unforeseen by the journalists who created them. The paired growth of audience and interpretive choices makes the press into incendiary material.[44]

NOTES

1. W. Sherman Savage, *The Controversy over the Distribution of Abolition Literature, 1830-1860* (New York, [1938; rept.]), 13, 92; Leonard L. Richards, *"Gentlemen of Property and Standing": Anti-Abolition Mobs in Jacksonian America* (New York, 1970).

2. Frank Otto Gatell, ed., "Postmaster Huger and the Incendiary Publications," *South Carolina Historical Magazine* 64 (Oct. 1963): 193-201; William W. Freehling, *Prelude to Civil War: The Nullification Controversy in South Carolina, 1816-1836* (New York, 1968), 327-60. Joe Williams, "Window on Freedom: South Carolina's Response to British West Indian Slave Emancipation, 1833-1834," *South Carolina Historical Magazine* 85 (April 1984): 135-44, esp. 141; Alison Goodyear Freehling, *Drift toward Dissolution: The Virginia Slavery Debate of 1831-1832* (Baton Rouge, La., 1982), 196-201; Larry E. Tise, *Proslavery: A History of the Defense of Slavery in America, 1701-1840* (Athens, Ga, 1987), 310-11.

3. *Niles' Register* 48 (29 Aug. 1835): 454-56; 49 (5 Sept., 3 and 10 Oct. 1835): 9, 73, 90.

4. Richards, *Gentlemen of Property and Standing*, 14, 69, 91-92, 95-99, 101, 110, 113; *Niles' Register* 49 (3 and 31 Oct. 1835): 78, 145.

5. *Niles' Register* 48 (22 Aug. 1835): 438; "The Fruits of Amalgamation," in David Grimsted, ed., *Notions of the Americans, 1820-1860* (New York, 1970), 104; Joseph C. and Owen Lovejoy, eds., *Memoir of the Rev. Elijah P. Lovejoy* (New York, 1838), 220; Richard M. Rollins, *The Long Journey of Noah Webster* (Philadelphia, 1980), 32-33, 127. See also Cynthia S. Jordan, "'Old Words' in 'New Circumstances': Language and Leadership in Post-Revolutionary America," *American Quarterly* 40 (Dec. 1988): 491-513.

6. See, e.g., [Calvin Colton], *Abolition a Sedition* (1839; New York, 1973), 31, 43-44, 104, 186. John C. Nerone, *The Culture of the Press in the Early Republic: Cincinnati, 1793-1848* (New York, 1989), 264-74, qualifies Richards's argument but emphasizes this town's fear that an antislavery paper would destroy Cincinnati's reputation.

7. See Richards, *Gentlemen of Property and Standing*, 56-58, for the Tyler speech.

8. Richard B. Kielbowicz, *News in the Mail: The Press, Post Office, and Public Information, 1700-1860s* (New York, 1989), 66; *Niles' Register* 49 (12 Sept. and 3 Oct. 1835): 20-21, 74, 77; *Richmond Enquirer*, quoted in the *Emancipator*, Oct. 1835; Richard Yeadon, *The Amenability of Northern Incendiaries . . .* (1835; Charleston, 1853), 17. Cassius M. Clay, the antislavery editor from Kentucky, held up his own new press as the perfect expression of a free labor system that the South could not match; see Grimsted, *Notions of the Americans*, 295.

9. Cincinnatus [William Plumer?], *Freedom's Defence . . .* (Worcester, 1836), 22.

10. *Manufactures of the United States in 1860 . . . the Eighth Census* (Washington, D.C., 1865), cxlii; Hinton R. Helper, *The Impending Crisis of the South: How to Meet It*, ed. George M. Fredrickson (1857; Cambridge, Mass., 1968), 390-92; Ottis C. Skipper, *J.D.B. DeBow, Magazinist of the Old South*, (Athens, Ga., 1958), 24-25, 50, 61-63, 83-84, 87-88, 125.

11. Fletcher M. Green, "Duff Green, Militant Journalist of the Old School," *American Historical Review* 52 (1947), 256-58. The *Emancipator* (Oct. 1835) praised Green for republishing more antislavery material than southern mobs had burned. See William S. Pretzer, "'The British, Duff Green, the Rats and the Devil': Custom, Capitalism, and the Conflict in the Washington Printing Trade, 1834-1836," *Labor History* 27 (1985-86), 5-30, esp. 13-15.

12. *Letters of Theodore Dwight Weld, Angelina Grimké Weld, and Sarah Grimké, 1822-1844*, ed. Gilbert H. Barnes and Dwight L. Dumond, 2 vols. (Gloucester, Mass., 1965), 2:717.

13. Katharine Du Pre Lumpkin, *The Emancipation of Angelina Grimké* (Chapel Hill, N.C., 1974), 171; Benjamin P. Thomas, *Theodore Dwight Weld: A Crusader for Freedom* (New Brunswick, N.J., 1950), 169; Thomas M. Owen, "An Alabama Protest against Abolition in 1835," *Gulf States Historical Magazine* 2 (July 1903): 26-34; *American Slavery as It Is: Testimony of a Thousand Witnesses* (New York, 1839), 172.

14. Louise H. Johnson, "The Source of the Chapter on Slavery in Dickens's *American Notes*," *American Literature* 14 (1942-43): 427-30; Thomas, *Theodore Dwight Weld*, 223; Harriet Beecher Stowe, "The Story of Uncle Tom's Cabin," *Old South Leaflets*, gen. ser.,4, no. 82 (1897): 6; Stowe, *A Key to Uncle Tom's Cabin* (Boston, 1853), 21, 109-10.

15. See Nehemiah Adams, *A South-Side View of Slavery* (1854; Boston, 1860), 94-96; A Citizen of Georgia, *Remarks upon Slavery* (1835), in *A Defence of Southern Slavery and Other Pamphlets* (New York, 1969), 18-19, 24; Bellinger's speech, the *Emancipator*, Nov. 1835; *The Proslavery Argument* (Charleston, 1852), 174-76; William M. Moss, "Vindicator of Southern Intellect and Institutions: The *Southern Quarterly Review*," *Southern Literary Journal* 13 (1980): 77, 84-85; Drew Gilpin Faust, *A Sacred Circle: The Dilemma of the Intellectual in the Old South, 1840-1860* (Baltimore, 1977), 90-95, 109, 112, 117; William Barney, *The Secessionist Impulse: Alabama and Mississippi in 1860* (Princeton, N.J., 1974), 47; Tise, *Proslavery*, 262.

16. August Meier and Elliott Rudwick, "The Boycott Movement against Jim Crow Streetcars in the South, 1900-1906," *Journal of American History* 55 (1969): 756-75.

17. Loudon Wainwright, *The Great American Magazine: An Inside History of "Life"* (New York, 1986), 174; James L. Baughman, *Henry R. Luce and the Rise of the American News Media* (Boston, 1987), 165; A.J. van Zuilen, *The Life Cycle of Magazines* (Uithoorn, Netherlands, 1977).

18. Anthony Lewis, *Make No Law: The Sullivan Case and the First Amendment* (New York, 1991), 34-45. CBS kept its crew out of Alabama during 1962-63 for fear of being served papers in a libel suit over a story it had broadcast on the abridgment of voting rights; see *Covering the South: A National Symposium on the Media and the Civil Rights Movement*, 3-5 April 1987, University of Mississippi (videotape), Robert Schakne, panel 1.

19. Fred Powledge, *Free at Last? The Civil Rights Movement and the People Who Made It* (Boston, 1991), 515-16; *Covering the South*, panels 1-2; Bob Warner, "The Southern Story," *Editor and Publisher* 94 (10 June 1961): 76, and 94 (17 June 1961): 55; Michael Dorman, *We Shall Overcome* (New York, 1964), 54.

20. Bob Considine, quoted in Philip Schuyler, "Panelists Agree: Journalistic Code Violated at Little Rock," *Editor and Publisher* 90 (2 Nov. 1957): 66; Claude Sitton in Howell Raines, ed., *My Soul is Rested: Movement Days in the Deep South Remembered* (New York, 1977), 380.

21. *Atlanta Constitution*, 24 Sept. 1957; *Editor and Publisher* 95 (6 Oct. 1962): 11, *Covering the South*, Charles Dunagin, Karl Fleming, John Lewis, and Charles Quinn, panel 2; *Editor and Publisher* 94 (10 June 1961): 13; Taylor Branch, *Parting the Waters: America and the King Years* (New York, 1988), 444-45, 559.

22. Benjamin Fine in "The Mob and the Newsmen," *Bulletin of the American Society of Newspaper Editors (hereafter BASNE)*, Nov. 1957, 2; "Newsmen Attacked as Police Look On," *Editor and Publisher* 96 (27 Feb. 1965): 15. On the alliance between mob and police in Birmingham, see Powledge, *Free at Last?* 273-74.

23. *Washington Post*, 20 Oct. 1962, 9; Wallace Westfeldt in "The Mob and

the Newsmen," 5; Stephen J. Whitfield, *A Death in the Delta: The Story of Emmett Till* (New York, 1988), 117-18; Powledge, *Free at Last?* 516; James Graham Cook, *The Segregationists* (New York, 1962), 266-67; Richard Lentz, *Symbols, the News Magazines, and Martin Luther King* (Baton Rouge, La., 1990).

24. Thomas Davis, Benjamin Fine, Walter Lister, Jr., Bert Collier, Robert S. Ball, Herbert F. Corn, Wallace Westfeldt in "The Mob and the Newsmen," 1-5 (Fine quoted, 2).

25. *Washington Post*, 24 Sept. 1957, A10; *New York Times*, 24 Sept. 1957, 18-19; Don Shoemaker, *BASNE*, Oct. 1957, 1; *New York Times*, 21 May 1961, 78. At the University of Georgia a KKK newspaper spread through the mob a short time before reporters came under attack; see *Atlanta Constitution*, 12 Jan. 1961, 1, and *New York Times*, 11 Jan. 1961, 1.

26. Dorman, *We Shall Overcome*, 58; Richard Valeriani in Raines, *My Soul Is Rested*, 371; Bob Warner, "Camera Is a Red Flag to Mob," *Editor and Publisher* 94 (10 June 1961): 13; Daisy Bates, *The Long Shadow of Little Rock: A Memoir* (New York, 1962), 92.

27. *Time*, 7 Oct. 1957, 24-25. Elizabeth Huckaby, *Crisis at Central High, Little Rock, 1957-58* (Baton Rouge, La., 1980), reproduces the photo of white school girls from the *Arkansas Gazette*; on the other photo Governor Faubus used, see *Life*, 7 Oct. 1957, 43; *Eyes on the Prize* (pt. 1) has a film clip of the governor holding up the picture of the bleeding agitator, C.E. Blake. See also *Covering the South*, Richard Sanders, panel 5; Nelson Benton in Raines, *My Soul Is Rested*, 385-86.

28. Howard Smead, *Blood Justice: The Lynching of Mack Charles Parker* (New York, 1986), 77; Warner, "Camera Is a Red Flag to Mob," 13.

29. Erik Barnouw, *The Image Empire: A History of Broadcasting in the United States* (New York, 1970), 3:65; Frank Luther Mott, *American Journalism: A History, 1690-1960* (New York, 1962), 682-83; Branch, *Parting the Waters*, 323; J. Fred MacDonald, *Black and White TV: African Americans in Television since 1948* (Chicago, 1992), 49-54.

30. *Covering the South*, panel 1.

31. Richard Lentz and Pamela A. Brown, "'The Business of Great Nations': International Coverage, Foreign Public Opinion, and the Modern American Civil Rights Movement" (paper read at the Western Journalism Historians Conference, University of California, Berkeley, 28-29 Feb. 1992), 4-7, 10; Branch, *Parting the Waters*, 184, 425-26; Hugh Davis Graham, *Crisis in Print: Desegregation and the Press in Tennessee* ([Nashville], 1967), 211; David Garrow, ed. *St. Augustine, Florida, 1963-1964: Mass Protest and Racial Violence* (Brooklyn, N.Y., 1989), 190-91.

32. *Covering the South*, John Lewis, panel 3; Papers of the Congress of Racial Equality, Swarthmore College.

33. On the iconography of lynching, see Ida B. Wells, *A Red Record* (1894), 55-56, Ida B. Wells-Barnett, *On Lynchings* (New York, 1969); Walter White, *Rope and Faggot: A Biography of Judge Lynch* (1928; New York, 1969), 27; Arthur F. Raper, *The Tragedy of Lynching* (Chapel Hill, N.C., 1933), 420; James R. McGovern, *Anatomy of a Lynching: The Killing of Claude Neal* (Baton Rouge, La., 1982), 84-85, 96.

34. Theodore H. White, *In Search of History: A Personal Adventure* (New York, 1978), 507; Edward Bliss, Jr., *Now the News: The Story of Broadcast Journalism* (New York, 1991), 321; Nelson Benton in Raines, *My Soul Is Rested*, 386.

35. Bob Warner, "Reporting Racial Strife in the South," *Editor and Publisher* 94 (10 June 1961): 76; Bob Warner, "Omens in Alabama," *Editor and Publisher* 94 (17 June 1961): 55 (quoting Hodding Carter); Bob Warner, "Violence and the News," *Editor and Publisher* 94 (24 June 1961): 15.

36. Bob Warner, "Omens in Alabama," 14.

37. *Montgomery Advertiser*, 29 March 1956, 4; 13 April 1956, 4; and 14 April 1956, 4.

38. "Tell It Not in Gath," *Time*, 23 April 1956, 62-63; Robert W. Brown, "Sage of Goat Hill," *BASNE*, Nov. 1956, 5-6; *Christian Science Monitor*, 10 April 1956, 7; Daniel Webster Hollis, *An Alabama Newspaper Tradition: Grover C. Hall and the Hall Family* (University, Ala., 1983), 107-8; Graham, *Crisis in Print*, 302-3; Harry S. Ashmore, *An Epitaph for Dixie* (New York, 1958), 158. Numan V. Bartley, *The Rise of Massive Resistance: Race and Politics in the South during the 1950s* (Baton Rouge, La., 1969), 179, finds that this series "was very likely the most successful of all deliberative southern efforts to influence northern opinion."

39. Grover C. Hall Papers, Alabama Department of Archives and History, Montgomery, folders 2, 9; Martin Luther King, Jr., *Stride toward Freedom: The Montgomery Story* (New York, 1958), 49, 85, 176; *Covering the South*, John Lewis, panel 3; Jo Ann Gibson Robinson, *The Montgomery Bus Boycott and the Women Who Started It: The Memoir of Jo Ann Gibson Robinson*, ed. David J. Garrow (Knoxville, 1987), 81-82, 106; Brown, "Sage of Goat Hill," 5.

40. Wayne Greenhaw, *Watch Out for George Wallace* (Englewood Cliffs, N.J., 1976), 116-17; Ray Jenkins, "Wallace Beats the Press," *Nieman Reports* 24 (1970): 6; Grover C. Hall, Jr., "Faust at Tuscaloosa," *Masthead* 15 (1963): 12-16.

41. George C. Wallace, *Stand Up for America* (Garden City, N.Y., 1976), 22-23; Bill Jones, *The Wallace Story* (Northport, Ala., 1966), 149, 201, 432; [George House], *George Wallace Tells It like It Is* (Selma, Ala., [1969]), 77-79; Jenkins, "Wallace Beats the Press," 3-8.

42. Marshall Frady, *Wallace* (New York, 1968), 25, 169; Jenkins, "Wallace Beats the Press," 4; E. Culpepper Clark, *The Schoolhouse Door: Segregation's Last Stand at the University of Alabama* (New York, 1993), 201, 215.

43. Jones, *Wallace Story*, is a compendium on the hypocrisy theme from the stump: 9, 109, 126, 146, 182, 201, 252. Wallace underscored this theme in his first network appearance before a panel of journalists, *Meet the Press*, in 1963; he took Hall along for this interview.

44. Civil rights scholars have rarely employed social science models to explain the role of media in changing attitudes. David J. Garrow, *Protest at Selma: Martin Luther King, Jr., and the Voting Rights Act of 1965* (New Haven, Conn., 1978), is an exception, drawing on the theories of E.E. Schattschneider. Todd Gitlin, *The Whole World Is Watching: Mass Media in the Making and Unmaking of the New Left* (Berkeley, Calif., 1980), is the most ambitious and successful attempt to fit theories to the practice of journalism in modern protests, but it does

not take up the first decade of civil rights coverage in the national media. William A. Gamson and Gadi Wolfsfeld, "Movements and Media as Interacting Systems," in *Annals of the American Academy of Political and Social Science* 258 (July 1993): 114-25, revived interest in "scope enlargement" and the "struggle over meaning," but these theories are untested in American racial discourse. There are superb narrative and institutional histories of the civil rights struggle, but the press has been gone over lightly. "We are on unploughed ground," Jack Nelson said in welcoming his fellow correspondents of this era to the conference *Covering the South*, in 1987. The same can be said today.

9

American Cartoonists
and a World of Revolutions
1789-1936

MARK W. SUMMERS

To judge by the rhetoric of two centuries, Americans seem to believe that revolution is too important to be left to the agitators. That a country formed in upheaval would take so active a dislike to disorder may be a matter demanding the talents not of a historian but of a psychologist. Yet the output of American cartoonists between the passage of a new Constitution and a New Deal leaves not the slightest doubt on this point.

Admittedly, the classical imagery associated with liberty, both the torch and the Phrygian cap, would become stock symbols of American freedom. Columbia herself wore the "liberty cap," and Bartholdi's colossus bore the torch. In a cartoon commemorating the October revolution, the *good* head of the Russian doubleheaded eagle would wear it, as well.[1] But other symbolic persons replaced Columbia in cartoons during the nineteenth century, and perhaps more significantly, the lady that cartoonists drew increasingly either went bareheaded or wore a crown of stars in place of her original headdress; Thomas Nast, the father of modern American political cartooning, actually decked her in feathers.[2] Very likely the cap's resemblance to the headgear of sans-culottes of the French Revolution explains the reluctance to retain it as a freedom symbol. Instead, the cap appeared most prominently in bedecking John Peter Altgeld, an Illinois governor to whom anarchist theories were imputed.[3] The torch too, except when relegated to the Statue of Liberty's clutch, became almost exclusively what it had been from the start, a symbol of chaos and nihilism. In that cause it would be wielded by everyone from czarist revolutionaries to dissident Democrats.[4]

A few cautions need to be made before advancing any generalizations about the image of revolution. First, unlike the English and the French, Americans produced no cartoons about the French Revolution itself. Nor did they treat the Latin American revolutions of the early nineteenth century; there was no George Cruikshank to comment on the upheavals in Spain in the 1820s, no Richard Doyle or John Leech to exalt the European uprisings of 1848. Napoleon III, the "Ratapoil" of Honoré Daumier, might as well not have existed. Only in one form did the Jacobins appear: as a reflection on the hidden designs of Thomas Jefferson and his followers.

Second, for all the antagonism that a vast majority of cartoonists showed, the United States did produce a tiny band of defenders of revolution, both in the abstract and in detail, in the first twenty years of this century. With the organization of the Socialist Party in 1901 and the proliferation of left-wing newspapers that followed, Marxism recruited a host of cartoonists of its own. Among the most important were Robert Minor and Art Young of *The Masses*, but they enjoyed the good company of social critics such as Boardman Robinson, George Bellows, and John Sloan. Their treatment of social problems was as diverse as socialism itself.[5] Among the crude prints that the Industrial Workers of the World (IWW) periodicals produced were ferocious appeals to sabotage and violence; Minor's stark, sardonic attacks on the capitalist order showed more humor and considerably more subtlety; best of them all was Art Young, whose sense of the ridiculous never deserted him and was even applied to the high-flown ideals of his own side.[6] Between liberal Democratic and conservative Republican responses to revolution, too, shades of differences are discernible. It was possible for Rollin Kirby of the *New York World* to deride the abuse of the Bolshevik as a Republican scare tactic and for Daniel R. Fitzpatrick of the *St. Louis Post-Dispatch* to mock the alarmists of the Senate, cowering in bed on being convinced that "Trotsky'll Get You If You Don't Watch Out."[7]

Third, there was one special exception to American cartoonists' distaste for the overthrow of government: czarist Russia. Whatever the Romanovs' symbolic services to the Union cause during the American Civil War, Russia remained in the public mind a benighted land, its prisoners in Siberia and pogroms against the Jews far more representative of the government's character than was Alexander II's emancipation of the serfs— which got no notice from cartoonists at all. The assassination of the czar in 1881 elicited scathing remarks at his expense.[8] In the uprising of 1905, American commentary was almost wholly on the side of the Duma and against the autocrats. Nicholas was depicted as a butcher of innocent women. "I have the honor to inform your royal and sacred Highness that the petition of your loyal subjects has been granted," an executioner informs the arrogant monarch in one characteristic cartoon, as before him he holds their appeal for liberty or death.[9]

Not very surprisingly, then, the overthrow of the czar in March 1917 elicited a storm of applause from cartoonists. The hand of the Duma shoved up from the ground to overturn autocracy's throne; a youthful Gulliver roused himself and snapped the tiny tyrants' chains. Jay N. Darling ("Ding") suggested that the trimming the czar got might be just the thing to make over the kaiser as well.[10]

These caveats do not change the picture in any basic respect. Even cartoonists who treated the Bolshevist threat with skepticism took pains to express their detestation of revolution in general. Their skepticism, too, flowed in uneven quantities. With little cause, but in keeping with a number of editorial writers, Kirby spotted the Red flag raised from a steel strike in 1919; "Bolshevizing American industry" was but the first step to Leninizing America.[11] As for the radical cartoonists, their audience was limited from the first and, with the Great War, further restricted by mob violence and government suppression. Minor, Sloan, Young, and others were indicted; *The Masses* and *Good Morning*, never able to attract commercial advertising, barely survived a troubled infancy and left no successor of equally wide appeal.[12]

These exceptions acknowledged, what can be said about the general image of revolution that cartoonists fostered? Details changed, but certain characteristics remained the same. First, and most important, revolution was negation, pure and simple: the undoing of something, the absence of institutions. The revolutionary's props were neither the hammer nor the sickle but, as noted, the destroyer's torch and the bomb, the latter stylized into a ball with a fuse—the antithesis and semblance of the orb that kings bear.[13]

That revolutions undid even the most widely accepted essentials of civilized society had been a standard allegation in English attacks on the first French republic; Federalists applied the same commonplace to their attacks on Jeffersonian Democrats. One allegorical print shows the French invasion of America; the landing party's first acts are to kill and eat the inhabitants. In another sketch, "Mad Tom" Paine, helped by a devil looking faintly like Thomas Jefferson, tries to pull down the pillars of government. In a third, only the eye of the Lord prevents Jefferson from burning the Constitution on the Altar of Gallic Despotism.[14]

Allegorical print showing the French invading America. Not reproduced here is the inscription below: "Triumph Government: perish all its enemies.—/Traitors, be warned: justice, though slow, is sure." "The Times: A Political Portrait," c. 1795 (source unknown).

It would be Nast who developed this theme to its extreme. Devising a skeleton in a suit to stand for the "dead-headism" of Communist ideas in the late 1870s, he made the figure the antithesis not just of democracy and private enterprise but of life itself.[15] Even where the skeleton did not appear, traces remained: the badge with a skull and bones, generally.[16]

Most Socialists in Progressive America might be native-born and northern European in stock—in real life. In cartooning, from Washington's time on, the imagery was entirely different and, ironically, developed to the fullest by artists who themselves were foreign-born: Nast (German), Joseph Keppler (Austrian), Bernhard Gillam (English). If revolution as negation was the first indispensable characteristic of the caricaturists' picture of revolution, its alien origin was the second. What could be expected, say, of a movement whose weapon was the guillotine and whose defenders lived on a diet of frogs? or whose American apologists expostulated in gutteral Swiss-French, "Stop de wheels of de Government"?[17] "Look On This Picture," one Federalist propaganda poster challenged readers, "And On This." Who could doubt the better man, when confronted with the smiling face of Washington, his portrait resting on books of Order, Law, and Religion, and beneath a snuffed-out candle the portrait of a wizened Jefferson atop tomes by Tom Paine, Condorcet, and Voltaire?[18]

"The emancipation of labor and the honest working people." From *Harper's Weekly*, 1874.

France was already embarked on a third republic before the imagery of the first had lost its power to discredit revolution. The guillotine and the military hats of Robespierre's day continued to stand for authoritarianism when Nast drew his attacks after the Civil War, and the crushing of the Paris Commune in 1871 gave added force to the connection of revolutionary doctrine and France. To the artist, as to most American editors, the Commune *was* Communism, and that doctrine in its most nihilistic form, "as much the foe of human nature and society as the terror of '93," said the editor of *Harper's Weekly*.[19] So Communism first appeared in *Harper's Weekly* as a skeleton with a pencil-thin French mustache and goatee on its lantern chaps.[20] Later, Nast would depict it as a frog offering panaceas (lest the ethnic joke of the choice of animals be missed, the frog too had the stereotypical French beard and mustache),[21] and as a frothy poodle making its home in the "Bier-Haelle," with the motto overhead "Vive La Commune! Beware, or the Lion will be Let Loose!"[22]

As the choice of doghouse suggested, however, cartoonists were already looking for another foreigner on whom to fix the blame for Communism. Nast himself led the way. Within weeks of the poodle's first appearance another cur replaced it: a spitz, living off beer, sausage, and pretzels.[23] It seemed a natural choice. As the editors of *Harper's Weekly* had pointed out a few weeks before, Communism had virtually died out in France; now

"Leave him alone, officer, he hasn't started anything—yet." From *Outlook*, December 25, 1919.

Germans were infected.[24] By 1886 the figures representing revolutionary movements had taken on the bristling beard of intemperate German agitators. In promoting this stereotype, Nast had help. As head of *Puck*, the most influential comic political weekly of the day, Joseph Keppler made much of the alien nature of radicalism. Then, with Keppler's passing, this image too gave way to another, from farther east still. As hordes of immigrants from Eastern Europe reached American shores in the 1890s, the image of the subversive was transplanted to the Slav, the Russian, and, occasionally, the Jew. And there it stayed, years after new laws closed the doors to the so-called New Immigration in 1924. By the 1920s the American revolutionary was the tramp of the globe, uttering his thoughts, if they could be so dignified, in gutteral pidgin: "Fine! Me fer dat America!" a Bolshevik announces, on reading P.T. Barnum's aphorism that there is a sucker born every minute.[25] Bearded Bolsheviks gave way to more clean-cheeked apparatchiks, but the image remained fixed on Russian agitators. Between the Communist tramp in a *New York Herald-Tribune* cartoon of 1936 and a Keppler creation, the family resemblance was unmistakable—and so hackneyed that it no longer had any resonance.[26]

The imagery, of course, had an obvious point. Revolution could not come from real Americans, certainly not from the working class, which had a stereotype of its own; nor could it originate in American conditions, which gave no just cause for complaint. The doctrine and the doctrinaire alike had to be imports, for which lax immigration laws deserved the blame.

Within these two crucial stereotypes—the apostle of negation and the alien—the imagery of revolution was permitted plenty of variation. It reflected the anxieties of its time more than the characteristics of a particular movement. Thus, for Federalist propaganda, revolution conjured up the dangerous skepticism toward institutions that conservatism associated with the French *philosophes*. For Nast, as an employee of a middle-class magazine in the Victorian age, the main threat of the revolutionary movements was to the family. In its cap the "dead-head" wore a ribbon endorsing "free love," and if it made its appeal to the workingman, wife and child were within arm's reach.[27]

But what, precisely, *was* this revolution, beyond annihilation and alienism? Quite a few artists were able to capture the essence of radical doctrine, if only to argue against it and in favor of liberty or capitalism. ("Workingmen that work must give their earnings to the lazy and drunken workingmen," one Nast cartoon summed it up. "That's Communism.")[28] But the closer they tried to reason about ideology, the more muddled a picture they made of it. Bolshevism was not nihilism, nor was anarchism the same as socialism. Between Leon Trotsky and Prince Kropotkin lay a broad spectrum of beliefs, and the communism of Fourier or Brook Farm was something very unlike the free love notions of Oneida or the economic determinism of *Das Kapital*. Outside the coterie of artists on the left, however, American political cartoonists found it impossible (or inconvenient) to distinguish one variety from the others. As long as all such causes could be depicted as efforts to overturn the present order, no further distinction seemed necessary.[29] For all the role ideology played in the October revolution, the Bolsheviks might as well have been Baptists. (News stories were no better, of course. In addition to killing Lenin or Trotsky off at regular intervals, they referred to the "Anarchists Who Rule Petrograd," or speculated that the Bolsheviks were a front for Czar Nicholas II, determined to regain the throne at all costs.)[30]

The reluctance to explore doctrine more fully, not to mention more fairly, was not really evidence of the cartoonists' intellectual laziness. Nor

From
*Philadelphia
Inquirer,* 1919.

was it simply a necessary limitation of the cartoon as a medium of political discourse (though, as will be noted, that was part of the problem). The very intellectual complexity of revolutionary ideology itself became one more black mark against it, a final proof of how alien it was to the plain-speaking of the practical members of America's working class. Even before the Russian Revolution, American Communism had been stereotyped as a weedy intellectual. By the 1920s the figure had become fixed in caricatures as a rough physical approximation of Trotsky: wild mustache and goatee, bushy hair, goggle eyes behind oversized spectacles.[31] With the New Deal the association of radical theory with academics—especially members of Roosevelt's "Brain Trust" such as Rexford Tugwell—became indissoluble. In attacks on the New Deal, rare was the American-born Communist who appeared without glasses and a physique in crying need of hearty break-fasts. One might as easily have found a visionary without a mortarboard as a "Pink" with perfect vision.[32]

For cartoonists, then, revolution was like pornography for Justice Potter Stewart: they might not have been able to define it, but they knew it when they saw it. The trouble was, they also knew it when they did *not* see

From *New York
Tribune*,
January 7, 1920.

it, for according to their descriptions it broke out on the least pretense just
about everywhere in the United States—curious action indeed for a phenomenon so alien to the American spirit. It bobbed up to explain any agitation that threatened class war—at least, of the poor against the rich. For
Nast, the Communist was the same as the "Fiatist," who believed in inflating
the money supply, or might even be a supporter of the coinage of silver
such as Senator Daniel W. Voorhees, an Indiana Democrat.[33] Most commonly, the cartoonists discerned revolution lurking behind labor union agitation. Strikes were the fuse to the bomb of Red rule, prepared for blowing
up the United States government; organized labor was the sheep-skin covering the Red wolf in the steel mills.[34]

　　Imprecision therefore had real advantages, but it permitted a sporadic
swelling of alarm among readers. Depicting Franklin Roosevelt's New Deal

as the precursor to Soviet Communism took a fevered imagination, the kind restricted to lunatics, editors, and the conservative wing of the Republican Party. Yet by 1936 alarmism had become the order of the day, and nowhere more so than on the *Chicago Tribune*, where proprietor Robert R. McCormick had not one but three cartoonists on his payroll.[35] Where other newspapers made the Red Scare one issue among many, McCormick gave it nearly exclusive and very nearly libelous coverage.[36] Indeed, the only subject for open debate, as far as the *Tribune* was concerned, was whether Roosevelt was Communism's advance man or its innocent dupe. Was he, as one picture suggested, an Alexander Kerensky, soon to be overthrown by wild men such as Tugwell and Felix Frankfurter?[37] Or was he the knowing enemy, thrusting Miss Democracy into a forced marriage with Communism over the objections of "Patriotic Democrats"?[38]

Simplification, it must be conceded, was almost essential to American political cartooning once it passed from the early engravings, suitable for long examination, to the newspaper sketch, glanced at and dismissed in an instant.[39] A readership less familiar than its ancestors with American political figures could hardly be expected to master foreign ones. Symbols became indispensable. So France came to be represented by a cosmopolitan smoothie in slick top hat and parted beard; the "Negro" stereotype did regular service to represent natives of India, the Philippines, the Caribbean, and Mexico.[40] That explains but does not efface the problems that arise when symbols take on a life of their own. Instead of standing in for the subject, a representation can bring along heaps of ideological baggage. It may suggest a set of assumptions about class or ethnicity. Any revolution in Latin America that was shown in cartoons, as the work of figures better suited to a burnt-cork minstrel show could never be taken seriously—not even enough to merit readers' disapproval. How much, indeed, could Americans fret at the turmoil in Kerensky's Russia, when, as was so often the case, the events were acted out on the editorial page by that tired old stereotype for Russia, the blank-faced comic peasant in a Santa Claus beard, baggy clothing, and frowsy bangs, the hayseed of the steppes?[41]

More perniciously, how far could one differentiate the demands of different groups in a diverse labor foce when the artisan stood in for them all? Long after the blacksmith had become an obsolete figure, outpaced in the era of machine tools and automobiles, cartoonists depicted Labor as a figure in leather apron, hammer in hand, at the anvil. A harmless image, it might seem, but it had delusive connotations built in: the laborer as an individual, independent and needing no collective bargaining; the worker as craftsman, for whom the work itself was compensation.[42] All the more dangerous

From *Harper's
Weekly,*
May 22, 1886.

for being needless, therefore, was the outside agitator, the walking delegate,
the Bolshevik skeleton, offering the poisoned bottle of "Strike" to the laboring man.

Up through the 1930s, then, American cartoonists did forceful if generally hostile work against revolution and, indeed, against agitation on behalf
of the working class. The evidence is clear; the explanation may be less so.
What could explain the essential conservatism of the artists' response to
revolution?

No answer is possible without understanding the way that "the ungentlemanly art" developed in the United States, for the process helped
define and confine the message it delivered. For one thing, political cartooning came late to the United States. It had no tradition to base itself on,
and only the most limited means of distribution for satire. From the woodcuts of Lucas Cranach in the Reformation to the engravings of William
Hogarth in the eighteenth century, European art was available on its own,
in print-shops, or distributed by propagandists to those incapable of reading complicated tracts. By the time of the French Revolution, political cari-

cature had found strong state support; a George Canning might make uneasy alliance with James Gillray and even suggest ideas to him. But where freedom existed, the cartoon became the monopoly of no party and no class. There was room for the subtle, upper-class conservatism of John Doyle's caricatures, and the scurrilous, radical penny woodcuts of Charles Grant—and a crowd of humor magazines. In the age of Gillray and George Cruikshank, one designer's cartoons bred others; one side's comments on public events spurred the other to appoint cartoonists of its own. London's urban culture allowed a profitable market for an army of printmakers. With politics so ill defined on the basis of rigid party lines up to the 1820s, the issues, rather than the leaders of each side, would be the main targets of discussion. Only as the broadside and engraving lost their privileged place, and magazines such as *Punch* became unrivaled sources of political comment, did English satire lose its diversity. Only in the 1840s did it grow dispiritingly "respectable."[43]

None of these conditions existed in the early American republic, and certainly not a heritage of pictorial satire. Before the writing of the Constitution perhaps half a dozen crude allegories in woodcut appeared in the press, and scarcely any more engravings. With no major cities outside of Philadelphia, New York, and Boston, a market for prints did not exist. One may even surmise that a society so marked with Puritan and Quaker suspicions of frivolity took badly to ribaldry at the expense of politics. Many prints commenting on the American Revolution do exist, but most of them were drawn, published, and sold in London, While London was producing a Gillray to dramatize the first French Revolution, and Paris a Daumier to depict the betrayal of the second, Philadelphia and New York found even hackwork beyond their capacity.[44]

Well into the 1820s, American cartooning had not become an integral part of political commentary. In vain the historian looks for extant copies, or even mention of a past existence, of cartoons related to the inauguration of George Washington, the Louisiana Purchase, the elections of 1800 through 1820, the Monroe Doctrine, the annexation of Florida, the Indian wars against Tecumseh's confederation, the Missouri Compromise, completion of the Erie Canal, or virtually any public event before 1831.[45] No such cartoons were drawn.

Instead, those pictures actually produced were tied from the start to the two-party system and concerned primarily with its contests.[46] There was no tradition of independent broadside cartoons, certainly no radical exploitation of the medium outside of mainstream politics. While Honoré Daumier's lithographs were assailing the French political leadership in the

Second Republic, American lithographs were distributed by Whigs and Democrats as campaign handouts and stuck to the contest of personalities every four years; between times, with no ready sponsor, the number of such prints dwindled to nearly nothing. A presidential race might inspire a spate of prints—after Andrew Jackson's elevation to the White House the national parties discovered the possibilities of lithographic lampoons distributed nationwide—but that meant that cartooning was of a campaign, by the campaign, and for the campaign. Events not related to Henry Clay's bid for the presidency or Jackson's war on the national bank had no market. How far the art had been absorbed by the political establishment was made starkly clear when Cruikshank's attack on England's hierarchy, "The House that Jack Built," found its American equivalent, a near-plagiarism, in a Whig party tract against President Andrew Jackson's meddling with the established order.[47]

Long before the Victorian age weakened the power of revolutionary art in England, then, American cartoonists had been put under close rein. There they stayed. When periodicals began to run political cartoons, they either modeled themselves on *Punch*, appealing to a readership far more interested in humor than in indignation (and almost invariably failing within a few years),[48] or they directed their articles at the middle-class reading public of late Victorian America and provided caricatures as one in a number of attractions.[49] By the 1890s, daily newspapers were supplementing and soon replacing the weeklies' contributions. But here, too, it would have been unthinkable to defend revolution. Those papers able to afford a cartoonist by the turn of the century were well-off, powerful businesses with a stake in the status quo. Cartoonists did not necessarily or even usually have the right to reflect any views but those of the paper they drew for. Some, such as John Tenniel of *Punch* and Joseph Keppler during his youthful apprenticeship on *Leslie's Weekly*, neither chose the topic nor originated the idea; all that was done by the editor.[50] A cartoonist who strayed from the editorial position could be dismissed as swiftly as was Robert Minor, whose radicalism and hostility to war brought about his departure from Pulitzer's newspapers in 1914; at best, one who was lucky might be permitted to avoid the topic altogether.[51]

Nor is it to be imagined that the indignation of the cartoonist necessarily would be directed against the established order. For the best artists, the returns could be prodigious—no inducement to doubt the basic merit of the American capitalist system. To stand against institutions generally accepted, even with gentle ridicule, could earn cartoonists notoriety and cut into their income from "respectable" publications, even when their

From *Literary Digest,*
April 13, 1918.

material had nothing to do with controversial subjects. Indicted for opposition to the First World War, Young found friends abandoning him and income evaporating. Worse than all was the contempt or pity bestowed by those from whom he would have hoped for respect. "The radical and big humanist movements in all lands have found some of their best champions among the lawyers and cartoonists," Art Young wrote sadly in his retirement. "But for one cartoonist, or one lawyer, who sees through the evils that permeate his profession, there are many more who are taken in by the glamour of big fees, and will do nothing that will not assure more cushions for their comfort, and a proud status among the elect."[52]

So much for hostility to revolution. But what about the indifference? How, say, could the October revolution pass without the *Los Angeles Times* devoting a single sketch to it? Here, a second point needs to be made about the nature of political cartoons. Since Nast's day, the artists' task has forced them to concentrate on the immediate, even the ephemeral, at the expense of events affecting their readers more remotely. Even cartoonists who publish daily will overlook events that lack evident consequences for their readership. Gillray or Richard Doyle might comment on upheaval in 1793 or 1848, but England was just across the Channel. Similarly, Americans took revolution seriously only when it affected them or threatened to do so. Latin American uprisings became comic opera events in which various swarthy stereotypes—generally dressed in Mexican sombreros, whatever country they happened to come from—battled one another to no visible effect.[53]

The cartoonists' initial reaction to the Socialists' campaign for office and the October revolution in 1917 was typical of this limited vision. When the Socialist Party fielded candidates for mayor in New York and Chicago in 1917, the cartoonists ignored their program. Instead, they stated the issue in simple and immediate terms: did voters support the country against German aggression or not? A vote for Socialism was a vote against the war effort, for "Mayor—of Berlin."[54] Flourishing the city ballot, Uncle Sam advised Chicagoans to put their cross in the Socialist ticket's circle if they were against him, "and it will be an Iron Cross."[55] As the Bolsheviks gathered strength in Petrograd, American cartoonists noticed only the third part of their appeal for "Bread, Land, Peace." As far as they were concerned, these were ten days that shook the *war.* How would the uprising affect Russian involvement against the Central Powers? More sympathetic than most to Russians' struggle for freedom, Daniel Fitzpatrick of the *St. Louis Post-Dispatch* nonetheless responded by showing the Russian holding up his arms and declaring himself "Free!" while through the dike behind him "Prussianism" gushes from the hole he is no longer plugging. Other cartoonists were less equivocal: the revolutionaries had stabbed Russia in the back while it fought the kaiser, or shoved the country out of its rightful possessions (Finland, the Ukraine, and the Caucasus). What could the "recent 'turn' of events" mean but a cannon swiveled away from Germany and aimed at the Allies?[56]

It was then that the confusion of terms betrayed cartoonists. Convinced that the new regime was nothing more than evidence of Russian chaos, that Bolshevism and anarchy were interchangeable terms, they predicted a swift dissolution of institutions with nothing to replace them. Let the Bolshevik take his place on the pedestal of the state, club in hand. At his feet was a cautionary reminder: the scepter, robes, and crown of the czars. King Mob was "Dressed in a Little Brief Authority," nothing more.[57] Within a week, the prophecies seemed fulfilled, as a bayonet prodded Trotsky out of power.[58] But however far artists confused anarchy and Bolshevism in their sketches, real life proved different; by 1920 the regular announcement of the overthrow of Trotsky and Lenin had become a cartoonist's joke. It would be in a far grimmer mode that Rollin Kirby would portray the effects of Communism in the Soviet Union the following year; indeed, he would win the first Pulitzer prize awarded to a cartoonist for those portrayals.[59]

The problem of revolution, then, exposes the limitations of political cartoons as reflections of public events. The first point, that newspapers are businesses and that an artist representing such institutions will reflect a business perspective, seems all too obvious—so much so that it obscures a second and third. Cartoonists do not simply comment upon events; they are confined by them and compelled to react to them instantly. They are also confined by the restrictions on their medium of expression: the momentary attention that their readers can give, the limitations in the knowledge that readers bring to bear on the subject, and the interest they take in the topic at all. The wonder, indeed, may be that so many cartoons have such lasting value. Handicapped as the medium is, a successful outcome may be as improbable as a successful revolution.

NOTES

1. "The Double-Headed Eagle of Russia" (William A. Rogers), *New York Herald*, 11 Nov. 1917, p. 19. Hereafter, where possible, the cartoon will be listed by title, with its artist in parentheses.

2. Or in a tiara. See "Thanksgiving-Day, November 26, 1863," *Harper's Weekly*, 5 Dec. 1863; "Election-Day," *Harper's Weekly*, 12 Nov. 1864; "The Plank—Hitting the Nail on the Head," *Harper's Weekly*, 23 Oct. 1875, all rpt. in Morton Keller, *The Art and Politics of Thomas Nast* (New York, 1968), 20-21, 50-51, 224-25.

3. As in Nast's "Quack Frog," *Harper's Weekly*, 25 May 1878, 413; or his "Iron and Blood—This 'Don't Scare Worth a Cent'" *Harper's Weekly*, 31 July 1875, rpt. in Keller, *Art and Politics of Thomas Nast*, 249.

4. For uses of the torch, see "Leader Altgeld and His Mask" (Rogers), *Harper's Weekly*, 18 July 1896, 697; "Give Them An Inch, and They'll Take An Ell" (Nast), *Harper's Weekly*, 8 June 1878, 452; "Trying to Start Something" (Winsor McCay), rpt. in *Nemo* 18 (April 1986): 40.

5. Richard Fitzgerald, *Art and Politics: Cartoonists of "The Masses" and "Liberator"* (Westport, Conn., 1973), pp. 15-40.

6. For Young's career and much of his art, see Art Young, *Art Young: His Life and Times*, ed. John Nicholas Beffel (New York, 1939); Art Young, *On My Way: Being the Book of Art Young in Text and Picture* (New York, 1928); Fitzgerald, *Art and Politics*, 42-78. For Minor, see Fitzgerald, *Art and Politics*, 79-120. On *The Masses*, see Young's recollections in *On My Way*, 274-92; William L. O'Neill, ed., *Echoes of Revolt: The Masses, 1911-1917* (Chicago, 1966). IWW cartoons may be found in Joyce L. Kornbluh, ed., *Rebel Voices: An I.W.W. Anthology* (Ann Arbor, Mich., 1965).

7. "I Wants to Make Their Flesh Creep!" (Rollin Kirby), *New York World*, 1924, rpt. in William Murrell, *A History of American Graphic Humor* (New York, 1938), 216; "Trotsky'll Get You If You Don't Watch Out" (Daniel R. Fitzpatrick), *St. Louis Post-Dispatch*, rpt. in Robert K. Murray, *Red Scare: A Study of National Hysteria, 1919-1920* (Minneapolis, Univ. of Minnesota, 1955), 96. Similarly, Democrats were more likely to stress the real human needs that gave rise to Bolshevism and to emphasize cures beyond simple repression. A

square meal and bread on the table, one cartoon argued, was "Poison to Anarchy." See *Literary Digest* (Nelson Harding), Brooklyn *Eagle*, 25 Jan. 1919, 12. See also "Why Peace Must Hasten" (Kirby), rpt. in *Literary Digest*, 22 March 1919, 17.

8. "A Russian Nocturne" (Joseph Keppler), *Puck*, March 1881. See also "Russian Freedom" (Frederick Opper), *Puck*, 1881; "The Coronation of the Czar" (Friedrich Graetz), *Puck*, 1883; "Preparing for the Czar's Coronation" (Graetz), *Puck*, 1883.

9. "I Have the Honor . . ." (Tyler McWhorter), *St. Paul Dispatch*, rpt. in *Literary Digest*, February 11, 1905. See also "The Little Father," *Literary Digest*, Feb. 4, 1905 rpt.

10. "The Scepter" (Oscar Cesare), *New York Evening Post*, rpt. in Arthur S. Link, *Wilson: Campaigns for Progressivism and Peace, 1916-1917* (Princeton, N.J., 1965), 395. For links to German autocracy, see "Something for You, Sir?" (Jay N. "Ding" Darling), 21 March 1917; "Next?" (Nelson Harding), *Brooklyn Eagle*, rpt. in *Literary Digest*, 17 April 1917, 970.

11. "Coming Out of the Smoke" (Kirby), *New York World*, rpt. in Murray, *Red Scare*, 140.

12. Stephen Hess and Milton Kaplan, *The Ungentlemanly Art: A History of American Political Cartoons*, rev. ed. (New York, 1975), 143-44, 212-14.

13. See, e.g., "Leave Him Alone, Officer, He Hasn't Started Anything—Yet" (Harding), rpt. in *Outlook*, 24 Dec. 1919, 531; "The Poison-Gas Attack" (Edward Brown), rpt. in *Literary Digest*, 5 April 1919, 19; "And I'm To Be President of the League, Mother; I'm to be President of the League!" (Milton R. Halladay), *Literary Digest*, 12 April 1919, 11; "An Unpopular Color" (Carey Orr), *Chicago Tribune*, 21 Oct. 1919, 21; "It's What It Leads to That's Dangerous" (Orr), *Chicago Tribune*, 3 Nov. 1919, 20; "A Bird That Can't Be Scared" (Kirby), *New York World* rpt. in *Outlook*, 18 June 1919, 277; "And One Thing Leads to Another" (H.I. Carlisle), *Cincinnati Enquirer*, 21 Oct. 1936, 4.

14. "The Times: A Political Portrait," in Frederic Austin Ogg, *Builders of the Republic*, vol. 8 of *The Pegeant of America* (New Haven, Conn., 1927), 198; "Mad Tom in a Rage," in Marcus Cunliffe, *The American Heritage History of the Presidency* (New York, 1968), 103; "The Providential Detection," in Margaret L. Coit, *The Growing Years*, vol. 3 of *The Life History of the United States* (New York, 1963), 38.

15. "Confusedism," *Harper's Weekly*, 27 April 1878, 325; "Turbulent and Dangerous Lunacy," 21 Sept. 1878, 752-53; "Very Social," rpt. in Thomas Nast St. Hill, *Thomas Nast: Cartoons and Illustrations* (New York, 1974), 139. The symbolism recurred, albeit rarely, in twentieth-century cartoons. See "Tempted" (Robert Day), *Los Angeles Times*, 22 Sept. 1919, sec. 2, 4.

16. As in "Natural History" (Nast), *Harper's Weekly*, 2 March 1878, 165; "The Quack Frog" (Nast). *Harper's Weekly*, 25 May 1878, 413. The symbol would be adopted by W.A. Rogers, Nast's successor on the magazine; see "On a Populistic Basis" (Rogers), *Harper's Weekly*, 12 Sept. 1896, 889.

17. Untitled, in Stefan Lorant, *The Glorious Burden: The American Presidency* (New York, 1968), 55; "The Times: A Political Portrait," in Ogg, *Builders of the Republic*, 198.

18. "Look On This Picture And On This" (poster, 1807, New York), in Cunliffe, *The American Heritage History of the Presidency*, 139.

19. *Harper's Weekly*, 22 June 1878, 487.

20. "The Emancipator of Labor and the Honest Working-People" (Nast), *Harper's Weekly*, 7 Feb. 1874, rpt. in Keller, *Art and Politics of Thomas Nast*, 130.

21. "The Quack Frog" (Nast), *Harper's Weekly*, 25 May 1878, 413; "The Reptile" (Nast), *Harper's Weekly*, 1 June 1878, 440.

22. "Every Dog Has His Day" (Nast), *Harper's Weekly*, 20 June 1878, 520.

23. "Alexander and Diogenes (Not By Landseer)" (Nast), *Harper's Weekly*, 6 July 1878, 528.

24. *Harper's Weekly*, 22 June 1878, 487.

25. "But Barnum Was Right!" (Walsh), *Los Angeles Times*, 28 Sept. 1919, 4. See also "They Are All Out of Step But Me" (Orr), and "Bolshevism Has Its Place—Even in America" (R.O. Evans), both in *Literary Digest*, 29 March 1919, 17; "The Object Lesson" (John F. Knott), *Dallas News*, rpt. in *Outlook*, 21 Jan. 1920, 97; "The Same Platform" (Kirby), *Outlook*, 18 Feb. 1920, 269.

26. "And One Thing Leads to Another" (Carlisle), rpt. in *Cincinnati Enquirer*, 21 Oct. 1936, 4; see also "The Last of the Mohicans" ("Ding"), *Cincinnati Enquirer*, 6 Oct. 1936, 4. Such an overworked visual cliché deserved to be made fun of, and was. In the 1920s the *New Yorker* offered "original drawings on standard themes," every one a chestnut of the political cartoon trade. Among them was "A Word to the Wise"; see *New Yorker Twenty-Fifth Anniversary Album, 1925-1950* (Wakefield, Mass., 1951), [17], fig. 1.

27. "Always Killing the Goose That Lays the Golden Egg" (Nast), *Harper's Weekly*, 16 March 1878, 205; "Home, Sweet Home! There's No Place Like Home!" (Nast), *Harper's Weekly*, 22 June 1878, 496; "Turbulent and Dangerous Lunacy" (Nast), *Harper's Weekly*, 21 Sept. 1878, 752-53.

28. "Always Killing the Goose That Lays the Golden Egg" (Nast), *Harper's Weekly*, 16 March 1878, 205; "Yes! It Cured Russia!" (William Ireland), *Columbus Dispatch*, rpt. in *Outlook*, 27 April 1921, 665; "Cutting Down the Tree to Get the Fruit" ("Ding"), rpt. in *Literary Digest*, 10 May 1919, 15.

29. Cartoonists were at a loss to figure out even what the revolutionaries looked like, much less spell their names correctly; they might draw Leon "Trotzky" as a tramp in military boots, looking like a prizefighter, square-jawed, short-haired, ill-shaven, with a bomb in one hand; or they might impose his features on a character supposed to be "Lenine," oversized military boots and all. See "Its Lair" (Edmund W. Gale), *Los Angeles Times*, 30 Sept. 1919, sec. 2, 4; "Trotzky!" (Fitzpatrick), *St. Louis Post-Dispatch*, 15 Nov. 1917, 26; "At the Council Table" (John T. McCutcheon), *Chicago Tribune*, 24 Nov. 1917, 1; and untitled (Fred Morgan), *Philadelphia Inquirer*, Nov. 1919, copied in Murray, *Red Scare*, 161.

30. "What Next?" (McCutcheon), *Chicago Tribune*, 9 Nov. 1917, p. 1; or see "The Double-Headed Eagle of Russia" (Rogers), *New York Herald*, 11 Nov. 1917, 19.

31. See "Something to Be Thankful For" (Fitzpatrick), *St. Louis Post-Dispatch*, 28, Nov. 1917, 16; "A Warning to Radicalism" (McCutcheon), *Chicago*

Tribune, 6 Nov. 1919, 1; "How About Just a Trial Treatment?" ("Ding"), *Cincinnati Enquirer*, 1 Oct. 1936, 4; "How Come?" ("Ding"), *Cincinnati Enquirer*, 7 Oct. 1936, 4.

32. See "Just Around the Corner" (Orr), and "But the Ceremony Continues" (Joseph Parrish), both in *Chicago Tribune*, 23 Oct. 1936, 1, 14; "A Dummy Target to Hide Their Real Aim" (Orr), *Chicago Tribune*, 8 Oct. 1936, 1; "Actions Speak Louder" (Orr), *Chicago Tribune*, 1 Oct. 1936, 16; "A Modern Version of An Old Story" (Parrish), *Chicago Tribune*, 10 Oct. 1936, 14.

33. "The Argonauts in Search of the Greenback Fleece" (Nast), *Harper's Weekly*, 16 Nov. 1878, 905; "Always Killing the Goose That Lays the Golden Egg" (Nast), *Harper's Weekly*, 16 March 1878, 205.

34. For a general study of labor cartoons in *Puck*, see Richard Marschall, "One Hundred Years Ago," *Nemo* 22 (Oct. 1986): 25-34; "It's What It Leads to That's Dangerous" (Orr), *Chicago Tribune*, 13 Nov. 1919, 20; "Uncovered" (Orr), *Chicago Tribune*, 16 Oct. 1919, 19. See also "The Only Use He Has For It" (Orr), *Chicago Tribune*, 22 Nov. 1919, 17; "Too Big For Him To Swing" (Orr), *Chicago Tribune*, 6 Oct. 1919, 21; "Riding A Good Horse to Death" (Orr), *Chicago Tribune*, 18 Oct. 1919, 17; "Always Ready to Strike" (Orr), *Chicago Tribune*, 24 Oct. 1919, 21. But for a rare reply, see "There Are Moments When Married Life Seems Quite Endurable" ("Ding"), rpt. in *Outlook*, 2 July 1919, 361.

35. George Wolfskill and John A. Hudson, *All but the People: Franklin D. Roosevelt and His Critics, 1933-39* (New York, 1969), 184-88.

36. "Choked Out" (Parrish), and "The Red Jam of Moscow" (Orr), *Chicago Tribune*, 14 Oct. 1936, 10, 1. For the same point, see "Actions Speak Louder" (Orr), *Chicago Tribune*, 1 Oct. 1936, 16; "The End of the Democratic Donkey" (Parrish), *Chicago Tribune*, 2 Oct. 1936, 16; "The Brave Step of a Truly Great American" (Orr), *Chicago Tribune*, 22 Oct. 1936, 1.

37. "His Real Role" (Parrish), *Chicago Tribune*, 5 Oct. 1936, 12. See also "A Modern Version of An Old Story" (Parrish), *Chicago Tribune*, 10 Oct. 1936, 14.

38. "But the Ceremony Continues" (Parrish), *Chicago Tribune*, 28 Oct. 1936, 14. See also "The American Forces Open Up on the Foreign Invader" (Orr), *Chicago Tribune*, 3 Oct. 1936, 1.

39. William Murrell, *A History of American Graphic Humor (1865-1938)* (New York, 1938), 130.

40. For ethnic stereotyping in general, see Charles Hardy, "A Brief History of Ethnicity in the Comics," *Nemo* 28 (Jan. 1988): 6-44.

41. As in "An Attack of Indigestion Comes at An Unfortunate Moment" ("Ding"), *New York Tribune*, 10 May 1917; "Next!" (Orr), *Chicago Tribune*, 11 Nov. 1919, 19; "Bolsheviki Thanksgiving" (Orr), *Chicago Tribune*, 29 Nov. 1917, 17; "The Bolsheviki's Dream" (McCutcheon), *Chicago Tribune*, 30 Nov. 1917, 1.

42. See, e.g., "One And Inseparable" (Nast), *Harper's Weekly*, 23, Nov. 1878, 936; "Tempted" (Robert Day), *Los Angeles Times*, 22 Sept. 1919, sec. 2, 4.

43. On the diversity of medium and viewpoint in the 1830s, see Celina Fox, *Graphic Journalism in England during the 1830s and 1840s* (New York, 1988), 74-90.

44. Hess and Kaplan, *Ungentlemanly Art*, 51-71.

45. Two exceptions are the several caricatures drawn about Thomas Jeffer-

son's Embargo in 1807-9; and William Charles's cartoons supporting the War of 1812.

46. Hess and Kaplan, *Ungentlemanly Art*, 74-79.

47. "The House That Jonathan Built, or Political Primer for 1832" (Philadelphia: P. Banks, 1832).

48. There were two exceptions, late in the century: *Puck* (1877-1918) and *Judge* (1881-1937). Both modeled themselves on the humor magazines of central Europe, with colored lithographs. See Richard Samuel West, *Satire on Stone: The Political Cartoons of Joseph Keppler* (Urbana, Ill., 1988), 279-88, 320-22.

49. Hess and Kaplan, *Ungentlemanly Art*, 81-83.

50. West, *Satire on Stone*, 66-69.

51. Fitzgerald, *Art and Politics*, 68, This caution does not mean that cartoonists thought one way and drew another. E.g., Carey Orr of the *Tribune* shared Colonel McCormick's viewpoint almost entirely. See Lloyd Wendt, *Chicago Tribune: The Rise of a Great American Newspaper* (Chicago, 1979), 572, 584.

52. Young, *On My Way*, 76, 103-4.

53. As in "No Time For Foolishness" (Page), *Nashville Tennessean*, 19 Nov. 1917, 6.

54. "Bolsheviki Art" (Rogers), *New York Herald*, 1 Nov. 1917.

55. "The Iron Cross" (McCutcheon), *Chicago Tribune*, 5 Nov. 1917. See also "The Socialist Vote," *Chicago Tribune*, 4 Nov. 1917.

56. "The Russian at the Dike" (Fitzpatrick), *St. Louis Post-Dispatch*, 9 Nov. 1917, 26; "The Foxy Trotzki" (McCutcheon), *Chicago Tribune*, 26 Nov. 1917, 1; "The Meaning of the Recent 'Turn' of Events in Russia" (Orr), *Chicago Tribune*, 28 Nov. 1917, 17. See also "He'll Get It" (Grover Page), *Nashville Tennessean*, 11 Nov. 1917, 6; "The Liberty Motor" (Page), *Nashville Tennessean*, 18 Nov. 1917, 6. The stress on the war-related aspects of Bolshevik success remained almost total for the next year. See "Why Russia Must Be Free" (Knott), *Dallas News*, and "The Wurst Is Yet to Come" (J.E. Murphy), *San Francisco Call and Post*, rpt. in *Literary Digest*, 20 July 1918, 8, 10; "Why Leave the Sowing to the Enemy?" (Edward Brown), *Chicago Daily News*, rpt. in *Literary Digest*, 10 Aug. 1918, 14.

57. "What Next?" (McCutcheon), *Chicago Tribune*, 9 Nov. 1917; "Out of the Russian Chaos, Which Will Arise?" (McCutcheon), *Chicago Tribune*, 19 Nov. 1917, 1; "Dressed in a Little Brief Authority" (Fitzpatrick), *St. Louis Post-Dispatch*, 26 Nov. 1917, 18.

58. "Trotzky!" (Fitzpatrick), *St. Louis Post-Dispatch*, 15 Nov. 1917, 26.

59. "The Light That Failed" (Bronstrup), *San Francisco Chronicle*, rpt. in *Outlook*, 11 June 1919, 227; "On the Road to Moscow" (Kirby), *New York World*, rpt. in Richard Spencer, *Pulitzer Prize Cartoons: The Men and Their Masterpieces* (Ames, Iowa, 1951), 14-15.

10

Pravda and the Language of Power in Soviet Russia, 1917-28

JEFFREY BROOKS

The press was a conspicuous emblem of Soviet society.[1] The revolutionaries honored it with a holiday, and central newspapers retained a recognizable likeness throughout the Soviet era. Yet there is much evidence that the newspapers, sprinkled as they were with unfamiliar foreign words and acronyms, were neither widely read nor readily understood by the semi-literate masses the revolutionaries often invoked.[2] Why then did the Bolsheviks prize them so?

The answer is surprisingly simple. The press provided the leaders and growing numbers of sympathizers and functionaries with the array of symbols, self-images, and mentalities, as well as the shared purpose, that they needed to fight the civil war and hold power over a diverse and unruly society. The scattered newspapers on the table in I.I. Brodskii's 1930 painting *Lenin in Smol'nyi*—perhaps the most famous representation of Lenin—testify to the power of this special meaning. A bias for true believers was evident throughout the Soviet press not only in *Pravda* and other "leading" newspapers for elites but also in "mass" newspapers such as *Krest'ianskaia Gazeta* (The peasant newspaper) and *Rabochaia Gazeta* (The workers' newspaper), which catered to a lower but still sympathetic audience.[3] Yet every society employs some kind of public language for the common consideration of common issues, and the Soviet press had this role as well. The Bolsheviks enthusiastically promoted their special language by establishing a monopolistic information system and silencing all rivals.

Pravda was important to this process. As the chief party publication it was the preeminent insiders' voice, but it was also an authoritative public source on almost every issue. The consummation of these two historic functions—the representation of elite self-purpose and the public redefinition of a wider social world—is my subject here. Therefore I am concerned with the daily information in the newspaper rather than the fleeting if momentous treatment of a few great issues. My argument is that the Bolsheviks did two things simultaneously in their newspapers. They wrote meaningfully for themselves and their supporters about their experience in governing and problem solving, however boring and repetitive these accounts seemed to outsiders. They also concealed and distorted the wider social world behind an increasingly inappropriate ideological grid to produce by the end of the 1920s a grandiose system of public lying that paralleled the genuine communication between leaders and followers in the same media.

The special quality of the press for the triumphant Bolsheviks and the new elites who supported them was evident in the layout on the page of all the central newspapers, including *Pravda*. Each paper contained several relatively distinct discourses.[4] First and most important were the leaders' own words in editorials, speeches, articles, and official announcements, together with signed commentaries by authoritative journalists who had a special role as trusted government spokesmen. To informed supporters of the system, these texts were a source of authority, inspiration, and explanation of policy. They account for roughly half the space devoted to domestic affairs in *Pravda* from 1918 to 1928, and a somewhat smaller proportion of all the articles.[5] Comments by revolutionary leaders and lead editorials alone constitute 10 to 20 percent of the space on domestic affairs in the period.[6]

The Bolsheviks incorporated lower-level supporters in an interactive portion of the paper dedicated to comments from below, in accord with Lenin's notion of the press as an organizer as well as an ideological compass.[7] Columns such as "Workers Life" or "Party Life," which sometimes began with instructions from above, contained signed commentaries from semi-official worker, peasant, or soldier correspondents, as well as other activists and participants in the construction of Soviet society. However genuine such reports, and some were probably fabricated by editors, they represented an approved localized version of the values promoted in the leading sphere of the paper. Similar but more authoritative were signed reports from special local correspondents. All such commentaries taken together represent between a fifth and a quarter of the space devoted to politics, economics, and society during the first decade of the revolution.

Unsigned informational articles lacking both the requisite ideological instruction of the first sphere and the insider conceits of the second were most often concerned with actual events taking place in the country. These were generally the least directive portions of the paper and presumably most intelligible and interesting to unsympathetic readers. They make up roughly a fifth of the total space allotted to domestic affairs.

This division among the three spheres of discourse held relatively steady in *Pravda* during the first decade of Soviet power. Largely absent were human interest stories and reports of diverse happenings—the crimes, natural disasters, and personal lives of prominent people—that were so important in the pre-Soviet press and the presses of other industrial societies.

The Bolsheviks often expressed their self-awareness and sense of power in the press during the first decade of their rule by the use of the pronoun "we." In his "Letter to Workers and Peasants of the Ukraine on the Occasion of the Victory over Denikin," Lenin wrote: "We are opponents of national isolation; we are internationalists; we strive for the close unity and complete merging of the workers and peasants of all nations of the world in one universal Soviet republic" (1/4/20).[8] He underlined the possessiveness of this usage at to the eleventh party congress, when he announced, "We are the state" (3/30/22). This device was common among the leadership. "We want not only riches but socialist riches; we want not only accumulation but socialist accumulation," declared Lev Kamenev in a speech to the military academy (8/6/25).

Editorials carried great weight in the Soviet press, and the editorial "we" echoed the leaders' voices rather than those of journalists or editors of the newspaper, even when the editors belonged to the leadership. "We broke the united front of capital," wrote one editorialist in 1922 (5/17/22). "Our industry wants to live and can live," explained another in a leader on the fuel crisis (1/19/22). "The basic defect of our campaign to aid the hungry is not lack of assistance but lack of clear organization," wrote a third (2/21/22). This usage was specific but also vague. It embodied the elite's cliquishness but left room for sympathizers as well. For the party elite the difference between leaders and followers was obvious. The future Stalinist E. Iaroslavskii referred to "our problem" in an article captioned "With the Force of the Working People Themselves" (7/28/21). Similarly, Lev Sosnovskii wrote: "Now when all the printing presses and all the newspapers are in the hands of the worker-peasant authorities, we cannot permit any encroachment upon the freedom of the workers' press; we did not make the revolution for that" (12/1/22).

Columnists at *Pravda* were insiders, and bylines in central newspapers meant responsibility rather than independence, as is the case for presses of market economies. Soviet columnists spoke with almost official authority in the 1920s, and their power to intimidate was often apparent. The columnists' "we" had an institutional flavor, particularly in *Pravda*, as in the phrase "our Communist view" of a columnist who argued, "We ought to try to strengthen our influence everywhere" (1/40/20). But references could also be purposefully ambiguous. A journalist observed that "our next and most important task is not stopping to discuss the state supply of grain" (1/19/22). The exclusive implications of such usage were usually clear.

Problems of identity were handled somewhat differently in the interactive portion of the paper. If local contributors used "we" to identify the national cause, they looked up, not down, the social scale. Students at Sverdlov Academy wrote: "The question of the restoration of our economy is a question of our existence; a question about whether we will exist or not exist" (6/25/21). Activists also used "we" in a local sense. "The main difficulty is that we seldom lead," wrote one contributor under the heading "Our Shortcomings" (2/12/24). Local elites differentiated themselves from the surrounding population in this way and affirmed their links to central authorities. "Up to this time the state farms have not carried out this task because our agricultural proletariat was too ignorant and unorganized," wrote Elena Blokina on a special women's page (10/30/19). A female activist sent to the village explained in the same issue, "Before us, Communists, is posed a new and urgent task [*zadacha*]—work among peasant women" (10/30/19). A correspondent in the Workers' Life section wrote two years later, "Our foreign comrades expressed their delight to the workers, sharing their impressions" (6/25/21).

Local correspondents also occasionally used "we" to speak for workers and peasants. An activist among the bakers complained that the cooperative store lacked underwear: "Workers don't change their underwear for months or more. We protest." (2/12/19). But such comments were uncommon. The revolutionary "we" was also uncommon in the informational section, except during the civil war, when there were frequent references to "our position" (10/30/19) and "our victories" (1/4/18) in the military conflict. Yet even here the pronoun expressed the great power of the early Soviet press, which lay primarily in its intimate partnership with its special audience.

The actuality of this partnership was expressed in the single most repeated story of the decade, which journalists retold again and again in thousands of variations during the 1920s: the story of how the leaders and their supporters confronted the issues and tasks before them. The subject was not events but the ongoing process of governing within the expanding Soviet system. These were real and important articles that carried great meaning for people involved in some aspect of administration, even at the lowest levels of society. Such articles constitute the vast majority of the domestic stories in the press from 1918 to the late 1920s.

On one level they represent the press's attempt to grapple with the central issues confronting the government, but on another they signify a bifurcation of society, since governing was the preserve of officials, and the concerns of the rest of society were largely overlooked. Key words in such stories were "question" (*vopros*) and "task" (*zadacha*). The word *vopros* carried an echo of pre-Soviet politics, since it had often been employed by socialists and liberals: "the woman question," "the labor question," "the agrarian question," and so forth. People struggled with such cursed "questions" well into the early 1920s, but they were not generally expected to answer them with any finality. The word was also used during the last years before the revolution and a few years afterward in the sense of an issue as in "a tormenting [*bol'noi*] question" or as in Lenin's phrase "various questions of life."[9]

Zadacha, "task," had narrower connotations. The great prerevolutionary lexicographer Vladimir Dal' defined it as "a question [*vopros*] for resolution," but it too was employed in the first years after the revolution to refer to perplexing problems without obvious solutions rather than, as in the late 1920s, assignments to be fulfilled. Sometimes "problem" (*problema*) was used as a rough equivalent to "question" (*vopros*) and the question was occasionally implied, as in articles with headings such as "About [*o*] Communal Education" (9/6/21). Less frequent and more specific was use of the word *delo*, an old official term for a case, as in a bureaucratic or criminal file, but also for a business, an issue, or a cause.

The word *zadacha* was sometimes also used to focus attention on large concerns. "The task of the party is to bring about a decisive shift in the attitude of the working mass to the campaign," wrote an editorialist (2/21/22). "Financial employees ought to understand that too much depends on the completion of this task," explained a columnist (10/22/22). Yet "task," with its pedagogical and sometimes military connotations, was often more restrictive, as in a journalists' comment about grain speculation: "Our task is to direct the maximum force to this [issue]" (1/19/22). An editorial explaining the return of market relations in the New Economic Policy was captioned "The Basic Task" ((5/6/21).

Revolutionaries used both terms during the periods of the civil war and the New Economic Policy to express their personal involvement in events and to represent the link between leaders and followers on which the success of the central press depended. "Before us stands a serious and critical task, whose correct resolution is necessary for the rebirth of our industry," wrote an official, referring to adolescent workers (2/21/22). "We have only begun to resolve economic questions in the White Russian village," noted an activist in the "Party Life" column (2/12/25). "Only the resolution of the basic question of the organization of the national economy and the free allotment of working force permits us to get down to those measures which are directed at lessening the calamity of unemployment," wrote V. Shmidt under the heading "On the Question of Unemployment" (2/9/18).

Journalists clarified failures as well as successes in this manner. "Many times in the past year we were concerned with the question of supply of the Donbas, but despite this, the Donbas was not supplied," wrote a columnist, who added pointedly, "And we are sure that comrades in the center are not content" (9/7/22). E. Iaroslavskii likewise described the difficulties of famine relief as "our problem" (7/28/21). The leaders easily conceptualized issues in this way because they saw themselves, their followers, and the institutions they created as the only positive actors in Russian society. And given their assumptions, this was true.

Just how fully the Bolshevik press focused on insiders was apparent in the peopling of the newspaper narratives. The leaders were chief actors on the revolutionary stage, and stories with headings such as "Comrade Dzerzhinsky's Farewell to Transport Workers (2/12/26); "Lenin and Children" (2/12/24); and "L.V. Kamenev at the Military Academy" (8/6/25) were common.[10] The leaders also put themselves in the news when they personalized their own contributions. Nikolai Bukharin highlighted himself and his own thinking with observations such as "and so we move to the question of dictatorship" and "we are finished" in an essay "Democracy or Dictatorship" (2/9/18). The prominent journalist and editor Lev Sosnovskii did the same thing in a speech about the murder by a worker of one of *Pravda*'s part-time local correspondents: "We would prefer to see our class enemies—landowners and capitalists—accused in the dock, but we come to judge someone of working-class origins" (12/1/22).

Most individual actors in the press, however, came from the gray army of functionaries, activists, and exemplary party members who sheltered under the protective umbrella of the revolutionary "we." Professional journalists and activists who contributed to the press portrayed members of this group as people who were accomplishing what needed to be done, or at least trying to do so. A local party member wrote: "Now the task [*zadacha*] of old party comrades is to merge together promptly into a single united Communist family to bring in new arrivals; and we are doing this" (10/30/19). An activist wrote to support a "model" factory manager: "Despite the fact that comrade Bergamon has already been cut off for five years from the work bench and occupies a high post, he has not turned into a bureaucrat" (10/22/22). The workers, so important in Bolshevik ideology, rarely appeared as agents of action, either individually or collectively, although they were often featured as the objects of action. Women suffered a similar eclipse; they were seldom active protagonists in newspaper stores or authors except on the special women's page that appeared occasionally.

More common than leaders or functionaries as actors in the daily narratives were the anonymous institutions of the expanding bureaucracy, ranging from the government itself and the Central Committee to local organizations of various sorts. Institutional agents appear in roughly half the sample stories in the period.[11] The revolutionary "we" was implicit in these accounts, and so was the exclusion of outsiders, since the use of these institutions as actors made the discourse opaque to those who did not share an insider vocabulary or values. The employment of the term "Soviet power" to describe the party-based government in which Soviets played a limited role is an example. "The next task of Soviet power is the complete destruction of illiteracy" reads one report (1/4/20). "Soviet power," the party leader Mikhail Kalinin explained, "recognized the business of providing for and bringing up children as one of its tasks from the first days of its existence" (2/23/21).

The party itself was also such an entity, and during the decade the central newspapers and particularly *Pravda* swelled with stories organized around party directives. "The Party's Task in the Area of Cooperatives" was a typical headline (4/2/21). There were also, however, myriad accounts of smaller institutions, which were equally rich in meaning for members of the bureaucracy. "Local economic organs basically ought to change their view of handicraft production" reads one account (8/6/25). Sometimes groups of employees were identified instead of institutions, as in the statement "All the work in gathering grain outright is to be fulfilled by the large village executive committees with the participation of tax and food inspectors" (9/6/21).

The absence of individualized people lent these stories a ghostly quality except for readers who found the tendrils of the state and party alive with meaning. A workers' correspondent, who signed in as "the Bee," wrote that "not one serious question, not a meeting, takes place without the participation of the trade union organization" (2/12/24). The rest of society was passive or invisible in this world of active institutions. "Every union in Moscow, Petrograd, Saratov, and everywhere ought to take the initiative for itself in the organization of its basic economy" wrote an official, who explained that "On the question [*vopros*] depends the whole business [*delo*] of the supply and the improvement of the workers' lives" (6/25/21). "All these decrees and decisions of Soviet power are dictated by a striving to raise labor productivity as quickly as possible," noted a correspondent (5/6/21).

Formulations of this sort signify not only the bureaucratization of the language of public life and the exclusion of a large portion of Russian society from political and economic decision-making but also a severe restriction of the very notion of citizenship in the public eye. On one level the old institutions and organizations that had composed civil society simply vanished or were repressed; on another the population was divided into those who were visible on the stage of Soviet public life and those who were not. The result was a style of journalistic narrative uniquely suited to the emerging Stalinist order.

The fact that the Bolsheviks were largely talking and listening to themselves and their sympathizers was apparent both from the tone of the reportage and the sources quoted or cited in the articles. The leaders often addressed readers in a tone that brooked few questions, and they sometimes used Marxism as a foundation for their authority. In an essay titled "Industrial Democracy," Trotsky began: "Every state regime is the organized rule of a definite class" (1/11/21). Army leader M.V. Frunze punctuated a speech with the observation that "the Red Army ought to be so strong in two or three years as to be unbeatable for the whole bourgeois world" (8/6/25). Less elevated commentators often foreclosed discussion by citing unchallengeable authorities such as Lenin or the party. They also framed their remarks in a way that did not invite questions. An activist writing about the low wages of factory students observed, "Here is an immediate task [*zadacha*] for the Komsomol under the direct leadership of the Communist Party" (2/12/25). A wire service reporter simply informed readers, "The 10th of February was the 25th anniversary of the first radio station in the world, invented by A.S. Popov . . . before Marconi" (2/12/25). This kind of authoritative narrative voice sounded in a third to two-thirds of all articles during the period.[12]

More important than the authors' imperious tone was the absence of contrary or questioning voices within the articles themselves. Those who contributed to the press seldom cited other opinions except to confirm their own positions or to contrast right and wrong thinking. Rarely were readers left with two unchallenged opinions on even trivial matters. The authors of roughly half the articles make no mention of any outside sources of information or opinion but merely relate their stories as if they were the sole sources of information.[13] Those who cited other opinions most often did so simply to corroborate their views.

Such confirming voices ranged from quotations of Lenin's words to statements by anonymous workers and peasants. Typically, an activist who described a meeting at a bust of Lenin after the leader's death quoted peasants saying to workers, "You comrade workers are more developed and organized than we peasants; teach us; give us your knowledge and experience inherited from the party of Il'ich" (8/8/24). Meetings were frequently reported in this way, as was a factory gathering at which the workers were quoted as having decided, "We will carry out the directives of the party firmly and without mistakes" (8/6/25). Summaries of decisions at meetings often served the same purpose, as when a reporter concluded that after some argument "they at last decided that women are necessary in the construction of our [Soviet] Union" (8/6/25).

Condemnations or illustrations of wrong thinking also shrank the sphere of public commentary, and Bolshevik journalists often quoted their political enemies to this purpose. One columnist cited "the peasant Messiah Victor Chernov," the leader of the Socialist Revolutionary Party that the Bolsheviks had crushed (5/6/21); another referred to a Menshevik statement that "the new economic policy will give positive results only under conditions of the democratization (?) of Soviet power" (10/29/21). This method of reducing opposing arguments was also applied to domestic disputes. A reporter ridiculed opponents of the confiscation of valuables from the Orthodox Church for famine relief with the remark that "only an insignificant handful of 'delegates' and a few kulaks tried to create an unhealthy mood at the conference with their demagogic shouts" (3/30/22). This selective representation of dissenting constituencies belonged to a style of reportage in which views could be described only as right or wrong, and no graduations of opinion were possible. Stalin damned his opponents in this way throughout the 1920s.

A monologic voice was perhaps to be expected in the coverage of Soviet politics, but it extended to other subjects as well. Whereas American newspapers of the period tended to contain several opinions of a fire or a political speech, *Pravda* generally offered only an unbroken authoritative narrative. This was particularly noticeable in news of science and technology. Without a single querulous aside, reporters described the marvels of a new electric plow. "In contemporary conditions, with energetic and correct application to the task, shining results are possible," reads one report (7/28/21). "Thanks to such colossal productivity, the plow at once solves the task of shifting from petty peasant farms to great mechanized cultivation," reads another (7/28/21). The plow obviously failed to fulfill this dream, but what was remarkable was that it disappeared from the press without any negative reports or further discussion.

Claims for a new type of telephone that operated without a central switchboard but was easy to manufacture in Russia and did not require "gold from an American uncle" were also published without a whisper of skepticism, and this too vanished from public view without a single critical comment (2/12/25). The failure to follow up rosy reports on inventions showed a contempt for the uninformed reader that pervaded the newspaper. Such self-indulgence undoubtedly cost the society dear.

Some critical voices were nevetheless to be heard within the system. Although the leaders and journalists often confronted their readers with an aura of authority, there were several notable gaps in this otherwise claustrophobic discourse. One was the leaders' willingness to argue publicly among themselves about certain topics, at least through the mid-1920s. There were disputes among the top Bolsheviks during these early years on a range of public issues that included democracy within the party, the role of trade unions in communist society, the overall strategy of economic development, and Soviet foreign policy, particularly toward China.

Such arguments involved lively polemics, declarations and petitions, and open letters in the press, particularly in the first few years after the revolution. There were even public disputes about relatively minor issues during these years. Yet although disagreements could be bitter, they were always arguments within the Bolshevik family, and as such they had little to do with those outside it. Thus Lenin attacked E.A. Preobrazhensky, a theorist of industrialization, for "not understanding what every intelligent worker understands" (3/30/22). A journalist summed up a dispute about trade unions by observing, "Both points of view represented at the meeting by Zinoviev and Bukharin sparked a clear exchange of opinions" (1/11/21). And Trotsky denounced one of his opponents ("publicists of the Larin type") for urging less pressure on industrial enterprises and thereby, in his view, threatening the repair of locomotives (9/9/20).

Stalin put an end to all public policy disputes in the second half the decade. The last echo of controversy among the titans of Soviet politics for almost half a century took place during the crushing of Trotsky and the United Opposition in 1927. The leaders' arguments among themselves had filled a relatively small space in the newspaper up until that time. These articles were undoubtedly interesting to party members and sometimes to the rest of the population, even though nonparty members were barred from political life.[14]

Critical comments or complaints about local general abuses or problems constituted another opening in Soviet public discourse and a remarkable feature of the early Bolshevik press. These were occasional features of *Pravda* and other leading newspapers. "We say that everywhere the economic situation is still weak," wrote a journalist in *Pravda*, adding that "a militiaman gets [only] 15 rubles" (8/6/25). A reporter complained about the difficulties faced by war veterans and appealed to the authorities: "Remember the pensioners in the name of truth and justice before it is too late" (9/7/22). A columnist wrote at the outset of the New Economic Policy about the decline of mass education, complaining that it was "usually pleasant for Soviet and Party . . . authorities to say that Soviet power has done and is doing very much in the arena of enlightenment" (1/11/21).

In another type of criticism, local reporters or activists sometimes found fault with the local authorities or protested local conditions. "The workers have complained many times about Commissar Timefed, but he continues to live peacefully," wrote one reporter (3/30/22). A local correspondent complained that while workers sacrificed themselves for national goals, local authorities ignored poor working conditions at the factory. "Losing their health," he wrote, "they have the right to expect that the most energetic measures will be taken to address this" (2/12/24). A local contributor similarly faulted social policy, noting, "The decree about switching to collective provisioning somehow completely failed to foresee the [necessity of protecting] factory adolescents from the danger that threatens them" (2/21/22).

Such remarks were a minor part of newspaper content, however, and a tone of self-confident affirmation generally held sway. The Bolsheviks created a discourse in which the sympathetic voices of insiders usually crowded out other voices. It was a system of public information that increasingly lacked the means to describe that part of society lying beyond the world of the bureaucracy.

If one aspect of this self-inflicted myopia was the exclusion of a whole realm of human activity from the purview of the press and the language of public life, a second was the representation of human motivations in increasingly schematic and arbitrary ways. Every narrative of human activity is held together by a web of motives that determine the characters' actions: that is, by a sense of the meaning of behavior or a notion of agency.[15] Agency in modern industrial societies is frequently pragmatic and based on rational expectations, often of material gain or loss. Early Soviet journalists frequently shared such assumptions, but Marxism offered an alternative motivational system based on class consciousness. Although both systems of motivation appear prominently in *Pravda* during the decade, narratives in which agents acted without reference to class consciousness were the more common.

Journalists often described actions that did not fit the kind of Marxism prevalent in those years and according to which all people were motivated by class consciousness. Although some legal cases were depicted exclusively in terms of class conflict, many were not. One journalist recounted under the heading "Rural Life" a man's murder of his mother-in-law when he failed to gain ownership of the women's farm (2/12/24). Similar was the case of a former Red Army officer who went over to the Whites but later returned to Russia to ask forgiveness and "to rehabilitate himself" (2/12/24). The author of the article explained that the man was sentenced to ten years at hard labor, but he did not discuss the role of class in the decision.

The very notion of a world divided in half by a barricade was undermined or at least substantively denied in a range of articles about the real problems of daily life. One reporter recounted meetings at which workers were unsure of what the Bolsheviks stood for and asked, "And don't you have a [party] program, comrade?" The reporter noted that the party program was "too learned for rank-and-file representatives of the laboring classes" who lacked "party literacy" (10/30/19). A local official even defended a bourgeois factory director against a *Pravda* critic: "The 4th auto factory has set off on the path to a decisive struggle on the labor front," he wrote. "Its director, a former bourgeois, works conscientiously for the creation of Russian production" (2/23/21).

Such articles were published beside others in which class consciousness appears to be the only motor of human activity. The most powerful formulation of class motivations and the one that served best to bridge gaps between new elites and the common people was the notion of class war. More than a quarter of the stories on economics, politics, and society published in *Pravda* from 1918 through 1920 were framed in this way.[16] Such articles were enhanced by military metaphors, the portrayal of opponents as class enemies, and the belief that society was kept in motion by class interests. Journalists routinely described revolutionaries as "soldiers of the revolution," and they invariably showed the masses allied with them against common enemies (2/12/19). In this way they swept aside many incongruities. "The peasants support the avant garde of the revolution, the proletariat, and equally . . . objectively they support the struggle of the proletariat for socialism," wrote one commentator, who added that the same peasants "know almost nothing about socialism or about the path to it" (2/9/18). Under the heading "Class against Class," a columnist admonished, "Remember, comrades, there is a thin line of bourgeois and generals against millions of workers and peasants" (10/30/19).

Journalists used Marxism as a glass through which to examine social interactions in early Soviet society, but it was a distorting one, and the distortion increased as the decade progressed. To see class consciousness as the individual's informing purpose meant to read individual actions in a very specific way. This was a rationalization of behavior in which all human conduct was predetermined so as to fulfill an ideological prescription. A Communist village organizer wrote of the women with whom she worked: "The first who decided to go to the meeting were the wives of Red Army soldiers, then the wives of poor peasants, and last of all the wives of middle peasants." She added, "Kulak wives stayed away" (10/30/19). Under this glass, political or personal disputes became class conflicts, locally and in high politics. A cossack mutiny in Krasnoiarsk had to be a bourgeois plot, for in this schema of motivations there was no other way to explain it (4/2/21). In another case, a local reporter wrote, "The kulak persecutes the rural correspondents, but the poorest villagers take them under their protection" (2/12/25). "Many homes have already been liberated from the bourgeoisie, and families of workers are already settled in their place," noted an observer, who concluded "Yes, long live the advanced detachments of the world revolution—the Red Army" (9/13/18).

The effect of this reading of social life was to stigmatize a portion of the population, despite the Bolsheviks' own bourgeois class origins, as in this appeal for proletarian nurses: "A bourgeois nurse is more stepmother than nurse. Her brother is with Denikin [a White leader in the Civil War], her thoughts and feelings are with them. She reacts with hatred to the suffering of those who bring defeat and death to the capitalist stooges. Let those who have left their units feel the solicitous hands of a loving nurse, a comrade and a friend. Our visits, our words of sympathy remind them that they are not forgotten, that the closely knit unit of the proletarian family is there with them" (10/30/19).

This primitive idea of class consciousness collided, however, with the

Bolsheviks' accent on their own elite role, which was both the most important truth expressed in the early Soviet press and the source of greatest distortion. Leaders, journalists, and activists who together created the new language of Soviet power were at pains to emphasize their special function, and so they portrayed political and social struggles not only as class against class but also as "them" against "us." Marxist class categories in this sense eroded from within, since they were useful only to obscure elite rule, not to confirm it.

The revolutionary lie inherent in the crude application of Marxist ideology to the realities of Russian life was manageable in the early 1920s but less so toward the end of the decade, when bureaucratic habits became more rigid. This probably explains the decline in articles framed by the idea of class war from a high of 25 percent in 1918-20 to 16 percent of the total in 1921 and 1922, 12 percent from 1923 through 1926, and only 8 percent in 1927 and early 1928.

From 1923 to early 1928 there was a shift in portrayals of motivation from pragmatism to a bureaucratic ethos. Representations of a bureaucratic logic in which orders from institutions replaced rational explanations of behavior became more common in these years. One sign of this was that journalists increasingly presented the myriad directives and reports of tasks to be accomplished without explanations of their purpose or discussion of alternatives. Articles about the bureaucracy itself and changing structures of state and party administration were other indications of this shift.

Journalists presented this logic of human behavior most forcefully in articles portraying institutions as actors motivating human beings. The editors of *Pravda* allotted this role to the newspaper: "*Pravda*, the organ of the Central Committee of the Russian Communist Party, ought to be the leader and friend of each member of the party" (2/12/24). A commentator expressed with particular vigor the notion that institutions make decisions, not people, in an article about the Worker-Peasant Inspectorate (RKI): "It is necessary to observe that up to this time the peasantry knows little and sometimes nothing at all about the RKI, while at this time the need for its work is established in almost every village" (8/6/25). "The locales are given all means; they are offered wide organizational initiative," wrote an editorialist under the heading "Tasks [*zadacha*] of Local Organs and Soviet Social Organizations" (8/8/24), an article about overcoming the consequences of famine. Just as the exclusion of a large portion of the population from public life narrowed the discourse, so also did the limitation of the range of possible motives. As orders from above became a chief motivation for action in the public imagination, the possible range of human behavior shrank.

Yet interest in practical issues of administration and government remained, and there was little evidence in the central press during the 1920s of the utopianism that is often associated with the revolution.[17] References to the coming of Communism or even descriptions of the future benefits of the Soviet system rarely appear in the newspaper except during the year of revolution and the two years of civil war.[18] From 1918 to 1920, references to a future society or to the benefits of world revolution appear, albeit fleetingly, in 20 percent of the articles. From 1921 to early 1928 this figure drops to less than 4 percent, and even when such references do appear, the promise of the future is usually mundane.

The apparent focus on the present was deceptive, however. The most powerful single metaphor governing the insiders' experience in the era of Lenin and Stalin was probably that of the path (*put'*).[19] Just as Trotsky dubbed those literati willing to maintain a friendly neutrality "fellow travelers" (*po putchiki*)—literally, "those on the path"—the Bolsheviks represented the revolutionary process as a path or journey toward a better future, as in the phrases "on the Leninist path" and "the path to socialism" (2/12/25; 7/22/27). The effect of this metaphoric construction was to deny the present except as a means to something else and to restrict attention in public life to those who moved ahead along this path, with the exception of those people who appeared as obstacles or enemies. This was the way of thinking the Bolsheviks chose for themselves when they formulated their unique language of public life. In this spirit, Minister of Health N.A. Semashko exalted Lenin for choosing "straight and true paths, leading to the establishment of those forms of social order, the coming of which he foresaw" (2/12/24). A mining professor paid similar homage to Lenin's legacy: "We go ahead along the paths established by these testaments" (2/12/24). Activists in Turkestan likewise hailed the students who sent them Lenin's works as "children of that class which step by step goes along the bloody path to the projected (planned) ends" (8/8/24).

The path was an appropriate metaphor for an avant-garde party, and it was illuminated by images of trains and marchers in Soviet posters throughout the Stalin era.[20] The meaning of literacy itself in the early Soviet years was linked with this image. "The Worker's Press is a Torch Lighting the Path to a New Life," reads one early slogan.[21] "Literacy is the Path to Communism," reads another.[22] The most famous of the early Soviet literacy posters, Aleksei Radkov's "The Illiterate Is Also Blind—Bad Luck and Misfortune Await Him Everywhere," shows a blind man, who has strayed from the path, stepping off a cliff.[23]

When journalists used the metaphor of the path, they generally looked beyond the world of daily life and turned the present into something to be overcome and forgotten. The metaphor spelled oblivion for those who stood by the wayside or proved an obstacle. This was the sense of Bukharin's nasty quip aimed at Karl Kautsky: "The living experience of the Revolution has passed him by" (2/9/18). More than thirty years later, V. Il'enkov titled his widely promoted Stalin-prize novel of 1950 *The Big Road*.[24] The "big road" was always the little road of oligarchy in Soviet Russia. That was the unpleasant fact of the Bolsheviks' revolution and of the press they created. The language of Soviet power was immediate and compelling for those engaged in the system, but it was obscure and deadening for those outside it.

What was peculiar to the informational system, even more than its monopolistic character, was its resistance to challenges and criticism from without. The Bolsheviks succeeded in centering their followers' attention on progress toward what they considered desirable goals, but in doing so they turned the lens of public perception away not only from the atrocities they condoned and perpetrated but from unintentional disasters and failures as well. During the 1930s the Soviet government managed to surmount such difficulties without changing the informational system; in the 1980s they did not. When social problems and economic shortfalls could no longer be concealed, the media were faulted, and *glasnost* was a logical response, even though it facilitated the collapse of Communism, to which the press had contributed so much.

NOTES

1. I thank Peter Kenez, Louis Galambos, and Karen Brooks for helpful comments.

2. I show how difficult the newspapers were to read and their limited distribution in Jeffrey Brooks, "Studies of the Reader in the 1920s," *Russian History* 2-3 (1982): 187-202, and "The Breakdown in the Production and Distribution of Printed Material, 1917-27," in Abbott Gleason et al., eds., *Bolshevik Culture* (Bloomington, Ind., 1985), 151-74. Peter Kenez, *The Birth of the Propaganda State* (Cambridge, 1985), 45, 232, finds the Bolshevik press more successful but also notes how dull the newspapers were.

3. Brooks, "Studies of the Reader in the 1920s"; and Jeffrey Brooks, "Public and Private Values in the Soviet Press, 1921-28," *Slavic Review* 48 (Spring

1989): 25-35. The Bolsheviks distinguished between guiding newspapers for elites and those directed at the masses.

4. I discuss this in Jeffrey Brooks, "Popular and Public Values in the Soviet Press, 1921-28," *Slavic Review* 48 (Spring 1989): 16-35; "The Press and Its Message: Images of America in the 1920s and 1930s," in Sheila Fitzpatrick et al., eds., *Russia in the Era of NEP* (Bloomington, Ind., 1991), 231-53; "Revolutionary Lives: Public Identities in *Pravda* during the 1920s," in Stephen White, ed., *New Directions in Soviet History* (Cambridge, 1991), 27-40; and "Official Xenophobia and Popular Cosmopolitanism in Early Soviet Russia," *American Historical Review* 97 (1992), 1431-48.

5. Comments on space and content in the press are based on a random sample of all articles on domestic politics, society, or economics (excluding high culture and foreign policy, which I treat elsewhere) in two issues per year for 1918-20, nine issues per year in 1921-22, two issues per year in 1923-27 and one in early 1928. A total of 721 articles were coded: 119 for 1918-20, 338 for 1921-22, 203 for 1923-26, and 61 for 1927-28. The sample was designed to pick articles from January or February and July or August, except in 1918-20 when those months were unavailable to me. Space was measured in square inches on the page.

6. Figures on space are 20 percent (1918-20), 12 percent (1921-22), 23 percent (1923-26), and 13 percent (1927-28). The figures are slightly less in foreign affairs for *Pravda* and such newspapers as *Trud* and *Krest'ianskaia gazeta*. See Brooks, "Official Xenophobia."

7. Kenez, *Birth of the Propaganda State*, discusses this in terms of mass mobilization.

8. The notation in the text indicates month/day/year of the issue of *Pravda* cited. All translations from *Pravda* are the author's.

9. *Slovar' Russkogo iazyka* (Moscow, 1957).

10. Leaders figure as agents of action in 12 percent of the articles in 1918-20, 6 percent in 1921-22, 7 percent in 1923-26, and 15 percent in 1927-28.

11. Institutional actors appear in 55 percent of the stories for 1918-20, 55 percent for 1921-22, 48 percent for 1923-26, and 52 percent for 1927 to early 1928. Such stories tended to be slightly longer than average and accounted for somewhat more space.

12. This tone is apparent in almost two-thirds of the articles in 1918-20, roughly 40 percent in the transitional period of 1921-22, less than 30 percent in 1923-26, and nearly half in 1927 and early 1928.

13. Articles in which no other voices or opinions were cited account for 66 percent of the sample in 1918-20, 43 percent in 1921-22, 55 percent in 1923-26, and 43 percent in 1927 to early 1928.

14. Such disputes fill a space too small to measure with my limited sample. They were more important in *Pravda* and *Izvestiia* than in other leading or central newspapers.

15. My use of the term "agency" is informed by the philosopher Kenneth Burke's discussion in *A Grammar of Motives* (Berkeley, Calif., 1945, 1969).

16. Here I apply the concept of schemata: that is, the notion that each story was packaged around a central concept.

17. This fits with an observation of Knei-Paz, "Lenin, Socialism and the State in 1917," in Baruch Knei-Paz, ed., *Revolution in Russia: Reassessments of 1917* (Cambridge, 1992), 301.

18. Reference to either the socialist future or world revolution appears in 18 of 97 sample articles in 1918-20, 6 of 319 articles in 1921-22, 3 of 193 articles in 1923-26, and 2 articles from 1927 and early 1928.

19. This does not mean that the metaphor was the most common in the press; rather, the sense of movement forward, progress, and marching ahead was embedded in many of the Bolsheviks' statements about what they were trying to do.

20. See, e.g., Stephen White, *The Bolshevik Poster* (New Haven, Conn., 1988), 99, 102, 118.

21. *Serdtsem slushaia revoliutsiiu —iskusstvo pervykh let Oktiabria*, ed. Mikhail German and Aleksandr Kokovkin (Leningrad, 1977, 1980, 1985), 78.

22. White, *Bolshevik Poster*, 11.

23. *Serdtsem slushaia revoliutsiiu*, 81.

24. V. Il'enkov, *Bol'shaia doroga* (Moscow, 1950). The novel was awarded a Stalin prize the year it was published.

11

Press Freedom and the
Chinese Revolution in the 1930s

STEPHEN R. MacKINNON

The Chinese press has been an integral part of the Chinese revolutionary process, which began early in the nineteenth century with the uprisings that mushroomed into the Taiping and Nian rebellions of the 1850s and 1860s, and continues today with Leninist parties still in power on mainland China and Taiwan. The closeness of the relationship is well illustrated by the fact that, like Ho Chiminh and Lenin, most of China's revolutionary leaders—such as Mao Zedong and Hong Xiuquan (founder of the Taipings)—began their careers as journalist-polemicists and not as political organizers. A modern press in China evolved from the Western-inspired treaty-port publications of the mid-nineteenth century into a chaotic array of daily newspapers, weeklies, and journals that flourished in the 1930s under various degrees of censorship, depending on geopolitical realities and financial resources. My focus here is on the 1930s, a kind of golden age for the Chinese press in its content, productivity, openness, and experimentation.

The history of the Chinese press is a relatively underdeveloped field. A few pioneering works were published in China and the West in the 1930s, and then the subject was dropped. To Chinese scholars the reasons are obvious: the subject was too controversial and dangerous.[1] Scholars outside China have been concerned with the institutional origins of the Chinese press in the late nineteenth century and the contributions of the dissident press to the Republican revolution of 1911-12. Recent works have related the press to the history of Chinese political thought, moving forward chronologically another decade to the Chinese enlightenment period around 1919 and the establishment of the two Leninist parties—Communist and Nationalist (hereafter Guomindang).[2] The most influential recent survey of the Chinese press is by Andrew Nathan, who focused on the formative period 1900-1920, tying the emergence of a critical press and the writings of polemicists such as Liang Qichao to contemporary Chinese notions of democracy as expressed in the late 1970s and 1980s.[3] Yet his analysis skips the 1930s, the crucial period when the press became more independent and assertive institutionally in an effort to create political discourse outside the state-dominated public sphere. It was the defining decade in terms of the historical alternatives available to the Chinese press in the twentieth century and hence the richest period for comparative analysis.

During the 1930s the Chinese press seemed to brim with potential in terms of variety, quality, and freedom of expression. The Guomindang and Chiang Kaishek (Jiang Jieshi) loosely governed from Nanjing a country that was mostly in the hands of warlords commissioned as generals. This made official censorship of the press erratic. Thus, in 1936-37, Xi'an (the capital of northwest China), could become an island of free expression. But overall, the best opportunity for experimentation and entrepreneurship in the press was in the more stable, foreign-controlled concession zones of Shanghai. Moreover, as the Japanese armies moved slowly south from Manchuria, nibbling away at coastal China, the Shanghai press was politically and institutionally strengthened by the protest movement against Chiang Kaishek over his hesitant response to the Japanese. Politically eclipsed until 1936 were the Communists, who after the Long March of 1934-35 were reduced in number and isolated at remote guerrilla bases in the rugged northwest.

Then in 1937 Chiang Kaishek declared war on Japan and formed a united-front government with the Communists. North China, Nanjing, and Shanghai fell quickly to the Japanese. What was left of Chiang's government retreated up the Yangzi River to Wuhan for a final stand. For ten months in 1938 the industrial city of Wuhan—or Hankou, as it was usually known at the time—became the political and cultural center of revolutionary China under a new Guomindang-Communist united front. The unusual absence of the repressive power of the state and the spirit of unity against the Japanese permitted the Chinese press a free hand in Wuhan. In productivity and variety the Chinese press exploded until the Japanese captured and burned the city in late October 1938. China's major publishers and editors had converged upon Wuhan: the number of dailies in 1938 shot from three to fourteen in three months, the number of weeklies from twenty to thirty, and journals from thirty to more than two hundred within ten months.[4] All factions and political parties were represented. Censorship was relatively ineffectual; no editors or publishers were arrested or assassinated. In the history of the Chinese press it was the acme of freedom in a Chinese capital, a golden age not surpassed before or since.

Four fundamental characteristics of the Chinese press in the 1930s are important for comparative analyses. First, the press operated within a political patronage system. Second, newspapers and some journals substituted for or acted like competing political parties in a polity that lacked an effective legislative forum. Because of this, the Chinese press was never able to perform an independent "fourth estate" function; it remained too close, too engaged as a player or advocate in the political system. Third, I argue that the Chinese press maintained a symbiotic relationship with the Western press, both inside and outside China. By the 1930s many leading Chinese editors had been trained in the West or at missionary schools, had traveled extensively abroad, had been employed by foreign-owned publications or worked closely with foreign journalists in China. Fourth, the press was plagued by censorship which the two competing Leninist revolutionary parties applied to Western as well as Chinese publications as relentlessly as possible. I take up each of these points separately.

Adequate political patronage seemed crucial to the success of major publications in China from the late nineteenth century to the present. A well-placed political patron bought protection from closure, arrest, or assassination as well as financial backing in some cases. The character of the patronage varied a great deal from period to period, region to region. Thus in the late Qing period, patrons of the press ranged from Manchu princes to senior military commanders like Yuan Shikai to merchant associations in Tianjin and Shanghai. By the 1920s, regional militarists and their followers provided essential protection as patrons. This state of affairs continued into the 1930s, with additional patronage coming from various factions within the ruling Guomindang, whose influence varied from city to city. The *Da Gong Bao* of Tientsin was probably the leading daily in the country. It was protected politically in the 1920s by the Anfu clique of Beiyang warlords. By the 1930s the paper's dominant figure was Zhang Jiluan, who in 1936 swung the paper in support of Chiang Kaishek after his kidnapping at Xi'an in December and took a strong stand against Manchurian warlord Zhang Xueliang.[5] Cheng Shewo, the publisher of the *Li Bao*, was one of the most successful newspapermen commercially in the 1920s and 1930s. He began in Beijing under warlord patronage in the 1920s but relied on key patronage in the 1930s from Ye Chucang and Li Shizeng, both cabinet-level officials in the Nanjing government, to operate papers in Nanjing, Beijing, and Shanghai. In Shanghai's foreign concession zones the press managed to operate more freely, and political patronage was less important. Thus Shanghai became the home of major publications, particularly those on the left which were sponsored by the Communist party or by coalitions of liberal intellectuals such as the group that spearheaded the National Salvation Movement (*Jiu guohui*) of the mid-1930s—a national campaign calling for war against Japan. But even in Shanghai political independence could go too far. The story of China's largest-circulation daily (estimated to be around 140,000 at its peak), the *Shen Bao*, was a sad case in point. The editor-entrepreneur behind the paper was Shi Liangcai, a wealthy man who had good connections with the Guomindang running back to the 1911-12 revolution. These began to break down in the early 1930s because of the paper's success and its criticism of Chiang Kaishek for softness toward Japan. Shi evidently thought of himself as too important to be in danger, and he paid the price: he was assassinated in 1934 in Shanghai. Thereafter, though becoming more oblique in its criticism of the Guomindang, the paper lost its voice and circulation.[6]

What is striking about the Chinese revolution in comparison with French and other revolutions is the bodily harm that Chinese journalists risked. The assassination of Shi Liangcai was not an isolated event. Journalism in China has always been a risky business because the journalist ipso facto became a political figure. The risk to life and limb was considerable. In one study limited to the history of the press in Wuhan and published in 1943, the author charted the age of death of twenty-six fellow journalists he had known personally since the first decade of the twentieth century. Of this group, three died in their fifties, seven in their forties, and the rest in their thirties and twenties—often violently.[7] What made these journalists vulnerable was their combined roles as publisher, reporter, editor, and often entrepreneur. Each one usually oversaw the entire process from reporting to distribution and was held accountable.

Thus, besides political protection, the other key to success was entrepreneurship on the part of the editor and publisher (usually one and the same). Cheng Shewo's and Shi Liangcai's entrepreneurial talents have already been mentioned. Restricted to Shanghai and politically more to the left was Zou Taofen, one of the seven gentlemen arrested in 1936 as leaders of the mass movement urging Chiang Kaishek to declare war on Japan. Crucial to Zou's success was the profitability of his *Shenghuo* (Life) string of publications. Zou made good use of advertising and a sizable chain of bookstores for distribution. He also recruited leading intellectuals such as

Mao Dun (in literature) and Tao Xingzhi (in education) to edit and distribute journals as they wished. Despite the protection of the foreign concession zone in Shanghai, Zou was threatened, harassed, and occasionally forced to close a publication; but he was not silenced. The financial support of Shanghai's fledgling professional "liberal" classes and attraction of students to his bookstores, plus Zou's skillful use of "events" such as Japan's encroachment upon north China made his publications politically unsuppressable.[8]

In 1938 there were few treaty-port protections in wartime Wuhan, yet the atmosphere was unusually conducive to a free press. No one party or warlord was in the ascendancy or able to exercise control over the press as a whole. The result was an unprecedented political range, running the gamut from left to right, from Trotskyist to pro-Fascist publications. Moreover, the figures cited earlier show that the proliferation of new publications meant a flowering of free expression, which is precisely how contemporaries have described it.[9] By mid-1938 Wuhan had four major daily newspapers. The _Wuhan Ribao_ and _Xinhua Ribao_ were operated by the Guomindang and Chinese Communists respectively. Between them politically was the _Da Gong Bao_, which had moved from Tientsin and was still under Zhang Jiluan. The _Sao Dang Bao_ was under the wing of the major military figures who controlled Wuhan at the time, Guomindang general Chen Cheng and Guangxi warlords Bai Zhongxi and Li Zongren (the latter were political opponents of Chiang Kaishek).

Patronage was critical to the survival of smaller publications in Wuhan as well. Recent interviews in Beijing and Taibei with two former editors, Hu Qiuyuan and Hu Sheng, who in 1938 were on opposite sides of the political spectrum, illustrated the point. Hu Qiuyuan's fledgling pro-Guomindang _Shidai Ribao_ was forced to close in July of 1938 because the lack of a political patron shut off access to paper and printing machinery. The crisis was occasioned in part by editor Hu's refusal to accept help from Wang Qingwei, then secretary-general of the Guomindang and a political rival of Chiang Kaishek.[10] Another young editor, Hu Sheng, had arrived in Wuhan as a refugee from Shanghai, where he had been working in left-of-center publications connected to the Communist Party under the patronage of Qian Junrui. In Wuhan, Hu edited three different publications—best known was _Jiu Zhongguo_, (Save China)—on a stop-and-go basis, depending on the wishes of the party. Financially, he relied heavily upon the relatives with whom he was living. At the end of the year, after Wuhan fell to the Japanese, Hu's job security dramatically improved when he and Qian Junrui were hired by militarist Bai Zhongxi to edit a new newspaper being published and distributed by Bai's army as it retreated south towards Guangxi.[11]

As for the second characteristic of the Chinese press in the 1930s, some publications served as surrogates for third-force movements that tried to challenge the competing Leninist parties. In the 1920s the political system had been dominated by warlords and the one-party "tutelage" of the Guomindang, which itself split into factions. Parliamentary institutions were not functional. Thus by the time the Guomindang came fully to power in Nanjing in 1928, the press was one of the few avenues left for political protest outside of mass demonstrations or the underground Communist movement. Despite the obstacles and risks, third-party movements did organize during the 1930s in opposition to both the Guomindang and Communists, but always on a small scale and never in the countryside. Usually their publications became the heart of the party by supplying leadership and organization.[12] (Mark Summers and other authors in this volume have noted similar roles for the press as party surrogates in other revolutions.)

At Wuhan in 1938, third-party movements reached peaks of activity for two reasons: first, the convening of a People's Political Council (parliamentary advisory body) offered a public forum for the first time; secondly, Wuhan had a free press. For example, the New Youth Party was resurrected in Wuhan around the daily *Xin Zhongguo Ribao* and the journal *Guoguang*, and Carsun Chang's National Social Party (*Guojia shehui dang*) around the journal *Caisheng*.[13] All together there were four important "third" parties in Wuhan. None had over a thousand members, but in their publications and in the People's Political Council, their leaders demanded a voice in government and denounced corruption and dictatorship. Although differences broke out over the degree to which all parties should subsume their interests to the will of the commander in chief, Chiang Kaishek, because of the war effort (the question they posed was, must democracy wait because of the war?), the voice the free press of Wuhan provided these small parties was unprecedented.

Less obvious is the third characteristic of the Chinese press in the 1930s: the symbiotic relationship that existed between Chinese and Western journalists in China. Earlier Japanese experiences had influenced the work of such major Chinese journalists as Liang Qichao, Shao Biaoping, Huang Yuansheng, and Hu Zhengzhi. During the 1930s major editor-publishers such as Cheng Shewo, Zou Taofen, and Shi Liangcai traveled widely in the West, studied the Western press, and published accounts of their experiences.

The foreign-owned English and Chinese press, especially in Shanghai, also exerted major influence on Chinese journalism. Many of China's top journalists apprenticed for a time at foreign-edited publications such as the *China Weekly Review* in Shanghai. The influence of the University of Missouri School of Journalism was also remarkable. In 1932 the school's dean, Frank Martin, played a major role in shaping the Journalism Department at Yanjing University in Beijing, in addition to hosting a stream of Chinese journalists in Missouri. But perhaps the best way to illustrate the intimate relationship between the Chinese and Western press is to look at the biographies of two leading journalists on the Communist and Nationalist (Guomindang) sides of the political equation.

Liu Zunqi became an underground Communist while an English major at the missionary-run Yanjing University in Beijing. In Shanghai in the early 1930s he worked on a number of Chinese- and Western-owned publications, including the *China Forum* edited by Harold Isaacs (later *Newsweek* correspondent in China). At one point Liu was arrested by the Guomindang; after being released, he made his way to Yan'an, the Communist guerrilla base. By 1938 Liu was in Wuhan as a special war correspondent for the leading Guomindang daily, *Wuhan Ribao*, and the military-controlled *Sao Dang Bao*. He was recruited in 1941 to join the American government's wartime press center in Chongqing as chief of Chinese staff for the Office of War Information. From this post he exerted a major influence on American wartime coverage of China until at least 1945.[14]

Dong Xianguang, or Hollington Tong, had received grade school education in English at a Shanghai missionary school. Before he departed for the United States in 1907 for further study, he tutored Chiang Kaishek for almost a year in English (both were from the same hometown, Ningpo). Dong graduated from the University of Missouri's School of Journalism in 1912, after which he worked in New York for a year as an assistant editor of the *Independent* and reporter for the *New York Times* and *New York World*. He returned to China in 1913 and worked on a variety of English- and Chinese-language publications in Beijing and Shanghai. By the early 1930s he was editor and publisher of *China Press*, a Guomindang-sponsored English weekly in Shanghai. Working under him were two young adventurers, Tilman Durdin and Harold Isaacs. By the mid-1930s Dong had joined the government, and by 1938 he was vice-minister of information in charge of overseeing the Chinese press and Western correspondents in Wuhan (a subject to which I shall return). For his staff in the Ministry of Information, Dong recruited young Western-trained Chinese like himself, a number of whom would become prominent later—as did Zeng Xubai, who edited the *Zhongyang Ribao* (Central daily news)—the Guomindang party organ—for over thirty years.[15]

Besides taking advantage of the training and background of individual figures such as Liu Zunqi and Dong Xianguang, the best Chinese publications maintained strong institutional ties overseas. Major dailies had a mixed pedigree of Western and Chinese ownership. For example, the *Shen Bao* in Shanghai had originally been British-owned but was bought out by Western-educated Chinese editor-publishers in 1915. In their layout the Shanghai papers also epitomized the Westernization process sweeping the Chinese press. Commercial advertising, photographs and cartoons, want ads, and letters to the editor came into full play in Chinese publications, following Western models. And turning a profit in the Shanghai market were a significant number of Chinese equivalents of specialized Western business, women, sports, and fashion magazines aimed at the newly emerging upper-middle class.

Paradoxically, the Chinese press grew more Westernized in appearance and cultural content at the same time that political content and subject matter were increasingly nationalistic and anti-foreign. This was particularly noticeable with publications on the left such as Zou Taofen's *Shenghuo* publications and Mao Dun's literary journal, which consciously imitate the *New Masses* of New York, including the cartoon work of Robert Minor and German political satirist George Grosz. Thanks to Lu Xun—twentieth-century China's most important writer—and his followers, woodblock prints were in vogue. Before he died in 1936 Lu Xun edited and annotated with the American writer Agnes Smedley a special collection by the German artist-lithographer Käthe Kollwitz. Guomindang publications were a little slower to adopt Western visual propaganda techniques, but by 1938 the publications edited by leading figures such as Tao Xisheng and Tao Baichuan were using political cartoons and woodblock prints just as effectively as their Communist-leaning competitors.[16]

The flow of influence between the foreign and Chinese press went both ways. It was a symbiotic relationship. Western correspondents in China relied heavily on Chinese journalists as sources and staff. Few Westerners spoke or read Chinese, and many developed close working ties with Chinese counterparts by serving together on such English language publications as the *China Weekly Review, China Press, China Forum,* and *Shanghai Post.* Tilman Durdin (later with the *New York Times*) and Harold Isaacs (later of *Newsweek*) worked for Dong Xianguang on more than one such publication. The UPI bureau chief for Wuhan in 1938 was McCracken Fisher, who had attended journalism classes at Yanjing University in the early 1930s with a whole generation of future Chinese journalists. His professors included Dean Walter Williams of the University of Missouri and a young man (also from Missouri) named Edgar Snow, who had just come north from Shanghai after working on the *China Weekly Review*. During World War II, Fisher led the U.S. government's Office of War Information in Chongqing, recruiting as his Chinese chief of staff Liu Zunqi, whom he had known at Yanjing University. Similarly, the British-American journalist Freda Utley relied heavily in 1938 on the young editor Hu Qiuyuan as a source for her stories written between 1938 and 1941. Leading correspondents for the *Da Gong Bao*—the sister and brother pair of Yang Gang and Yang Chao (also Yanjing graduates)—worked closely with Chris Rand of the *New Yorker* and John and Wilma Fairbank of Harvard. And finally, the two best-known China reporters today from the 1930s and 1940s, Edgar Snow and Theodore White, relied heavily on Chinese counterparts—Snow working with Huang Hua (a Yanjing graduate) and White with Li Bo-ti.[17]

In other words, Chinese journalists shaped the environment and usually provided the key sources for Western journalists reporting in China. The young missionary-educated Chinese journalists who worked for reporters such as Snow, White, and Utley were highly nationalistic and increasingly impatient, first with Chiang Kaishek's reluctance to fight Japan and, after 1937, with his conduct of the war itself. Not surprisingly, wartime China reporting by Westerners was highly colored or sympathetic to Chinese nationalism and openly anti-Japanese. In the end, the relationship between the Chinese press and the Western correspondents became so intermeshed that it is impossible to conclude who influenced whom the most.

The relationship was symbiotic in another sense as well. Just as it does now, domestic Western press coverage of visiting Chinese intellectuals and politicians, and translations of their writing, empowered these figures at home. In the 1930s Lin Yutang was such a writer, wielding influence in the United States and Britain, where his books sold well, and in China through his journal *Yu Feng* and other publications. Similarly, Lao She, Zou Taofen, Xiao Qian, Yang Gang, and other prominent Chinese sojourners in the West were read widely in China, with enhanced authority. Edgar Snow's *Red Star over China* had greater impact inside China (in Chinese translation) than outside. Snow's presumed objectivity as a foreign journalist gave the work credibility as the truthful inside story on the Communist movement, its history and leadership. Finally, as is well known, Henry Luce's Time-Life media empire openly backed Chiang Kaishek and his wife, Song Meiling, in feature articles, photo stories, and directly authored appeals for aid to China. Madame Chiang's frequent wartime trips to the United States became major media events, including her addresses to joint sessions of Congress. Historians have long agreed that Chiang Kaishek's wartime recognition in the West (participation in the 1943 Cairo conference of the Big Four and so on) greatly enhanced his political stature in China.

Cross-fertilization between the Western and the Chinese press in the 1930s was all the more extraordinary considering the divergent paths China and the West would soon follow. By the mid-1940s the Chinese press grew increasingly nationalistic and conscious of class and relative poverty. Calls for drastic social change were accompanied by growing ambivalence about the West and criticism of bourgeois society generally. This is abundantly clear in the dispatches from the United States of Yang Gang, for example, written for the influential *Da Gong Bao* during the middle and late 1940s. Western reporters in China, on the other hand, remained sympathetic to the revolutionary nationalist thrust of the Chinese press and even to the Chinese journalists' social agenda. Take Theodore White's reporting for Times-Life on the Henan famine of 1943; his 1946 book, *Thunder out of China* (with Annalee Jacoby); and Jack Belden's *China Shakes the World* are examples. To say the least, for Western correspondents the coming of the Cold War to Asia in the late 1940s was a shock, a personal trauma that either cut off China reporters from friends and sources or forced them to choose sides between the revolution of the Chinese Communist Party and the counterrevoltution of Chiang Kaishek and the Guomindang.

Censorship, the fourth fundamental characteristic, defined the environment in which the Chinese press has operated since the late nineteenth century. During the last decades of the Qing dynasty (ending in 1911) the state exercised direct control by closing publications, arresting and often executing their editors, as well as banning overseas publications. The closing of the *Su Bao* in 1903 and the trial of its editor, Zhang Binglin, is considered a major event in the history of the revolutionary movement that led to the overthrow of the dynasty in 1911-12.[18] When the risks arc so high, political patronage becomes a necessity. During the early republic in 1912-16, Yuan Shikai attempted to control the press by terror. He even had Huang Yuansheng, an editor in San Francisco whom he did not like, assassinated in 1915. There was an upsurge in new publications around the protest events of May 4, 1919, because warlord controls were more haphazard than those of Yuan Shikai or the Qing. With the birth of Leninist parties in the 1920s (rebirth in the case of the Guomindang), competition for control of the Chinese press intensified and grew more ideological. Once the Nanjing government of Chiang Kaishek was firmly established in 1928, the situation worsened as the Guomindang attempted to apply the controls on a Yuan Shikai or late Qing scale. As indicated earlier, however, the effectiveness of Nanjing's policing powers varied depending on geography and local commanders, with Shanghai remaining the most open until it fell to the Japanese in late 1937.[19]

For a moment in 1938 the interior city of Wuhan became interesting because suddenly the playing field for the Chinese press became much more level. The united-front government in charge of Wuhan, made up of countervailing political and military forces, resulted in a commitment to a free press as long as it was anti-Japanese. In whipping up anti-Japanese fervor, both Leninist parties had to compete not only against each other but against other parties and voices for the hearts and minds of the populace. Even so, the behavior of both Leninist parties showed that they were interested in exercising control of Wuhan's press, and not in promoting free speech or a free press.

In the spring of 1938 the Guomindang military government passed a series of regulations aimed at control of the press, but enforcement proved impossible when a publication had a solid political patron with a position in the united-front government. Still, by August a number of publications had been closed down as was Hu Qiuyuan's *Shidai Ribao*. When possible, Guomindang officials tried to obstruct distribution of Communist publications outside of Wuhan—especially at the front—and they were partially successful.

The Communists likewise attempted to exercise control over the Wuhan press, in two ways. First, they infiltrated Guomindang publications as much as possible. There is no question that journalists such as Liu Zunqi and Sa Kongliao softened the anti-Communist tone of many Guomindang newspapers in 1938 and later.[20] Second, Communist thugs halted distribution of small, virulently anti-Communist publications by buying up copies and intimidating shopkeepers. Defectors from the Communist camp such as Chen Duxiu and Zhang Guotao aroused Communist ire the most, and a considerable effort was made to counter their statements and hinder their publication. Eventually, life in Wuhan became too uncomfortable and threatening for both men, forcing them to retreat upriver to Chongqing by the midsummer of 1938.[21] Moreover, the Communists seemed as irritated as the Guomindang by the third-party press; they tried to limit circulation and counter statements, especially when the small parties supported the positions of renegades Chen Duxiu and Zhang Guotao.

In short, Guomindang and Communist attitudes toward a free press in the relatively open atmosphere of Wuhan in 1938 did not augur well for the future. Not surprisingly, in 1939 after the fall of Wuhan, Chiang Kaishek and Dong Xianguang succeeded in reimposing draconian controls on the press in Chongqing, Chiang's capital, until the end of the war. At the same time, under the influence of Kang Sheng and Mao Zedong, the Communists cracked down on dissident voices in areas they controlled. Turning points were Mao's *Talks on Yanan Forum* and the sweeping Cheng-feng or Party Rectification campaign from 1942 to 1944, after which a prominent writer, Wang Shiwei, was executed.[22]

Finally, censorship is the most relevant theme, unfortunately, for a discussion of the 1950s, when Leninist revolutionary regimes reshaped the press in mainland China and Taiwan. In both places the journalists who suffered most were often those with strong Western connections or a grounding in the freer press of the 1930s.

The situation in the People's Republic of China was the most serious. In Beijing, Liu Zunqi became a founding editor of the *Guangming Ribao*, a national paper aimed at intellectuals, and Yang Gang became associate editor of the *People's Daily*, the party's flagship newspaper. But by 1958 Liu was in disgrace as a "rightist," ostensibly because of his earlier connections with the West and the Guomindang. A year earlier, Yang Gang had committed suicide under mysterious circumstances.[23] Later, journalists such as *People's Daily* editor Deng T'o became major targets of the Cultural Revolution in the 1960s, while radical Shanghai journalists Yao Wenyuan and Zhang Junqiao rose rapidly as willing instruments of Mao, ultimately wielding absolute power as members of the infamous "Gang of Four." The tragedy of the situation is told with extraordinary candor and understanding by China's most important living journalist, Liu Binyan, in his memoir, *A Higher Kind of Loyalty* (1990).

In Taiwan, the Guomindang under Chiang Kaishek was also able to impose tighter press controls than ever before. Senior figures such as Cheng Shewo stayed in retirement, never able to restart the *Li Bao* publications or open a journalism school until after Chiang Kaishek died. Dong Xianguang's close colleague and one of the most able men in Chiang's government, George Yeh (Ye Kongchao), was forced to resign as ambassador to the United Nations and lived out his life under island arrest. Dong himself found Taiwan's atmosphere suffocating; he moved to the United States in the late 1950s and died there. In the 1960s the closure of the *Wen Xing* string of publications and the arrest of writer-owner Li Ao was a major event, traumatizing a generation of Taiwan intellectuals. It was not until the late 1980s, long after Chiang Kaishek's death, that major political changes began occurring in Taiwan, sparked by the Guomindang's much greater tolerance for freedom of the press and the realization by leaders that they had to accommodate the Taiwanese majority.

In the 1990s the press and revolution remain intertwined in China, particularly on the mainland. Within this context a tradition of striving toward a freer press, rooted in the 1930s, also exists. This striving was expressed in the rapid liberalization of the press in the spring of 1989, which led to the extraordinary events of May and June.[24] Thus the press remains at the center of the political stage in revolutionary China, as either a symbol of political repression or the key to change. The continuities are important. As Liù Binyan's memoir makes clear, political patronage remains critical for any publication's success. And interestingly enough, sensitivity to Western journalism and coverage of China has come to have an important place in Chinese politics in the 1980s and 1990s, not unlike the role it played in the 1930s and 1940s.

NOTES

1. Ge Gongzhen, *Zhongguo Baozue shi* (History of the Chinese press), (Shanghai, 1927); Roswell S. Britton, *The Chinese Periodical Press, 1800-1912* (Shanghai, 1933); Lin Yutang, *A History of the Press and Public Opinion in China* (Chicago, 1936); Fang Hanqi, *Zhongguo jindai baokan shi* (History of modern Chinese press) (Taiyuan, 1981). The last work is considered today in China to be definitive yet its coverage ends in the 1920s. For an important recent article on the 1930s, see Chang-tai Hung, "Paper Bullets: Fan Changjiang and New Journalism in wartime China," *Modern China* 17 (Oct. 1991): 427-68.

2. Adrian Bennett, *John Fryer: The Introduction of Western Science and Technology into Nineteenth Century China* (Cambridge, Mass., 1967); Mary C. Wright, ed., *China in Revolution: The First Phase, 1900-1913* (New Haven, Conn., 1971); Chow Tse-tsung, *The May Fourth Movement: Intellectual Revolution in Modern China* (Cambridge, Mass., 1960); Vera Schwarcz, *The Chinese Enlightenment* (Berkeley, Calif., 1986).

3. Andrew Nathan, *Chinese Democracy* (New York, 1985), and "The Beginning of Mass Culture: Journalism and Fiction in the Late Ch'ing and Beyond," in David Johnston, Andrew Nathan, and Evelyn Rawski, eds., *Popular Culture in Late Imperial China* (Berkeley, Calif., 1985), 360-417.

4. Yuan Jicheng, "Kangzhan shuqi Wuhan di baozhi kanwu" (The press at Wuhan during the early anti-Japanese war period), *Hubei Xinwen shiliao huibien* (Serial collection of materials on the press in Hubei), no. 11 (1987): 26.

5. Liang Jialu, Han Song, Zhong Si, Zhao Yuming, *Zhongguo Xinwen Yeshi* (Business history of Chinese journalism) (Nanning, 1984), 249-55; and Zhang Jiluan, *Jiluan wencun* [Selected writings of Zhang Jiluan], (Tianjin, 1944).

6. Parks Coble, *Facing Japan: Chinese Politics and Japanese Imperialism,*

1931-37 (Cambridge, Mass., 1991); Liang Jialu et al., *Zhongguo Xinwen Yeshi*, 255-59, 339-42, 349-51.

7. Cai Qiao, *Wuhan Xinwenshi* [History of Wuhan journalism] (Wuhan, 1943), 29-30.

8. The literature on Zou Taofen is extensive; sources are given in *Taofen wenji* (Collected works] (Beijing, 1955). See, in English, Margo Spiesman Gewurtz, "Tsou Tao-fen: The Shenghuo Years, 1925-1933" (Ph.D. diss., Cornell University, 1972); and more recently, Wen-hsin Yeh, "Progressive Journalism and Shanghai's Petty Urbanites: Zou Taofen and the Shenghuo Enterprise, 1926-1945," in Yeh and Frederick Wakeman, eds., *Shanghai Sojourners* (Berkeley, Calif., 1992) 186-238.

9. Yuan Jicheng, "Kangzhan shuqi Wuhan di baozhi kanwu," 26.

10. Interview, 21 June, 1992, in Taibei, Taiwan; *Shidai Ribao* editorials for the period at Sichuan Provincial Library, Chengdu, PRC.

11. Interview, 3 June 1992, in Beijing. Hu Sheng is currently president of the Chinese Academy of Social Sciences.

12. Roger Jeans, ed., *Roads Not Taken: A Struggle of Opposition in Twentieth Century China* (Boulder, Colo., 1992).

13. Yuan Jicheng, "Kangzhan shuqi Wuhan di baozhi kanwu," 41, 55, 66.

14. Harold R. Isaacs, *Reencounters in China: Notes of a Journey in a Time Capsule* (Armonk, N.Y., 1985), 95-110; Li Hui, *Jianyu Yinyingxia dirensheng* (Biography of Liu Zunqi) (Zhangsha, 1989).

15. Dong Xianguang, *Dong Xianguang Ziquan* [Autobiography] (Taibei, 1973); Zeng Xubai, *Zeng Xubai Ziquan* [Autobiography] (Taibei, 1988); and Hollington Tong, *Dateline China* (New York, 1950).

16. See for example the 1938 monthlies *Xuelu* (ed. Tao Baichuan) and *Minyi* (ed. Tao Xisheng).

17. Stephen R. MacKinnon and Oris Friesen, *China Reporting: An Oral History of American Journalism in the 1930s and 1940s* (Berkeley, Calif., 1987).

18. Mary B. Rankin, *Early Chinese Revolutionaries* (Cambridge, Mass., 1971); Fang Hanqi, *Zhongguo jindai baokan shi*, 230-675.

19. In English the standard work is Lee-hsia Hsu Ting, *Government Control of the Press in Modern China, 1900-1949* (Cambridge, Mass., 1974). See also Fang Hanqi, *Zhongguo jindai baokan shi*; and "Chinese Editors Defy Censorship, Preserve Best Traditions of Free Press," *China Weekly Review* 855 (16 July 1938).

20. See *Xinwen yanjiu ziliao* [Quarterly studies and sources on journalism], nos. 25-29 (Beijing, 1984-85), for memoir accounts by Sa Kongliao and others. The *Da Gong Bao* would be a case in point.

21. Lee Feigon, *Chen Duxiu: Founder of the Chinese Communist Party* (Princeton, N.J., 1983); Chang Kuo-t'ao, *Autobiography of Chang Kuo-t'ao* (Lawrence, Kan., 1972), vol. 2.

22. MacKinnon and Friesen, *China Reporting*, chap. 5; Frederick Teiwes, *Politics and Purges in China* (New York, 1979), 64-78. The best recent work on Kang Sheng is John Byron and Robert Pack, *The Claws of the Dragon: Kang Sheng* (New York, 1992).

23. On Yang Gang, see *Yang Gang Wenji* [Collected works] (Beijing, 1984), and *Meiguo Zhaji* [Rough notes on America] (Beijing, 1950).

24. Stephen R. MacKinnon, "The Role of the Chinese and U.S. Media," in Jeffrey N. Wasserstrom and Elizabeth J. Perry, eds., *Popular Protest and Political Culture in Modern China: Learning from 1989* (Boulder, Colo., 1992), 206-14; Judy Polumbaum, "Tribulations of China's Journalists after a Decade of Reform," introduction to Chin-Chuan Lee, ed., *Voices of China: Politics and Journalism* (New York, 1990).

12

Mass Media and Mass Actions in Urban China, 1919-1989

JEFFREY N. WASSERSTROM

The aim of this chapter is to see what the history of Chinese student activism can tell us about the connections between media revolutions and patterns of popular protest.[1] My main conclusion is that even though technological innovations in fields such as communication are bound to have profound effects upon certain features of the political process, they do not necessarily change the structure and meaning of public expressions of discontent. Since 1919, Chinese city life has been transformed in many ways, thanks in part to the introduction and growing importance of various forms of mass media, including radio and television. Nonetheless, when students took to the streets in 1989, their protests were strikingly similar to those that accompanied the May 4th Movement of 1919, both in their basic style and in the kind of threat they posed to those in power. The Chinese case thus suggests that although media revolutions and political revolutions may indeed go hand in hand, it is dangerous to assume that technological innovations inevitably alter the basic dynamics of street politics.

In light of my concern with culture continuity and my interest in features of revolutionary politics that seem to be affected very little by developments related to modes of communication, it is easy to see why Jeremy Popkin and Jack Censer draw a sharp contrast, in their insightful introduction, between my chapter and those such as Pierre Rétat's that focus on themes of disjuncture and stress the importance of media-related political turning points. It is worth noting, however, that the contributors to this volume treat the relationship between technologies of communication and revolutionary politics as a complex and ambiguous one, and as a result the differences between us are usually matters of degree and emphasis. The contrast between Rétat's chapter and mine is significant, but it is not the kind that results from two opposing scholars taking extreme positions on a common issue; rather it is the sort that emerges when authors who agree about many things approach a topic from very different angles.

There is an extreme, technologically determinist position in the debate on media and revolution, however, that I *do* seek to challenge. This position was not taken by any participant in the Lexington conference, but it has become increasingly popular of late among some journalists. Thus, for example, during each of the crises of the last few years that involved mass actions such as demonstrations, we have seen a flurry of newspaper articles and reports by network anchors present these "telerevolutions" as completely unprecedented political events.[2] One of the most notable recent book-length studies to champion this and related notions is a work by former *New York Daily News* editor Michael J. O'Neill. Revealingly subtitled "How Television and People Power Are Changing the World," O'Neill's book contains fascinating tidbits of information about a variety of recent political upheavals, including the 1989 occupation of Tiananmen Square, and is shaped by a vision of the power of media that owes a great deal to the work of such theorists as Marshall McLuhan. This combination makes for stimulating reading, but it often leaves one with the unsettling feeling that the only really important question to ask about any revolution is whether it was covered by CNN.[3] Most interesting to me are the contrasting ways that he and I view the parallels between the protests that accompanied the May 4th Movement and those that took place in the same parts of Beijing seventy years later. Where I am struck most by the physical and symbolic similarities between these two sets of events, which affected everything from the way marches were structured to the kinds of slogans that were shouted, he is most interested in two basic contrasts: unlike their predecessors of 1919, the students of 1989 took to the streets after watching and learning tactical lessons from newscasts showing protests taking place elsewhere in the world; and the only footage of the May 4th Movement seen by foreign audiences was silent newsreel film shown long after the events in question took place, whereas the occupation of Tiananmen Square was broadcast around the world via satellite almost instantaneously.[4]

The preceding caution against overemphasizing media-related innovations notwithstanding, it is important to note at the outset that the history of Chinese student activism would seem at first glance to have a great deal to offer those seeking to show that technological and political revolutions tend to be very closely related indeed. This is so because many of the key turning points in this history can be linked quite directly to important changes in fields such as mass communications. The period lasting from roughly 1905 until 1925 is a clear case in point, for these decades witnessed both the birth of a new type of student movement and a range of major technological transformations relating to communication and also transportation. In the events leading up to and immediately following the May 4th Movement, one sees the isolated bouts of protest that had typified earlier periods of student activism being replaced by nationwide mass movements led by educated youths who were based in (and traveled freely between) cities scattered throughout China. It is no mere coincidence that these events occurred at the same time that newspapers and telegrams were rising to importance as media for political communication and a railway system linking major urban centers was being completed.[5]

The year 1989 also stands out as a watershed mark, of course, both for those interested in tracing the rising political importance of new (or newly widespread) technologies of communication and transportation in Chinese political life, and for those concerned with the history of student activism. Just as technological advances of the early twentieth century paved the way for the *nationalization* of student protests, we cannot understand the recent *internationalization* of Chinese youth activism (its global impact and cosmopolitan character) without taking into account a variety of developments in telecommunications (relating to everything from faxes to satellite-assisted broadcasting systems) that allowed images and information to travel to and from (and within) China with unprecedented ease and speed.[6] One can even argue that improved aeronautic capabilities were as important in 1989 as the new railways were in 1919, since airplanes played a key role in facilitating the flow of people (including the members of international news crews) and objects (such as videocassettes) between Beijing and the rest of the world.

While focusing on the shifts from localized protests to national movements to struggles with global impact helps draw attention to the importance of technological changes, however, the importance of media revolutions appears in a much more ambiguous light if other issues are foregrounded. Most notably, if one emphasizes tactical issues and basic goals as opposed to questions of scope, it is the continuities rather than disjunctures between the student movements of different eras that seem most striking. For example, in looking back to the events of 1919, one sees participants in the May 4th Movement relying heavily upon many of the same forms of collective action (such as ritualized marches to government offices) and using many of the same methods to publicize their struggle (such as drafting and pasting up wall posters denouncing corrupt officials) as those employed by their predecessors of earlier centuries.[7] The basic motivation and rationale for the May 4th Movement were also time-honored ones: students of previous generations too had been angered by foreign threats to China's sovereignty and the misbehavior of domestic officials, and had claimed (like the protesters of 1919) that it was their right and duty as intellectuals to speak out against these abuses and thus serve as the conscience of the nation.[8]

If we move from looking backward from 1919 to looking forward, we see striking continuities also between the student movements of the Republican (1912-49) and Communist (post-1949) eras, some of which I have already alluded to. Even though both the Red Guards of the 1960s and the student activists of the Dengist period (1978-) have been able to take advantage of a wide range of communication technologies that were unavailable to their Republican-era counterparts, throughout the Communist epoch dissatisfied students have continued to present handwritten petitions of complaint to officials. And even though air travel performed novel functions in 1989, the most important method of student transportation (in both symbolic and pragmatic terms) remained the least technologically sophisticated: marches from campuses to central gathering places such as Beijing's Tiananmen Square and Shanghai's Bund. In addition, although some of the grievances that have motivated student activists to take to the streets in recent decades are distinctive to the Communist era, here too there have always been links to earlier eras. For example, despite basic differences between the students involved in Republican-era mass movements and the Red Guards, relating to such things as the latter's anti-intellectual stance and devotional loyalty to Chairman Mao, it is important to remember that anger over official corruption played a central role in motivating many campus activists of both the pre-1949 and Cultural Revolution periods to take to the streets. Student protesters of the Dengist era have also stressed this theme, as well as a variety of others (most notably, the need for a more open political system) that have clear Republican-era precedents.

In fact, the transition to the era of telecommunications and rapid transcontinental travel notwithstanding, almost all the most important mass actions and slogans of 1989 had historical precedents of one sort or another. When they gathered to swear collective oaths to persevere until death if necessary to protect the nation, when they divided into groups on a school-by-school basis and marched behind banners emblazoned with the names of individual institutions, when they held rallies in central squares and shouted out *"Minzhu wansui"* (long live democracy)—in each of these cases, the youths of 1989 were improvising upon scripts that had been firmly entrenched parts of the Chinese student protest repertoire for at least half a century.[9] Finally, it is worth noting that the youths of 1989 saw themselves as carrying on a time-honored tradition: just as some May 4th activists drew connections between their cause and that of patriotic student martyrs of the Song Dynasty (960-1279), some participants in the most recent protests paid homage to the legacy of 1919 by dubbing their struggle the "New May 4th Movement."[10]

It is possible, of course, to acknowledge the importance of these continuities and still leave room for discussion of the novelties associated with technological change. No history of the mass movements of either the Republican or Communist eras would be complete, in fact, without some attention being paid to both the unprecedented features of these events and the influence of protest traditions. The most persuasive and effective histories of these movements would have to go even further and look at the subtle interplay of new and old within specific actions and communications. For example, a 1919 petition written in a style reminiscent of the protest memorials of an earlier era, yet designed to be printed in mass circulation newspapers rather than delivered to a single official, is a document that can be understood fully only with reference to both previous events and contemporary technologies. Similarly, as familiar as many of the wall posters created in 1989 looked, the novel technologies that people used to record the contents of these handbills (reading them aloud into portable tape recorders, filming them for news broadcasts) made them texts with ties to both the modern and postmodern eras.

Is it enough then simply to adopt a kind of mix-and-match strategy to come to terms with the subject, using references to historical precedent to temper moves in the direction of technological determinism and references to specific technology-related novelties to undermine interpretations that place too much emphasis upon tradition? As tempting as it would be to say "yes," this kind of scattershot approach begs too many important general questions about the connections between technology and revolution—questions that appear increasingly significant in light of the emerging literature on Chinese and Eastern European events of 1989. It is too soon to speak about any kind of broad scholarly consensus on these events, and some issues (such as why the Chinese struggle of that year ended so differently from the Czechoslovakian one described in Owen Johnson's chapter) seem destined to remain the subject of intense debate for years to come. Nonetheless, the general analytical frameworks that are likely to define future discussions of 1989 have already started to take shape, and one of the most prominent of these is based on the assumption that telecommunications capabilities generally, and the advent of satellite television in particular, have played midwife to the birth of a new genre of revolution distinctive to this particular technological age.[11]

This kind of vision of 1989 as a watershed is worth taking seriously, both for its own sake and because it fits well with the general arguments that some scholars have been making for decades about the political impact of the telecommunications revolution. There is considerable disagreement among scholars who are interested in assessing the consequences of this media revolution, of course, but some of the strongest voices in the debate have always belonged to those who, like Daniel Boorstin, claim that the introduction of new technologies of communication trigger sea changes in the way power is exercised and contested within a society. According to this school of thought, the telecommunications era is one in which coverage has become more important than content in determining the impact of speeches and confrontations, and orchestrated "media events" or (to use Boorstin's more loaded term) "pseudo-events" designed to please the camera have increasingly come to be accepted as substitutes for more authentic forms of public political action.[12]

All of this suggests that for those interested in the study of comparative revolutions there may be a great deal at stake in assessing the novelty of the Chinese protests of 1989. If we are to grapple seriously with the kinds of issues that Jeremy Popkin and Jack Censer delineate in their opening chapter, then at some point we have to ask the following kinds of questions. Does the introduction of new technologies (of communication, of transportation, and, as the role of tanks in the recent Chinese movement's suppression reminds us, of destruction) change fundamentally or merely modify the basic structure and character of the revolutionary process? Does it make sense to continue to compare contemporary revolutions (abortive or successful) with those of 1789, 1917, and 1911-49, which occurred before the purported rise of the "media event"? Does television coverage of an uprising change the dynamics of mass action profoundly enough that we should limit ourselves to comparing protests like those of 1989 to other street actions of the telecommunications era, such as the Chicago demonstrations of 1968, so often cited as an early example of a struggle that unfolded when the "whole world was watching"?[13] In short, we need to ask

whether recent technological changes have shaken up basic political equations so dramatically that the strategies useful for shedding light on popular
movements of the past are no longer helpful for making sense of contemporary struggles for power.

As someone who has argued in previous works that the same kinds of
interpretive strategies can be used to understand Chinese student protests
of the Republican and Communist eras, I have an obvious stake in the debate over questions such as these. In those same works I also claim that
methodological and theoretical insights offered by scholars working on
times and places far removed from twentieth-century China (such as eighteenth-century England) can help us make sense of modern Chinese student
movements, and this makes my stake in the debate over comparability
greater still. In light of these tidbits of scholarly autobiography, it should
come as no surprise that the main thesis of this chapter is that technological
changes have *not* fundamentally altered the basic nature of certain key political equations.[14]

My central claim here is simply that despite the many important novelties of the contemporary era, the student protesters of 1989 gained much
of their power from the same source as their predecessors of the pre-
telecommunications era: their ability to stage symbolically charged acts of
subversive political theater. This claim is based on the assumption that in
China (as elsewhere) government-sponsored spectacles and ceremonies
remain important vehicles through which ruling elites assert and defend
their claims to hegemony, and that student activism is feared not only (or at
times even primarily) because of the physical threat to the running of the
state posed by groups of educated youths but also because of the potential
of student protest to undermine the efficacy of what Sean Wilentz calls
official "rites of power."[15] Technological changes have certainly served, in
a variety of ways, to change the pace of and up the ante involved in the
part of the struggle to maintain or subvert hegemony that is played out via
competing performances of political theater and official ritual. I argue,
however, that the basic dynamics involved in such public contests have
nonetheless remained fairly constant over time.

Whether one will still be able to say this after the next round of Chinese upheavals takes place is not a primary concern here. Nonetheless, the
arguments that follow suggest that all claims about technological developments ushering in completely new forms of public politics should be taken
with a large grain of salt. This is true not only of the notion that the 1980s
witnessed the birth of a completely novel form of "people power" but also
of Mark Poster's very different yet related presentation of the events of

1989 as part of the death throes of an outmoded form of politics. What I have to say suggests that there is good reason to be skeptical about Poster's suggestion that "the image of the people in the streets, from the Bastille, in 1789, to the Sorbonne in 1968 and Tiananmen Square, Beijing in 1989 may be the images that will not be repeated in the forms of upheaval of the twenty-first century and beyond." [16]

Although this chapter can be read as an attempt, in part, to defend and even extend my earlier claims that any attempt to understand contemporary and perhaps even future Chinese student protests has to pay close attention to continuities with and similarities to much earlier events, this does not mean that preparing for and taking part in the Lexington conference did nothing to alter my views on 1989. Familiarizing myself with works in communications theory, reading studies of China's recent crisis that focus on the unprecedented roles played by new technologies, and listening to conference presentations that stressed ruptures between past and present media systems—these experiences have led me to look at my first publications on 1989 (which were written in the immediate aftermath of the June massacres) with a much more critical eye. I now feel that some of these writings do indeed place too much emphasis upon continuities with the past and pay too little attention to the novel constaints and possibilities of the contemporary era, and that they are open to the criticism that they ignore the ways in which developments in telecommunications (particularly the rise of television) have altered the processes through which information about collective actions is transmitted to differing audiences. I remain convinced, nonetheless, that (with only minor modifications) strategies that help shed light on Chinese mass actions of the pre-telecommunications era can also be used to illuminate the meaning of the perplexing events of 1989. I discuss some of the more significant novelties of the current age at the end of this chapter, but the pages that follow are devoted primarily to making the case for the importance of basic continuities. [17]

The method used to explain and defend this position may seem a roundabout one at times, since it involves moving back and forth chronologically and geographically, but it is actually quite simple. I begin by presenting a series of brief descriptions of some of the Republican-era mass actions analyzed in my book on Shanghai student protests, and then use these descriptions as a jumping-off point to discuss the interpretive strategies I have found most useful for analyzing popular protests and rites of power, as well as to introduce the theoretical and comparative works that have shaped my approach. After that I return to the events of 1989 in an effort to demonstrate that the same kind of approach is still a valid and potentially valuable one.

Antigovernment demonstrations and loyalist spectacles of the Republican era often took remarkably similar forms. The mass movements that rocked Shanghai throughout the warlord era (1916-27), which almost always involved students and members of other classes taking to the streets to protest imperialist aggression or domestic misgovernment, provide some of the best examples. During the May 4th Movement, for example, even though foreign interference in China's affairs was a central issue, Shanghai protesters routinely staged demonstrations that involved symbols and actions reminiscent of mass gatherings organized by the leaders of the local Western community (such as Empire Day celebrations). And even though May 4th activists were highly critical of the Chinese authorities (whom they viewed as repressive and insufficiently patriotic), the student protests of 1919 often bore more than a passing resemblance to officially sanctioned parades held on holidays such as October 10, the anniversary of the 1911 revolution.[18]

Protesters of the Nationalist era (1927-49) also staged mass actions that looked a great deal like official ceremonies, as the case of the parades held to welcome General Marshall to Shanghai in 1945 illustrates. Long before the general set foot on Chinese soil, local representatives of the Nationalist regime had drawn up and publicized plans for a gala welcoming march and reception. When the great day arrived, however, these official spectacles had to compete with a alternative, pro-democracy welcoming demonstration, which involved almost all the basic elements (down to columns led by marchers carrying American and Chinese flags) found in the government parade.[19]

These examples can be read ironically as instances in which Shanghai protesters learned how to stage effective mass actions by watching and participating in official gatherings. But the situation was actually a good deal more complex than one in which dissidents simply imitated the authorities they opposed. In some cases, such as the holding of almost identical types of funeral processions to honor fallen leaders, it is likely that neither side was (intentionally or even subconsciously) imitating the other but rather that both were drawing from a common repertoire of religious and civic rituals. In still other cases, moreover, the government seems to have "learned" from the protesters, rather than vice versa.

Some of the clearest illustrations of this last phenomenon come from the protests against Japanese aggression of the 1930s. Throughout the decade following Chiang Kaishek's rise to power in 1927, Japan's military activities in northern China placed his regime in an awkward position. His Nationalist Party's original claim to legitimacy derived largely from the leading role it had played in the Northern Expedition, the twin goals of which were to free the Republic from the oppression of both domestic warlords and foreign imperialists. But once in control he steadfastly maintained that the nation could not afford to challenge the Japanese directly until the Chinese Communist Party (CCP) had been destroyed. Whenever new "incidents" involving Japan (such as the Manchurian invasion of 1931) revived popular anti-Japanese sentiment, therefore, he and other Nationalist officials had to choose between two potentially dangerous courses. They could ignore popular calls for action and move swiftly to suppress mass mobilization, but to do so was to run the risk of compromising both Chiang Kaishek's status as a militant foe of imperialism and the party's position as heir to the patriotic traditions of the 1911 revolution and the May 4th Movement. Alternatively, they could try to harness popular anger and steer it in a loyalist direction but once the people were mobilized, the movement could all too easily take on a radical hue. There was also a constant danger that groups within the divided Nationalist Party would use mass actions to serve factional ends.

The party's leaders often disagreed over which course of action to take, but those favoring attempts to channel mass enthusiasm generally won the day. Local and national officials thus ended up sponsoring a variety of "protests" that were clearly intended to be reminiscent of famous mass movements of the past. There were, however, two distinctive features of these Nanjing Decade "protests": they generally ended with ritualized expressions of support for the government, and local police forces were unusually tolerant of them. Although these gatherings succeeded at times in bolstering the legitimacy of the regime, at other points official fears regarding such events proved justified, as (thanks in part to the actions of Communist organizers and partisans of out-of-power Nationalist factions) officials proved unable to keep manifestations of discontent within acceptable bounds, and chants attacking the political status quo came to supplement or replace pledges of fealty.[20]

The situation became still more complex in the middle to late 1940s, when Shanghai's citizens were exposed to a bewildering variety of look-alike events, particularly on certain international holidays (such as Women's Day and May Day) and commemorative dates associated with the Chinese Revolution (such as October 10 and May 4). Along with staging competing mass actions on these dates, defenders and opponents of the particular Nationalist group in power each laid claim to the May 4th legacy of patriotic mass action: loyalists invoked the imagery of 1919 to mobilize support for agitations against "Red" imperialism in 1946 and 1947; critics of the regime (including members of the CCP underground) invoked the same symbols in more successful 1947 and 1948 rallies (triggered by incidents such as the alleged rape of a Chinese student by two American GIs) that sought an end to "white" imperialism.[21]

In previous attempts to shed light on the events described above, I have drawn upon several types of comparative and theoretical studies, including works by historians and social scientists interested in the political significance of officially sanctioned public spectacles. Thus, for example, I have argued that recent studies of French revolutionary festivals, which interpret these events as rituals that were designed to transfer sacrality from an old regime to a new one and to simultaneously acknowledge and defuse "radical aspirations," can be used to help place China's Republican era ceremonials in perspective.[22] Official gatherings staged on October 10 and May 4 were, after all, clearly intended to associate the sponsors with political events that had almost immediately acquired a "sacred" status and were designed both to remind people of past acts of defiance and to discourage them from militant action in the present.

A variety of sociological and anthropological studies of official ceremonials also have a great deal to offer the student of Shanghai street politics. For my purposes, the most useful of these has proved to be an insightful essay by Clifford Geertz, "Centers, Kings, and Charisma: Reflections on the Symbolics of Power." In this piece Geertz uses descriptions of several very different types of monarchical porcessions (including those of Elizabethan England and nineteenth-century Morocco) to argue that the power of ruling elites is always derived largely from practices that link them with a numinous "political center," which is composed of the symbols and values that the members of a community hold sacred. The essay's main claim is that all governing elites "justify their existence and order their actions in terms of a collection of stories, ceremonies, insignia, formalities, and appurtenances" that "mark the center as center" and make people feel that "what goes on there [is] not merely important but in some odd fashion connected with the way the world is built."[23] According to Geertz, even the rulers of the most seemingly secular and rational of states depend on symbolic actions to legitimate their authority, a point he drives home by arguing that public appearances during American presidential campaigns serve the same function as monarchical processions, for they too are ritual events that give a numinous quality to wielders of political power.

Geertz's ideas have an immediate appeal for historians of China, since a variety of influential works on the Chinese imperial system, by authors ranging from Confucian philosophers to Western social scientists, highlight the close links between rulership and ritual under this particular *ancien régime*. Emperors seldom took part in public processions of the sort Geertz describes, but they were masters of using the "ceremonies" carried out within the Forbidden City to "mark the center as center" and to identify themselves with "insignia" and other sacred symbols of power. Few members of the "public" personally witnessed the various annual rituals in which the emperors supplicated heaven on behalf of the people, but this intentional mystification may have added to rather than detracted from the power of these rites. In any case, the rites were far from "private" acts, since a complex set of practices (ranging from the issuance of edicts describing events within the Forbidden City, to local performances of equivalent rites, in which magistrates and local gods served as counterparts to the emperor and the highest deity) helped keep the populace informed about and in awe of the spectacles that took place behind the gates of the palace. Transmitting information about the emperor's activities to the public was considered essential, in fact, since one thing that could cause natural catastrophes and lead a dynasty to lose the heavenly mandate, it was said, was a ruler's failure to perform the proper rituals and sacrifices.

Rulers of the Republican era were not emperors, of course, and both of the famous aborted attempts at monarchical restoration by warlords that took place after the 1911 Revolution ended as parodies rather than genuine revivals of old rites.[24] But Republican-era leaders were heavily influenced by the imperial tradition, and in their efforts to create a new "political center" defined by revolutionary symbols, many familiar rituals reappeared in altered form. The interplay between novelty and tradition in Republican spectacles dates back to ceremonies that marked the ascendancy of the first post-dynastic regime in 1912. Less than two months after elaborate inaugural ceremonies designating Sun Yat-sen the first president of a new republic were held in Nanjing at the beginning of January, Sun took part in a highly publicized visit to that same city's Ming Dynasty (1368-1642) tombs, during which he adopted forms of speech and behavior that were more imperial than revolutionary.[25]

Soon after Sun's death in 1925, moreover, Chiang Kaishek instituted a variety of ritual practices that were designed to establish an image of the first president (who was now known officially as the *Guofu* or "National Father") as a modern equivalent to the semidivine sages given credit for founding China's most famous dynasties. Chiang's own roles in official ceremonies of the Nationalist era also came to bear more than a passing resemblance to those of traditional monarchs, even though (as Alexander Woodside points out) he was a much more public figure than any Chinese emperor of the past, and the devotion accorded him by his most committed followers was much more personalized than the role-specific awe inspired by imperial figures.[26] The celebrations held in Shanghai in 1945 to mark Chiang's sixtieth birthday illustrate this point. Prior to 1911 the birthdays of gods and emperors were the only ones celebrated publicly, and statues of ordinary mortals were virtually never carried through the streets. Yet in these 1945 parades not only do we see a living secular personage being honored publicly, but we also find an enormous effigy of him figuring prominently in the march.[27]

Just how greatly the warlords or Nationalists depended upon ceremonies of this sort to sustain their rule is hard to document. I have tried elsewhere to show, however, that such rites of power should not be dismissed as mere window dressing for these Chinese regimes, and that comparable rituals were also important to the foreign authorities who controlled sections of treaty-port cities such as Shanghai prior to World War II.[28] Here I limit myself to a single piece of suggestive (though admittedly fragmentary) evidence on this point, which has to do with the fact that in the fall of 1947 Shanghai officials broke with tradition and decided not to hold large-scale gatherings to mark either National Day or Sun Yat-sen's birthday.

To understand the significance of this decision, it is important to know that the spring of 1947 witnessed the eruption of a series of protests known collectively as the Anti-Hunger, Anti–Civil War Movement, which looked for a time as if it would culminate in a nationwide general strike of workers and students. The Nationalist regime used a campaign of terror to put an end to the movement in early June. Nonetheless, fear that something would happen to reignite the flames of protest continued to run high for several months, and this undoubtedly had something to do with the decision to scale back anniversary celebrations. This at least was the claim of a radical leaflet, distributed on Sun Yat-sen's birthday, which argued that the Nationalist Party was afraid to allow mass gatherings of any sort and insisted that this inability to celebrate key revolutionary dates in the ordinary fashion proved that Chiang's "evil designs" had alienated the masses from his regime. Without actually mentioning the term *Tianming* (mandate of heaven), the leaflet directed the attention of its readers to the recent appearance of two of the omens that traditionally foreshadowed the fall of a dynasty: outbreaks of popular unrest, and ritual irregularities.[29]

As helpful as the kinds of comparative and theoretical works discussed above are for putting official spectacles of the Republican era in perspective, they have relatively little to say about either the internal dynamics and public meanings of popular protests or the links between official rites of power and acts of resistance. Most notably, in his essay on political centers, Geertz encourages us to focus so intently on ritualized expressions of shared values that it becomes all too easy to forget the kinds of fissures and tensions, present within all political communities, and which periodically inspire acts of protest.[30] To create a comprehensive framework for linking official rituals and collective unrest, one must look to works that focus on protest as well as to those that concentrate on more consensual forms of mass action, and to writers who take more of their cues from Marx and Gramsci than from Durkheim or Weber.

For the purposes of this essay, E.P. Thompson's studies of the tensions between the "patrician society" and "plebeian culture" of Hanoverian England are among the most illuminating and suggestive works to focus on the activities of protesting crowds.[31] Thompson argues that throughout the eighteenth century the British gentry relied heavily on gestures of benevolence to assert their authority over those they dominated. He stresses, however, that this "theatre of hegemony" did not go unchallenged, for ordinary people continually attempted to subvert its claims through a "counter-theatre" of "threat and sedition," which would "twist the tail" of the gentry by mocking or appropriating elements of official symbolism.[32] As concerned as Thompson is with the material underpinnings of gentry hegemony, he insists that the "contest for symbolic authority" should not be dismissed as merely "a way of acting out ulterior 'real' contests" but should rather be seen as "a real contest in its own right."[33] Thompson claims, moreover, that "the weakness of other organs of control" gave political theater a "peculiar importance" in the Hanoverian period, and that as a result close attention should be paid to the ways in which powerholders used ritual displays (in the law courts, at funerals, during coronations) to defend their legitimacy, as well as to the actions ordinary people took to "strip power of its mystifications."[34]

Nicholas Rogers's important work on the competing celebrations of Jacobite and anti-Jacobite anniversaries, which defined public politics in early eighteenth-century London, lends support to Thompson's claims.[35] According to Rogers, supporters and opponents of the newly inaugurated

Hanoverian regime used similar street displays and celebrations in their efforts to raise doubts about the other side's legitimacy and claims to popular support. Rogers is sensitive to the many specific differences between the gatherings the two sides held, but a recurring theme in his work is the interplay between radical and loyalist forms of public action. He notes, for example, that on different but roughly equivalent political anniversaries, Hanoverian and Jacobite groups could be counted on to stage parades that centered on almost identical types of ritualized public desecration of symbols that the other side held dear.

Charles Tilly's studies of French protest traditions complement these discussions of the British case. In *The Contentious French*, for example, Tilly argues that the tendency for crowds to improvise upon official rituals was a dominant feature of the "collective action repertoire in France from the seventeenth to the mid-nineteenth century." Improvisations of this sort tended to take one of three forms, he claims: satire (displaying an inappropriate symbol during an authorized gathering in order to "mock delinquent powerholders"), subversion (turning a public execution into a "declaration of official iniquity"), or substitution (taking on official roles during bread riots in order to inventory and then distribute seized grain). One attraction of using "authorized procedures to press unauthorized claims" was that the familiarity of the forms saved participants from having to "plan, organize and practice the routine." Another was that "the adoption or mockery of powerholders' procedures sends an unmistakable message to those powerholders; they see opprobrium coming their way."[36]

Works such as these suggest that the connection between official spectacles and protest gatherings found in Republican Shanghai was no mere fluke but, rather, one manifestation of a fairly common phenomenon. The competing celebrations of May 4th and other revolutionary anniversaries, for example, seem less strange once we know that something quite comparable occurred in early Hanoverian London. Comparing preindustrial Europe to Republican China may initially seem farfetched, but on closer inspection it does not seem terribly problematic in this case. The two contexts were very different in obvious ways, but the legacy of the imperial order and its collapse left the warlord and Nationalist regimes as dependent upon symbolic action as the British gentry Thompson describes.

The "Popular Tribunal Incident" of 1931 illustrates the relevance that Thompson's and Tilly's discussions of subversive "countertheatre" and improvizations upon official procedures can have for interpreting Republican protests. This incident occurred in Shanghai at the height of a mass movement triggered by Japan's invasion of Manchuria and the Nationalist regime's decision not to go to war over the issue. The popular tribunal was formed when local students, protesting the arrest of visiting campus leaders from Nanjing and Beijing, seized control of the local municipal government buildings, held the mayor hostage, and performed a series of dramatic public acts of satire, subversion, and substitution that mocked the Nationalist regime's efforts to use the spectacle of the courtroom and the language of legality to defend its use of force against dissidents. During the course of the Popular Tribunal, protesters took on roles ordinarily reserved for government figures and even went so far at to issue a warrant for the arrest of the local Public Security Bureau chief.[37]

It may seem at first that the essay by Geertz and the works by Thompson pull in quite different directions, since the former is concerned primarily with acts contributing to a consensus that power is being exercised in a legitimate fashion, while the latter focus on public manifestations of discontent. It is worth stressing, however, that there is some important common ground. Most notably, all the scholars mentioned above are interested in the symbolic dimensions of public displays, and all of them consider it dangerous to lose sight of the fact that ritual and theater can play central roles in very "real" political struggles.

Can this common ground be expanded to create a kind of "unified field theory" of politically and symbolically charged mass actions? Social theorist Stephen Lukes suggests one strategy for doing so.[38] In attacking what he refers to as "neo-Durkheimian" approaches to political rituals, Lukes argues that we should never expect a general consensus within any society on basic issues, and that as a result we should treat all mass gatherings as attempts to gain support for a particular *interpretation* of what holds a community together. Thus, whereas the most famous study of the British coronation treats this ceremony as an instance in which "society reaffirms the moral values which constitute it as a society and renews its devotion to those values by an act of communion."[39] Lukes claims that both this kind of official spectacle *and* protest marches are best viewed as "symbolic strategies used by different groups . . . to defend or to attain power vis-a-vis other groups."[40]

Although there is a great deal to be said for the approach Lukes outlines, it has one important shortcoming: it does not explain why the mass actions of competing groups so frequently take similar forms and involve invocations of the same symbols. This problem can be solved, however, if we combine Geertz's conception of a "political center" and Durkheimian notions of sacrality with Thompson's vision of an ongoing struggle between interconnected acts that in one case assert and in the other challenge elite hegemony. Judging by the slogans they shouted and the way they structured their demonstrations, there seems to have been a great deal of consensus among Republican era political actors about the kinds of symbols, values, stories, and so forth capable of conferring legitimacy. And the fact that both loyalists and dissidents tended to treat certain terms ("The Revolution," "The Republic," "New China") with similar reverence suggests that some kind of transference of sacrality had indeed been accomplished (at least among some important sectors of the urban population). But while the look-alike nature of their street displays and common idealization of key symbols and concepts suggest that there were broad areas of agreement relating to the composition of the political center, the contentious aspect of mass actions shows that the community remained deeply divided on the question of whether those currently in power had a right to occupy that "center."

What all this means is that Chinese officials never had the luxury of casually using ceremonial forms to remind the people of their right to rule. Instead, these spectacles were part of an intense and often desperate struggle to impose, defend, and then reimpose a hegemonic view that would locate the regime in this numinous spot. Hegemonizing, as Stuart Hall notes, is always "hard work," but in Republican Shanghai—thanks to the frequency and effectiveness of student demonstrations and such other forms of dissident "countertheater as workers' rallies and rice riots—it was especially tough going.[41] To sum up, then, many urban mass actions of the Republican era can best be understood as battles within an ongoing war for legitimacy, in which opposing forces used strikingly similar types of symbolically charged public displays either to defend or to attack the idea that those in power should be seen as representing the sacred ideals of the Republic and the revolution, and hence deserved to speak in the name of New China.

The next question to take up is whether more recent political struggles can be placed within a similar analytical framework. There is good reason to think so, as even a quick overview of some key events of 1989 indicates. Not only have recent protests and rites of power been strikingly similar in form to specific events of the Republican era, but the relationship between official spectacles and dissident demonstrations has remained essentially the same. A survey of selected mass actions taking place in 1989, starting with the ceremonies marking Hu Yaobang's death that launched the student movement of that year, illustrates this point.[42]

When the former CCP general secretary died in April 1989, the party leadership faced a painful dilemma reminiscent of those the Nationalists confronted so frequently before 1949. On the one hand, to downplay the death of this famous figure (who had been demoted because of the lenient way he handled the student protests of 1986-87), to ignore dissident wall posters praising Hu, and to clamp down on any unofficial mourning ceremonies could be dangerous. At best, doing so would simply increase Hu's status as a martyr for the cause of democracy. At worst, it could trigger massive demonstrations like those that occurred in the spring of 1976, when thousands of Nanjing protesters and then millions of their Beijing counterparts defied the Gang of Four's proscriptions against holding public gatherings to honor the recently deceased Zhou Enlai. On the other hand, to bury Hu with the public fanfare due a fallen revolutionary hero would risk creating a mass movement that could spin out of control. This was precisely what had happened in 1931, when the Nationalists tried to harness anger over Japan's invasion of Manchuria by sponsoring anti-imperialist rallies, only to have protesters combine criticism of Japanese imperialism with criticism of Chinese governmental inaction.[43]

Members of the current regime should have been well aware of both the Communist and pre-Communist historical parallels for their predicament, since the April 5th Movement of 1976 had laid the groundwork for Deng Xiaoping's rise to power, and many of today's leaders gained their first initiation into the world of street politics as participants in Republican-era struggles such as that of 1931. As it turned out, fears of a possible repetition of 1976 took precedence over fears of a replay of 1931, and official ceremonies honoring Hu were held. From the moment these events began, however, there were clear signs that (as in 1931) urban discontent (this time relating not to imperialism but to grievances associated with official corruption, inflation, and the slow pace of political reforms) was strong enough that mass actions could easily take on an antigovernment tone. Thus, for example, the students who took part in events honoring Hu Yaobang did not limit themselves to expressing regret for his premature death but also used the opportunity to suggest that it would have been better if some who continued to hold power had died in his place.[44]

The regime soon began to put most of its energy into discrediting and intimidating the students by issuing official statements branding the protests acts of "turmoil" (a term that serves in contemporary Chinese politics as a code word for Cultural Revolution extremism). Then, of course, the government started to back up its rhetorical assault with force, an evolution that culminated in the June massacres. If the authorities quickly lost hope of keeping mass actions from turning into expressions of dissent, however, this did not stop them from continuing to use theatrical and ritualistic displays of benevolence and devotion to the revolution as part of their effort to defuse popular unrest and buttress the legitimacy of the political status quo. The grandest of these displays, the National Day celebrations held in Tiananmen Square on 1 October 1989 to mark the fortieth anniversary of the founding of the People's Republic of China, took place several months after the protests had ended and was designed to show the people that order had been restored to the site in which so much student "turmoil" had been created. But the regime also sponsored mass actions during the movement itself, ranging from officially sponsored celebrations of the seventieth anniversary of the May 4th Movement to state receptions welcoming Mikhail Gorbachev to an early June "anti-turmoil rally" (complete with "protesters" who blamed the West for stirring up trouble in China again).

These official displays are interesting for various reasons, including the fact that each had Republican-era predecessors. It is also worth noting that (as often happened in the Republican era) these gatherings tended to be at best only partially successful events, in large part because of the competing spectacles that student protesters staged. The unauthorized student demonstrations held in Tiananmen Square on May 4, for example, overshadowed the authorized ceremonies taking place simultaneously inside the Great Hall of the People. And the students of 1989 proved even more adept than their predecessors of 1945 when it came to turning the arrival of a foreign dignitary to their own advantage. Whereas the protest parade Shanghai students staged to greet General Marshall was a modest affair that had little impact on the official welcoming ceremony, massive popular demonstrations timed to coincide with Gorbachev's arrival stole the thunder from (and in some cases precipitated changes in the venues of) government spectacles meant to capitalize on the Soviet leader's visit.

The 1989 competition for control of the streets, reminiscent of the Republican era, makes it tempting to argue that whatever interpretive strategies help make sense of the pre-1949 period also help shed light on the events of 1989. Before taking such a daring step, however, it is important to examine the differing ways in which information about and images relating to the events of these two eras were disseminated. We need, in other words, to take a closer look at media-related novelties of the contemporary period and ask to what extent they should lead us to modify the analytical schema outlined above.

One novel feature of the current political scene worth considering is the unusually elaborate system the CCP has developed for controlling the flow of political information. Although censorship has a long history in China, this system is even more intrusive and comprehensive than its predecessors. This fact is directly relevent to the topic at hand, because the system can be used to minimize the spread of information about potentially subversive political events.

This said, however, the differences between the Republican and Communist eras relating to communication networks and controls should not be exaggerated. When CCP authorities closed down the *World Economic Herald* for showing too much sympathy for the protests of 1989, they were doing the same thing that Nationalist censors had done to Shanghai newspapers that presented the Anti-Hunger, Anti-Civil War Movement of 1947 in a favorable light. When the official media tried to minimize the impact of the 1989 movement by pretending that certain protests had not occurred, they were likewise following a long-standing precedent: Nationalist newspapers of the late 1940s routinely failed to mention dissident commemorations of revolutionary holidays that competed with government ceremonies. And the official media's efforts to discredit the recent protests also has its precursors. There was nothing new about its use of either negatively charged code words (both "turmoil" and "counterrevolutionary" were equally popular with the Nationalist press) or foreign conspiracy theories (although Nationalist spokesmen tended to blame the Soviets rather than the Americans for fomenting unrest).

It is also important to remember that the CCP censorship system, elaborate as it is, proved unable to control completely the flow of information in 1989. Here again, several parallels with the Anti-Hunger, Anti-Civil War Movement are worth noting. First, as the case of the banned newspapers alluded to above illustrates, in both 1947 and 1989 some journalists and editors working for independent or semi-independent periodicals took the risk of questioning or contradicting the official line. Second, in both 1947 and 1989, factional struggles within the ruling party created uncertainty as to the final form the official line would take. Some of the reporters who described the initial protests of these years sympathetically were not committed critics of the ruling party but journalists who hoped that expressions of popular discontent would benefit or embarrass particular factions within the party. Factional divisions also go a long way toward explaining why official censors have occasionally turned blind eyes toward seemingly subversive reports, such as the surprisingly frank accounts of 1989 events that appeared in the May issues of the CCP's official English language magazine, *Beijing Review*.

A final parallel between 1947 and 1989 relating to censorship has to do with foreign journalists. Although Deng Xiaoping has tried to manipulate and control some aspects of Western media coverage of Chinese affairs, like Chiang Kaishek and the warlords before him, he has proved unwilling or unable to subject foreign reporters to the same controls as those exercised on their domestic counterparts. Thus Western journalists continued to carry sympathetic interviews with 1989's student leaders long after the official media had begun its campaign of disinformation, just as in 1947 participants in the Anti-Hunger, Anti-Civil War Movement confounded Nationalist censors by writing letters for publication in the American-owned *China Weekly Review.*

Another novelty that deserves attention is the prominence of television as a purveyor of information about protests and rites of power. The growing importance of this visual medium has certainly introduced new elements into the struggles that officials and protesters wage to convince the populace that their version of events is the most authentic one. Since visual reports carry a different weight from written ones, any increase in a population's reliance on television broadcasts as opposed to newspaper accounts is bound to have an impact. Just as skillfully made films can impart a greater sense of verisimilitude than even the most descriptive novels, television reports have a special power to shape an audience's memory of how a particular event unfolded, and they can be particularly effective when it comes to eliciting certain kinds of emotional responses, such as horror at an act of violence.[45] There can be no question, therefore, that the rising importance of television made 1989's governmental campaign of disinformation different from its Republican-era counterparts, during which officials relied upon simpler technologies (ranging from newspaper editorials denigrating all protests as Soviet plots, to phonograph recordings of anti-Communist messages played at village meetings) to reach and convince the people.

Visual images can also certainly play a special role in distorting popular perceptions of official spectacles. For example, reports of the National Day celebrations of 1 October 1989 that appeared in publications based outside the PRC tended to present these events in a negative light, stressing that the regime's fear of untoward incidents had forced it to limit participation to carefully screened (and mostly military) groups.[46] Whereas foreign journalists cited the irony of the "people's" exclusion from ceremonies marking the anniversary of the founding of a "people's republic," however, China's television stations and pictorial magazines presented viewers with positive images (smiling officials, happy crowds, elaborate fireworks displays) designed to show as words alone could not that "order" once again reigned in the square.[47]

Even more noteworthy in illustrating the power of television as a tool of official propagandists were the artfully crafted documentaries of the protest movement shown and reshown on Chinese television stations in the summer of 1989. These documentaries derived much of their force from the fact that actual shots exist of crowds killing individual soldiers and then displaying their remains in a gruesome fashion. With careful editing, isolated outbursts of crowd violence of this sort were molded into chilling tales of urban chaos, which ignored or disguised the fact that such killings were generally responses to threats or actual acts of state-sponsored terror. Official documentaries even gave a special reading to the famous confrontation between the lone protester and the armored personnel carrier by claiming that this stand-off illustrated the saintly patience shown by members of the People's Liberation Army in the face of adversity.

But if visual documents could be used to aid the government in its quest to convince the public that its version of events was correct, the same new media could also be used to subvert the official message. No matter how skillfully its documentaries are put together, the CCP will never be able to convince many of those who have seen foreign television broadcasts that the protesters were the initiators and main perpetrators of violence in 1989. This audience, moreover, is not composed solely of foreigners; it includes citizens of the RPC who were studying or working abroad during 1989, those residents of Guangdong Province able to pick up Hong Kong stations, and all the Hong Kong locals who will become citizens of China in 1997. Thanks to photographs and videotapes smuggled into China, other groups of Chinese have also been exposed to foreign visual coverage of 1989 that undermines official claims.

It is important to remember that no matter how powerful the media involved, the key to any kind of communication's persuasive power is still determined largely by whether the recipient believes the purveyor of information to be reliable.[48] There are undoubtedly Chinese whose only sources of information concerning Beijing or Shanghai (let alone the world beyond China's boundaries) are the official media, and such people—as some post-June 4th Western newspaper reports suggest—have little reason to question the story told in government documentaries.[49] But we have no reason to think that the Republican-era equivalents of these villagers were any more or less skeptical of the stories of urban mass movements they heard from Nationalist Party phonograph records. Conversely, many Chinese urbanites are so suspicious of everything they see or read in the official media that they are unlikely to be influenced by even the most powerful visual images purveyed by the government. Such viewers were quite capable of constructing their own ironic readings of official broadcasts of the October 1 celebrations, especially because savvy Beijing residents were well aware of the changes in the program the regime had made to ensure that the fortieth Communist National Day was marked by an uneventful media event.

Another novelty of the contemporary era worth keeping in mind is the extent to which, thanks to the rise of telecommunications, protesters and officials engaged in planning and carrying out mass actions are now aware of and interested in cultivating world opinion and free to look beyond their own borders for inspiration when it comes to deciding what kind of public display to stage. There is no doubt that one thing making the events of 1989 different from their Republican predecessors was a consciousness on all sides that images of Chinese mass actions were being sent around the world almost instantaneously. It is also clear that at least in the case of the protesters there was a great deal of interest in mass actions that had recently been staged in other parts of the world.

Here again, however, the importance of this disjuncture between the Republican and Dengist eras should not be overstated, for the public actions of the former were not as free from external influence or their contemporary equivalents as dominated by global concerns as one might think. It is worth remembering, for example, that long before television ushered in the age of the global community, Chinese protesters and officials had already shown an interest in enlisting foreign public opinion of some sort. For example, some participants in the May 4th Movement compared their efforts to a variety of events in Western history (one student publication aimed at foreign readers mentioned the Magna Carta, the Declaration of Independence, and the French Revolution), and placards with English-language slogans could be seen in Shanghai and even Beijing (which had a much smaller number of foreign residents) during 1925's May 30th Movement.[50] Thus, though the prevalence of such banners in 1989 may have been a novelty for which we can thank television, neither their appearance nor a general interest in drawing symbolic connections between Chinese and Western protest was without precedent. It is also worth noting that, as concerned with foreign public opinion as protesters and officials were in 1989, participants in mass actions remained most intent upon influencing the views of key members of the Chinese urban populace. Not surprisingly, therefore, banners and wall posters that spoke to specifically domestic concerns (such as inflation) and invoked symbols associated with

Chinese history (such as portrayals of Deng as a new "last emperor") great-ly outnumbered those whose rhetorical cosmopolitanism so fascinated the Western media.

Similar points can be made about student interest in foreign forms of collective action. Yes, some of the protesters of 1989 were keenly aware of international traditions of remonstrance, thanks in large part to newscasts depicting recent upheavals in countries such as South Korea and the Phil-ippines. And, yes, there is some evidence (the prevalence of headbands emblazoned with slogans, the prominence of group hunger strikes) to sug-gest that foreign events helped introduce new twists into the Chinese pro-test repertoire, much as the protests at Tiananmen Square certainly influ-enced subsequent events in Eastern Europe. Once again, however, neither the novelty of the situation nor the influence of the outside world should be stressed too much. After all, earlier generations of Chinese dissenters also drew inspiration from foreign movements. Some participants in the May 4th Movement, for example, were quite keenly aware of the March 1st Movement in Korea that same year. And even in 1989 most of the mass actions Chinese students staged were adaptations of scripts from their own nation's protest repertoire. The links to the past of some pieces of 1989 street theater (such as the presentation of petitions on bent knees with ac-companying *ketous* or "kowtows") were clear. And even the events that journalists treated as heavily influenced by foreign traditions were often more firmly rooted in indigenous traditions of protest and ritual than most Westerners thought.

The Goddess of Democracy's appearance in Tiananmen Square illus-trates this last point in a particularly relevant way. The image was certainly designed in part to remind people of the Statue of Liberty, but it was not the simple imitation of a foreign icon that Western journalists described. This large white statue was also reminiscent of both the figures in socialist realist monuments and representations of Chinese folk deities. Most signifi-cantly for my purposes here is the way in which it was carried to and set up in Tiananmen Square. A large white statue of Chairman Mao figured prom-inently in some National Day rallies held in the same spot in the 1960s, and a similar statue of Chiang Kaishek was carried through the streets of Shanghai in the 1945 birthday parade I described earlier. If we want to understand the Goddess of Democracy's meaning for Chinese as opposed to Western audiences, therefore, we need to see its exhibition as an act of subversion that (to borrow E.P. Thompson's description of eighteenth-century English protests) gained much of its power from its ability to "twist the tail" of the authorities.

The Goddess of Democracy is thus, ironically, both a distinctively contemporary symbol and a suggestion that important long-standing equations relating to political street theater have survived the transition to the age of telecommunications unscathed. Just as first the Nationalist and then the Communist Party combined elements drawn from Chinese folk religious practices and imperial rituals with elements drawn from Soviet personality cult spectacles, to establish a new set of rites of rulership designed to help them define and defend the revolutionary political center, the creation and placement of the Goddess of Democracy needs to be seen as an eclectic challenge to the Dengist regime's claim to that numinous area. Like much of the street theater of 1989, the scenes involving this new deity were ones in which contemporary students tried (as their Republican precursors had before them) to use variations on official scripts to cast doubt upon the legitimacy of current leaders.

My goal here has not been to suggest that the telecommunications revolution has had no impact on Chinese mass actions. The events of 1989 were very different in many ways from their Republican-era predecessors, and changes in mass media capabilities have had a great deal to do with this process. But the most profound differences have tended to involve international as opposed to domestic audiences. Changes in the international sphere are important, since for decades China's rulers and their critics have been intently concerned with the outside world in various ways. Throughout the Republican and Communist eras, participants in loyalist and dissident mass actions have been influenced by foreign models and interested in winning the support of foreign audiences, and diplomatic events have determined the timing of government spectacles and dissident rallies alike. Anything that affects international perceptions of Chinese politics will thus have a significant impact on domestic struggles for power. Nevertheless, in the popular movements of both the Republican and Communist eras, domestic considerations have ultimately tended to take precedence over international ones. Both the June 1989 massacres and the (less bloody but still severe) campaign of repression that Chiang Kaishek used to crush the anti-Hunger, Anti-Civil War Movement bear witness to this fact. In 1947, Chiang Kaishek knew that his actions would be viewed with displeasure by some of the foreign officials whose favor he had courted in the past, just as Deng Xiaoping had good reason to think that the Western world would not condone the use of tanks in 1989. In each case, however, the regime proved willing to risk a loss of carefully cultivated international goodwill.

Developments in mass media capabilities have influenced the domestic sphere as well as the international one, of course, but I have tried to show that in this case the changes have not been as fundamental. They have tended to be changes in degree rather than kind; changes that upped the ante of symbolic and physical battles but otherwise had little impact on the basic dynamics of such struggles. Critics of media events like to single out major turning points (the spread of daily newspapers, the invention of radio, the first televised news conferences) after which political life became less spontaneous and authentic. These turning points can indeed be significant, but it seems dangerous (in the Chinese case, at least) to draw sharp distinctions between eras on the basis of the presumed authenticity of mass actions, for these events (whether rituals within the Forbidden City or public gatherings at Tiananmen Square) have always been performed with an eye toward producing reports of some kind that will influence people who are not actually present. They have thus, in an important sense, always been "media events," and there have always been two audiences: eyewitnesses and those exposed to representations.

That the media through which members of the latter group have learned of popular protests and official rituals has changed over time (from edicts to newspaper reports to radio and television broadcasts) is certainly significant in many ways. I am not convinced, however, that they have altered the basic rules of this particular (and vitally important) political game. In 1989 both sides certainly made use of new technologies, but they also relied heavily on familiar forms of mass action, and they did so for the same reason as their predecessors of the Republican era. Mobilizing large groups of people to take to the streets, gather in central squares, and participate in symbolically charged performances remains an effective way to challenge or defend the legitimacy of those who claim to embody the political center.

NOTES

1. I thank Michael Curtin, Lisa Holstein, and Jeffrey Gould for offering me valuable advice concerning this piece. None of them should be held responsible in any way, however, for the views expressed here.

2. The term "telerevolution" is taken from Timothy Garton Ash, *The Magic Lantern* (New York, 1990), 94. I hasten to add, however, that although Ash does emphasize technological developments, his handling of the connections between media and revolution is too nuanced to be associated with the kind of technologically determinist position I have in mind here.

3. Michael J. O'Neill, *The Roar of the Crowd: How Television and People*

Power Are Changing the World (New York, 1993). The footnotes to this book refer to a variety of publications that take similar positions on the issue.

4. Ibid., 39, 93-94, 100.

5. The most comprehensive histories of the 1919 protests are Chow Tse-tsung, *The May 4th Movement* (Cambridge, Mass., 1960); and Peng Ming, *Wusi yundongshi* (A history of the May 4th Movement) (Beijing, 1984). A good comparison of pre- and post-twentieth-century student movements, one that highlights important factors (such as the changing nature of the Chinese educational system) not discussed in this chapter, is John Israel, "Reflections on the Modern Chinese Student Movement," in Seymour Lipset and Philip Altbach, eds., *Students in Revolt* (Boston, 1969), 310-33. Some specific examples of how travel between cities helped establish contacts among student activists in different parts of China and how protesters and their supporters used telegrams and newspapers during the May 4th Movement are provided in Jeffrey N. Wasserstrom, *Student Protests in Twentieth-Century China: The View from Shanghai* (Stanford, Calif., 1991), 52-55, 62-63.

6. Three interesting discussions of the Chinese events of 1989 that highlight media-related themes are Craig Calhoun, "Tiananmen, Television, and the Public Sphere: Internationalization of Culture and the Beijing Spring of 1989." *Public Culture* 2, no. 1 (1989): 54-71; He Zhou, "The Role of the Chinese National News Media and the Voice of America in the 1989 Chinese Pro-Democracy Movement" (Ph.D. diss., Indiana University, 1991); and James Lull, *China Turned on: Television, Reform, and Resistance* (London, 1991). For the impact of one new technology that receives little attention in the works cited above, see Tiger Li, "Computer-Mediated Communications and the Chinese Students in the U.S.," *Information Society* 7 (1990): 125-37, which examines the part that e-mail networks played in keeping information flowing and a sense of community alive among Chinese intellectuals outside of China. Michael Curtin, "Electronic Imaginings: Collective Identities and the Global Reconfiguration of Space" (unpublished, cited with author's permission), an insightful and provocative think piece on the "transnational flow of media imagery," places several recent political phenomena (including the events at Tiananmen Square) within a broad theoretical context.

7. A detailed version of this argument appears in Jeffrey N. Wasserstrom, "The Evolution of the Shanghai Student Protest Repertoire," in Frederic Wakeman, Jr., and Yeh Wen-hsin, eds., *Shanghai Sojourners* (Berkeley, Calif., 1992), 108-44.

8. For information concerning pre-twentieth-century student activism, see Lin Yu-tang, *A History of the Press and Public Opinion in China* (1936; New York, 1968); and Tsing Yuan, "Urban Riots and Disturbances," in Jonathan Spence and John Wills, eds., *From Ming to Ch'ing* (New Haven, Conn., 1979), 271-320.

9. For more details, see David Strand, "Protest in Beijing," *Problems of Communism* 39 (1990): 1-19; and Joseph Esherick and Jeffrey N. Wasserstrom, "Acting Out Democracy: Political Theater in Modern China," *Journal of Asian Studies* 49, no. 4 (1990): 835-65.

10. Han Minzhu, ed., *Cries for Democracy: Speeches and Writings of the*

Chinese Democracy Movement of 1989 (Princeton, N.J., 1990), 135-37. The life of the most famous Song Dynasty student martyr is discussed in Lin, *History of the Press*, 48-50; and a reference to this figure in an important speech of the May 4th era is cited in Wasserstrom, *Student Protests*, 86.

11. This is, of course, a central theme in O'Neill, *Roar of the Crowd*; see also the various contributions to Steve Banks et al., "Seizing the Moment: Harnessing the Information Technologies," special issue of *Information Society* 8, no. 1 (1992). Several contributors use the Chinese events of 1989 to draw attention to the special political role now being played by television even in less developed parts of the world, and many works specifically focusing on China's crisis touch on similar themes. Some of the pieces cited above in note 6 fall into this category; see also Mark Hopkins, "Watching China Change," *Columbia Journalism Review*, Sept.-Oct. 1989, 35-40.

12. Daniel J. Boorstin, *The Image: What Happened to the American Dream* (New York, 1961). The most comprehensive discussion of media events and the debate concerning their meaning can be found in Daniel Dayan and Elihu Katz, *Media Events: The Live Broadcasting of History* (Cambridge, Mass., 1992). For a good brief introduction in which Katz and Dayan clearly differentiate their more positive vision of media events from that of critics such as Boorstin and authors such as Walter Benjamin, who focus on the way technological change has facilitated the rise of totalitarian regimes, see Elihu Katz with Daniel Dayan and Pierre Motyl, "In Defense of Media Events," in Robert Haigh et al., eds., *Communications in the 21st Century* (New York, 1981), 43-59.

13. An interesting comparison of the role of mass media in these demonstrations and the Chinese protests of 1989 can be found in Frank Reuven, "On Tiananmen Square, Echoes of Chicago in '68," *New York Times*, 4 June 1989, 27. The term "the whole world was watching" slightly modifies the title of Todd Gitlin's seminal study of the coverage of 1960s American protests, *The Whole World Is Watching: Mass Media in the Making and Unmaking of the New Left* (Berkeley, Calif., 1980). Interestingly, although Gitlin insists that various forms of mass media (including the increasingly dominant medium of television) should be seen as key players in (rather than passive reporters of information about) recent American mass movements, he cautions against drawing too sharp a distinction between the way visual and print media operate, stressing the continued centrality of the "verbal story" in most television newscasts (264-65).

14. It is worth noting that several illuminating recent works in communications studies take a cautious approach to assessing the significance of technological developments and hence present arguments that fit in well with those I outline here. Important examples, which typically downplay the importance of events that are presented elsewhere as dramatic media-related "breakthroughs," include Carolyn Marvin, *When Old Technologies Were New: Thinking about Electronic Communication in the Late Nineteenth Century* (New York, 1988); and James Carey, ed., *Communication as Culture: Essays on Media and Society* (Boston, 1989).

15. Sean Wilentz, ed., *The Rites of Power* (Philadelphia, 1985).

16. Mark Poster, *The Mode of Information: Poststructuralism and Social Context* (Chicago, 1990), 154.

17. I should note at least two important issues relating to television coverage that deserve some attention but will not be dealt with here. The first is that Western media coverage distorted foreign perceptions of Chinese events—e.g., by leaving viewers with the impression that (a) little of importance was taking place outside Beijing (when in fact there were protests, in some cases very large ones, in cities throughout China), and (b) the main victims of June 4 massacre were students (when in fact most of those killed were members of other social groups). The second is the role of media coverage in the rise to power within the movement of certain dissident leaders, who benefited from the attention of foreign journalists. Good discussions of these questions can be found in the Joan Shorenstein Barone Center on the Press, Politics, and Public Policy, *Turmoil at Tiananmen: A Study of U.S. Press Coverage of the Beijing Spring of 1989* (Cambridge, Mass., 1992). See also Gitlin's discussion of comparable themes in relation to American protests of the 1960s, in *The Whole World Is Watching*. As important as these two issues are for understanding China's 1989, extended discussion of them here would not alter my main conclusions about essential continuities between contemporary events and those of the pre-telecommunications era.

18. For more details and relevant citations, see Wasserstrom, *Student Protests*, 72-86.

19. Ibid., 242-47.

20. Ibid., 171-99.

21. Ibid., 240-76.

22. Lynn Hunt, *Politics, Culture, and Class in the French Revolution* (Berkeley, Calif., 1984), 60, 99. See also Mona Ozouf's seminal study *Festivals and the French Revolution*, trans. Alan Sheridan (Cambridge, Mass., 1988).

23. Clifford Geertz, "Centers, Kings, and Charisma: Reflections on the Symbolics of Power," in Wilentz, *Rites of Power*, 13-38, esp. 15.

24. See Joseph Levenson's seminal discussion of Yuan Shikai's "imperial" rituals, in *Confucian China and Its Modern Fate: A Trilogy* (Berkeley, Calif., 1965), 2:3-7.

25. The two ceremonies are described in *North China Herald*, 2 Jan. and 24 Feb. 1912; I am grateful to Andrew Cheung for providing me with these citations and drawing my attention to the contrasting tones of the two rituals in question.

26. Alexander Woodside, "Emperors and the Chinese Political System," in Kenneth Lieberthal et al., eds., *Perspectives on Modern China: Four Anniversaries* (Armonk, N.Y., 1991), 5-30.

27. *Wenhuibao*, 31 Oct. 1945, 2.

28. Wasserstrom, *Student Protests*, 277-94; Esherick and Wasserstrom, "Acting Out Democracy."

29. *Shanghaishi xuelian* (Shanghai Student Union), "Shanghaishi xuelian wei jinian zongli zhengchen gao jie tongbao shu" (Shanghai Student Union announcement to comrades of all classes on the anniversary of the president's birth), a 1947 leaflet held at the Shanghai Municipal Archive.

30. It is important to point out, as Robert Darnton usefully reminded me at the Lexington conference, that many other essays by Geertz do in fact draw at-

tention to just these sorts of fissures and tensions. E.g., several chapters in one of his most influential works—Clifford Geertz, *The Interpretation of Cultures: Selected Essays* (New York, 1973)—suggest that many symbolically charged ritual events involve fierce struggles for power. It is also worth noting places in which both Ozouf and Hunt stress that we should never assume that "sacrality" can be transferred from an old order to a new one in an uncontentious manner, and that symbolic acts of dissent (such as, in the French case, the chopping down of liberty trees) are bound to take place. See esp. Ozouf, *Festivals*, 259; and Lynn Hunt, "The Sacred in the French Revolution," in Jeffrey Alexander, ed., *Durkheimian Sociology: Cultural Studies* (New York, 1988), 25-43.

31. His general interpretation of the central issues is sketched out in Edward Palmer Thompson, "Eighteenth-Century English Society: Class Struggle Without Class?" *Social History* 3, no. 2 (1978): 133-65; and Thompson, "Patrician Society, Plebeian Culture," *Journal of Social History* 7, no. 4 (1974): 382-405. My discussion here is based both on those works and on the chapter "The Patricians and the Plebs" in Thompson, *Customs in Common* (London, 1991), 16-96, in which he expands upon the themes raised in those two pathbreaking essays and provides additional citations to recent scholarship on related issues.

32. Thompson, "Patrician Society, Plebeian Culture."

33. Thompson, "The Patricians and the Plebs," 74.

34. Ibid., 75.

35. Nicholas Rogers, "Popular Protest in Early Hanoverian London," *Past and Present* 79 (1978): 70-100.

36. Charles Tilly, *The Contentious French* (Cambridge, Mass., 1986), 116-18.

37. For details and citations, see Wasserstrom, *Student Protests*, 184-88.

38. Stephen Lukes, "Political Ritual and Social Integration," *Sociology* 9, no. 2 (1975): 289-308.

39. Edward Shils and Michael Young, "The Meaning of the Coronation," *Sociological Review*, n.s., 1 (1953): 63-81, esp. 67.

40. Lukes, "Political Ritual." It is worth noting that although Lukes does not discuss Geertz's work in this particular essay, "Centers, Kings, and Charisma" is open to some of the same criticisms as those Lukes calls "neo-Durkheimian" studies. This is true in spite of the fact that Geertz's position on monarchical rituals is by no means identical to that of Shils and Young, and in spite of the fact that he presents "Centers, Kings, and Charisma" as an attempt to extend a Weberian project (that of explaining the creation and replication of charisma) rather than a Durkheimian one. An interesting though in some ways controversial assessment of the intellectual debt both Shils and Geertz owe to Durkheim, which notes that no debt of any sort is acknowledged in key works by these two contemporary scholars, is Jeffrey Alexander, "Introduction: Durkheimian Sociology and Cultural Studies Today," in Alexander, *Durkheimian Sociology*, 1-21.

41. Hall's quotation and a useful brief discussion of related issues can be found in George Lipsitz, "The Struggle for Hegemony," *Journal of American History* 75, no. 1 (1988): 146-50. The best treatment of Shanghai labor unrest during the Republican era is Elizabeth J. Perry, *Shanghai on Strike* (Stanford, Calif., 1993).

42. Detailed description and discussion of these mass actions can be found in dozens of recent publications, including Han, *Cries for Democracy*; Yi Mu and Mark V. Thompson, *Crisis at Tiananmen: Reform and Reality in Modern China* (San Francisco, 1989); and various chapters of Tony Saich, *The Chinese People's Movement* (Armouk, N.Y., 1990).

43. For details and citations, see John Israel, *Student Nationalism in China, 1927-1937* (Stanford: Stanford University Press, 1966); and Wasserstrom, *Student Protests*, 171-99.

44. See, e.g., the elegiac couplets translated in Han, *Cries for Democracy*, 6-8.

45. For a fascinating discussion of this point, see Jeffrey Alexander, "Culture and Political Crisis: Watergate and Durkheimian Sociology," in Alexander, *Durkheimian Sociology* 221-22.

46. See e.g., David Holley, "Under Tight Wraps, China Marks 40th Anniversary of Communist Rule." *Los Angeles Times*, 2 Oct. 1989, 6.

47. Chun Ge, "National Day Celebrations in Beijing," *China Pictorial* no. 12 (1989): 2-5.

48. Alexander, "Culture and Political Crisis," 221-22.

49. Nicholas Kristof, "Outside China's Cities, the Crackdown and the Outrage Are Watered Down," *New York Times*, 22 Feb. 1990, A3; and Kristof, "Far from Tiananmen: T.V. and Contentment," *New York Times*, 7 Oct. 1990, A1.

50. See Wasserstrom, *Student Protests*, 237, and the photographs following 124.

13

Mass Media and the Velvet Revolution

OWEN V. JOHNSON

T here have been at least four revolutionary periods in the history of Czechoslovakia. In none of them did the mass media play a dominant role. In each of them, however, the revolution assigned a new role to the mass media. In most cases the new role was more instrumental than the one it replaced, despite the fact that it was usually the ineffectiveness of the press in the previous period that helped create the revolutionary movement.

Communication did influence the "Velvet Revolution" of 1989, but in a complex and indirect way, delegitimizing the old regime before the revolution because of its failure to persuade its audience, and then mirroring rather than instigating the events of November. Media did not significantly change the terms of the debate, bring crowds into the street, or destabilize the government. The dissidents who came to head the new government anticipated that the mass media would take a leading role in the new regime as tribunes of the new democracy, in a manner similar to what Pierre Rétat describes earlier in this volume as having happened in France two centuries earlier. The market made sure that would not happen.[1]

The modern history of the Czech press dates from the 1860s; the modern Slovak press began around the turn of the century. From those times until 1918, when Czechoslovakia was founded, the Czech and Slovak presses helped create a sense of Czech and Slovak national identity. The availability of newspapers in their own language helped people decide who they were, often not by political persuasion but by helping create a sense of shared experience that extended beyond the parish, the county, or the region.[2] The early modern papers had little of the objective, fact-based, middle-class form of reporting. Newspapers owed their first allegiance to the political parties that supported them.[3] Around the turn of the century some of the Czech parties began to support urban, sensationalist, nonpolitical dailies, which not only attracted large numbers of readers and helped develop the habit of reading newspapers but provided funds for the publication of the more limited-circulation political newspapers. Only one such newspaper, *Slovenska Politika*, published by the Agrarian Party, emerged in Slovakia, and its success did not come until the 1930s. *Lidove Noviny*, a Czech newspaper founded in Brno in 1893, was an exception in the newspaper world, being neither directly political nor commercial, but it developed into the most influential paper in the interwar period.

Amid the collapse of the Habsburg Empire at the end of World War I, the Czechoslovak National Council, led by Thomas G. Masaryk, Edvard Benes, and Milan R. Stefanik, waged a tireless campaign for political and military recognition. At home, the heavy hand of Austrian war censorship limited the activities of both press and politics. Because of the long uncertainty about the future of the map of Europe, the close ties of Czech newspapers to political parties, and the increasingly difficult economic situation, the press played little part in the revolution that brought about the new Czechoslovak state, though some newspapers did foster closer cooperation and ties between Czechs and Slovaks. From the turn of the century until the outbreak of war, some groups of Czechs had provided news and economic support to the nascent Slovak press, and a small group of Czechs and Slovaks—the most prominent of whom was the Czech Karel Kalal—also worked together to assist Czech newspapers in obtaining information about Slovakia.[4] When the war broke out, some of these Slovaks moved to Prague and continued to write about Slovakia.

The new Czechoslovak Republic was established 28 October 1918 after a small group of Czechs announced that they were taking control of the Corn Exchange in Prague.[5] They had the cooperation of Austrian authorities who sought to prevent a collapse of civil authority. Czechs and Slovaks in the interwar period referred to these events as a revolution (*prevrat*), and related as it was to the redefining of international boundaries, it was not a velvet revolution. In Slovakia, heavy fighting involved local militias, the developing Czechoslovak Army, and the invading troops of the Hungarian Soviet Republic.

The Czech press overnight was transformed from an oppositional one to a "state-creating" one. Most of the newspapers took on an educational role, changed their national identity from Czech to Czechoslovak (although in reality changing only the adjective and the geography but little in national content), and plunged into vigorous political debate, discussion, and vituperation. As one Western observer of the time noted, anyone who wanted to follow the political debate had to read the newspapers of all the main political parties.[6] Significantly, however, most Czechs, particularly outside the city of Prague, did not read the political press; most political papers had circulations of less than 10,000. Political power was centered in the party leaderships, and in four major parliamentary elections between 1920 and 1935 there were only modest shifts in outcome. Because members of Parliament owed their seats to slating by party leaders, there was limited opportunity or need for democratic interaction between the media and the citizens.

Slovakia entered the new state with only a few thousand nationally conscious intelligentsia. Its major cities were often Hungarian strongholds. The establishment of Bratislava as the administrative center of Slovakia led to the establishment of most Slovak newspapers there, and media penetration outside Bratislava was limited. That began to change in the 1930s under the impact of the emergence of large numbers of Slovaks from the high schools, and slowly improving economic and transportation conditions. Still, most media operations were small: sometimes only four or five journalists worked on a daily paper, and there were no more than one hundred journalists on all Slovak newspapers. Often they were only politicians in waiting.

The collapse of Czechoslovakia following the signing of the Munich agreement in September 1938 and the occupation of the Czech Lands in March 1939 was in some senses a revolution. Slovakia chose independence within shrunken boundaries; the Czech Lands had no choice and became a Nazi protectorate. The numbers of newspapers in both territories shrank dramatically. In the Czech Lands the restriction of political life was reflected in the elimination of newspapers as political instruments. Overt Czech political life was combined into two political parties. Underground Czech political life was modest.[7] In Slovakia most of the parties formed a political union dominated by the Hlinka Slovak People's Party. Four daily newspapers promoted in varying degrees the strengthening of Slovak statehood. Independence brought with it, too, the establishment of many scientific and professional periodicals, replacing those previously shared with the Czechs. In other words, the national revolution in Slovakia strengthened Slovak sociocultural development, helping prepare the way for the establishment of separate Czech and Slovak republics in 1993.

To some degree the period 1945-48, from liberation from Nazi rule to the Communist seizure of power, meant a restoration of the politics and journalism of the interwar period. The continuing education and urbanization of the population had led to an increase in newspapers' circulation and a broadening of their content. The uncertain political and economic situation prevented the press from assuming any kind of independent role, however. When the Communist Party of Czechoslovakia seized control in February 1948 by a combination of legal procedures and street power, most independent or opposition newspapers were shut down; only a few continued as representatives of emaciated political parties. The Communists saw the press as a mass mobilizer, herald of world revolution, but its initiative was hamstrung by party control and power. Only after the death of Stalin and riots in Plzen in 1953 did the press begin to change. The liberalization was modest compared to what took place in neighboring Poland and Hungary, however. In Communist dogma journalists were still soldiers in the building of Communism. What was not eliminated in this process was language. Even though newspaper content temporarily became socialist, the form remained national, a reserve that could be drawn upon when the international climate improved.

Among the most visible elements of the Prague Spring in 1968 were the mass media. The names, faces, and ideas of the leading reformers manifested themselves in print and, significantly, on radio and television. While journalists specifically had a lesser role in the development of events, this revolution from below found the people consuming newspapers and broadcasting, using the media in a revolutionary way to function as independent individuals as they had never done before. They lined up to buy newspapers as a political statement. They voted for democracy by listening to the radio newscast in the evening, a newscast they viewed as independent (television's impact was smaller, since only about half the households had it, and they were unevenly distributed across the country). As is the case in liberalizing movements in most totalitarian countries, calls for freedom of the press were an important plank in the reform platform. In fact, the organized professional activity of journalists was oriented chiefly in this direction, especially because liberalization of press controls had been on the journalists' public agenda since 1963, when the last of the Stalinists were removed from the Communist Party leadership.[8]

Having become such visible elements of opposition, the mass media were subjected to particularly severe repression when troops from the Soviet Union and other members of the Warsaw Pact invaded Czechoslovakia in August 1968. Hundreds, perhaps even thousands of journalists lost their jobs.[9] Repression was particularly severe in the Czech Lands. Although the crackdown was dictated by the party diehards, some journalists themselves helped to push their colleagues out.

As was the case with most of the quashed reform movements in Eastern Europe during Communist rule, the party was able to regain control of journalists and journalism, but only at the expense of its ability to gain the trust of the people. The party wanted to reestablish the mass media as an instrument of influence, a force that would help the party down the road of success. Dozens of books and hundreds of articles were written on how to make the press more effective and influential within society.[10] The reality, however, was that the press could become more effective and influential only at the expense of party influence and control. In Poland this lesson was learned anew in each successive reform effort until finally a popular rallying cry not only among people who actively sought reform but also in the public at large became "The press lies!"

The result was a graying of the media, a writing style that was generally dry and ponderous. Most party leaders must have recognized before long that the system was not working, but they were trapped between the dogmatism of the increasingly sclerotic leadership in Moscow and hardline careerists in their own country. Consequently, an "as-if" society gradually evolved. The popular epigram "We'll pretend to work if you'll pretend to pay us" was only the most obvious element of this state of affairs.

The events of 1968 and their tumultuous aftermath did bear one important fruit whose significance was insufficiently noted at the time but whose ripening contributed mightily to the course of events in Czechoslovakia after 1989. One of two reforms to survive the postinvasion crackdown was the establishment of a Czechoslovak federation: two individual sovereign Czech and Slovak republics were established within the confines of the larger federal state. For the Czechs this was an insignificant state, largely ignored by the populace. But the existence of the Slovak Socialist Republic brought about a Slovak Ministry of Culture, a Slovak Ministry of Education, and self-sufficient Slovak sociocultural development. Although the party remained subject to centralized control, the fact that the party leader (until 1987) and the president (from 1975 to 1989) were Slovaks was not insignificant. Society in Slovakia, perhaps more than in the Czech Lands, behaved as if it respected and trusted the party, but it did not. More important, the citizens of Slovakia turned inward. In a remarkable poll conducted in September 1992, the people of Slovakia chose the years of Communist rule as one of the two best periods in their national history.

Czech and Slovak contacts had been among the forces that had helped to drive the Prague Spring reform movement.[11] For that reason and others, the party made little effort to foster ties and contacts between the two parts of the country. Like the citizens, Slovak media turned inward, focusing their attention on Slovak issues and concerns. In the mid-1980s, Slovak mass media began to carry dialogue about the place of Slovakia in the joint state. Czechs, whose national self-identity had been secured in the previous century and whose state, they thought, had been established in 1918, had no such concerns.

Before 1968 the Communist Party had sought to increase the penetration of Czech newspapers in Slovakia. For a period there was even a Slovak mutation of *Rude Pravo*, the central Czech-language Communist Party daily. Slovak newspapers were far less often available to Czechs. After 1968, Czech newspaper penetration in Slovakia diminished, limited mostly to *Rude Pravo*, whose reading was still a daily requirement for party and societal leaders. Slovak newspapers became practically unavailable in the Czech Lands except at a few kiosks in Prague or by subscription. It should not be surprising that by 1990 Czechs and Slovaks no longer knew each other very well and by 1992 had decided to go their separate ways.

Contributing to the successful execution of the Velvet Revolution in 1989 and the collapse of the old Communist power structures was the internal life of the journalism community after 1969. When so many journalists were expelled from the professional ranks in the postinvasion crackdown, the regime was left with hardline leadership and careerist followers. Young journalists in particular faced the choice of joining the system and playing by its rules or undertaking a career change. Most of them joined the system, following a rule established a generation earlier that the only way to influence the system was to join it. They saw what had happened to the people who had challenged the system in 1968; they saw such challenges as unnecessary. Rewarding salaries and extensive privileges helped these young journalists make their decisions. But unlike the earlier generation, most had no illusions about the nature of Communist power. Eventually the pressures of professionalism would make themselves felt in the souls of many of these journalists. Some party leaders had already begun to tinker with the system in the late 1970s, trying vainly to make it more effective and more believable by making it more open. But both journalists and leaders were spooked by the memory of 1968. Both had too much to lose by pushing too far. Both drew back.

Journalists, therefore, were not the leaders of the nascent reform movement that received inspiration from the Soviet reform effort led by Mikhail Gorbachev. Instead, they focused on making their journalism more professional and less political, constantly balancing their wish to be more objective with the awareness of the power and control that could be exercised by the state and the Communist party. As an exiled critic noted, *Rude Pravo*, the Communist party daily, was not full of lies; much of what it printed consisted of truth.[12] The most interesting criticism appeared in fictional form, not on the news. A television drama, *The Grass Is Green* (named after the theme song of a soccer program), took aim at corruption within the world of soccer. Lubos Jurik, a Slovak writer, investigated limitations on journalistic criticism in his novel *Novinari* (Journalists).

The boundaries of what was acceptable media content slowly expanded after 1985. There should be "a more open and informative mass media," the seventeenth congress of the Communist Party of Czechoslovakia resolved in 1986, but "no one will be allowed to undermine our socialist order." In October 1987 the party leadership issued a policy document, "The Application of the Leninist Principle of Openness of Public Information in the Press, Radio, and Television," which said nothing terribly different from the policies that had characterized the party outlook for nearly two decades.[13] Its failure to address contemporary media issues was reflected in the fact that the party presidium had to return to the issue in July 1989.[14] The new thinking still reflected an instrumental understanding of the media: it called for "better information about the work of the party" and "more comprehensive information" about socioeconomic change.[15]

The regime needed the information the media provided so as not to be out of touch with the reform movements swirling about East Central Europe, however, and the regime also clung to the wish that it by now knew was vain: that greater openness could satisfy the populace. But openness did not mean freer expression of individual views.[16] That there could be, as Jeffrey Brooks mentions elsewhere in this volume, "no graduations of opinion, only right and wrong views," effectively limited the impact of *glasnost.* The regime could not afford to give up its monopoly on the media, because doing so would destroy the ideology that said the Communist Party should be the leading force in society. Its lack of formal censorship, if anything, limited the openness of the media, for journalists were unable to test the boundaries of the permitted. With only a few exceptions, they erred on the side of caution.

To some degree, the policy was a success. Beginning in the early 1980s, viewership and readership of domestic media increased. People read more papers and watched more television, engaging in a search for news and information about what was going on. Although they remained skeptical and sometimes confused about what they found in the domestic mass media, the greater transparency of news content meant that people no longer had to work so hard to discern what was happening. This gave them more time and reason to search other sources of information. One additional source was *samizdat,* but its circulation was very limited. Another source consisted of radio broadcasts from abroad (television from abroad, available to about 40 percent of the population, was less a source of news than of entertainment). Foreign radio broadcasts provided supplemental information, but by helping to fill in the gaps, they reduced the demand for change within the domestic media system (a situation which, ironically, continues today). Foreign radios did not persuade people that the Communist system was bankrupt; listeners who tuned in to foreign radios had already decided that their domestic system had failed. Dissidents applauded (and still applaud) foreign radio because under Communist rule they found there some confirmation that their activities were being noticed. Many others continue to applaud foreign radio today because the stations appear to represent continued foreign interest in the fate of the two republics. In the late 1980s there was no need for dissidents or anyone else to conduct propaganda to persuade Czechs and Slovaks that the Communist system was bankrupt and should be replaced. But the memory of 1968 ensured that few people would express their ideas in public forums. It was this interplay between the liberalizing domestic and foreign media, therefore, that helped delegitimize the governing regime.

As the domestic media became more open, the regime's credibility declined. The media, in effect, became weathervanes, measures of the possibility of change. In the eyes of foreigners the changes were modest, especially compared with what was happening in neighboring Poland and Hungary. What most foreigners could not see was the increasing number of open-discussion meetings taking place behind closed doors in factories and institutions across the country.[17]

The system of media command and control remained in place to the end. Curiously, though there was considerable room for maneuver and assertion by journalists, they did not use it. The executive director of the journalists' union remarked to me in March 1989 that journalists could be much more aggressive than they were, could work on a much wider range of stories and in much greater depth, but they still remembered the journalists of a generation earlier who had taken such words to heart and paid dearly for it. Ironically, some of the journalists of the 1980s would later pay dearly for their failure to take advantage of the opportunities that the reform movements offered. But even those who might have been inclined to pursue news more actively often found the doors to information shut.[18] The only journalists who would play leading roles in the Velvet Revolution were those who had contributed to the underground *Lidove Noviny* beginning in 1987, such as Vaclav Havel, Jiri Dienstbier, Vaclav Klaus, and Rita Klimova. For them, however, *samizdat* journalism had been only a political alternative until such time as they could enter the public arena.

The Velvet Revolution of November 1989 broke out without benefit of domestic media, when police clubbed marchers commemorating the fiftieth anniversary of the Nazi closure of Czech universities. Foreign broadcasts provided some information about the suddenly revolutionary situation, but the crucial source was word of mouth. Television images from CNN (not widely available) or from German or Hungarian television (more available) were not as influential in changing people's minds as their having seen, earlier in the year, East Germans (or their abandoned cars) in the streets of Prague seeking visas.[19]

Czechs had been going to the streets themselves, beginning with a demonstration on 21 August 1988, the twentieth anniversary of the Soviet invasion that ended the Prague Spring. A United States diplomat in Prague related to me later his surprise at hearing about that demonstration. Apparently, it was primarily the work of students and young people with little knowledge of the fear that had kept their parents off the street for those twenty years and with little thought of communicating beyond the student body. Students returned to the streets from time to time over the next fifteen months as the regime dithered over what response to make to their protests. As word of mouth carried news of these demonstrations, they served as a kind of communication, similar to what had occurred in England in the seventeenth century. This function may have been particularly important to members of the intelligentsia who, if not strong supporters of the regime, had made their peace with it, for the benefits of protesting were beginning to outweigh the benefits of cooperating with the old regime. In addition, all those taking part in one demonstration could tell their friends about plans for succeeding demonstrations.[20] From the street, the revolution spread to the theater.[21]

The Velvet Revolution was revolution from the bottom up. It broke out without the benefit of domestic media and, though foreign broadcasts provided some information about the suddenly explosive situation, information spread chiefly by word-of-mouth communication. These reports helped explain the peculiar address by a leading Czech Communist on Czechoslovak television, 19 November 1989, two days after the police attack.[22] In that address, the leader, Frantisek Pitra, a member of the Communist Party presidium, appearing on the screen forty-eight hours after the student demonstrations, blamed the students for the unrest, which up to that time had not even been mentioned in the mass media. Handbills, posters, and slogans took the place of mass media. Even before Vaclav Havel arrived at the Magic Lantern, people were going to Wenceslaus Square in the center of Prague to demonstrate. The crowd was calling, "Live broadcast, live broadcast."[23] When journalists at Czechoslovak Television finally succeeded in broadcasting part of the demonstration of 20 November it was a confirmation that the revolution had already occurred. By 25 November, under continuing pressure from the growing protest and its leaders, demonstrations were being broadcast in their entirety. Newspapers conveyed the same message, but television had a greater impact because it was visual, it reached the largest audience, and it penetrated the countryside. The 20 November issue of the Socialist Party's *Svobodne Slovo* had carried a joint statement by the party leadership and the paper's editors attacking the Communist Party's failure to enter into a dialogue with the protesters and condemning the attacks on demonstrators. Authorities stepped in and stopped the printing presses after only 1,000 copies had been printed.[24] But on the same day that the television breakthrough occurred, some four hundred journalists called for unlimited freedom of the press.[25] The mass media proved to be the weakest of the regime's cornerstones.[26]

In the months that followed the most discredited old journalists left their jobs, and the most active of the new journalists, less professionally oriented, became leaders of the new government and political parties. Many of the revolution's leaders continued to believe that the media were a powerful factor, but that was because they had been heavy information consumers. They did not realize that their own hunger for printed and broadcast sources did not extend to the public, which—distrustful after nearly a half-century of restricted media—remained wary and critical of the reoriented but still political press.[27] Intellectuals sought to recreate the politics of the interwar period, but the public was not interested. Near the end of 1992 public consumption of the media and its political content was down sharply. People concentrated more on securing their own economic and social future—a subject on which many publications provided only modest independent information—or preferred less demanding content and features. The most widely sold newspapers in both the Czech and Slovak republics were tabloids. As news became much more readily available, readers and viewers were no longer so actively involved in finding out what was going on. The revolutionaries had won the right to say what they wanted, but the public was not so interested. The politics and public sphere of the press and broadcasting again moved into the private sphere, but this time for individual gain, rather than communication.

In Slovakia after 1989 the press strengthened its focus on issues of national concern, and the media remained a representative voice of Slovak national assertion. Czechs found such a focus nearly incomprehensible, which in turn further strengthened the Slovak drive toward independence.

In summary, the Czech and Slovak mass media were marginalized and lost their political influence during a half-century of Nazi and Communist rule, except for brief periods of reform. Unlike the French Revolution, the Velvet Revolution was not a conflict of discourses, because by 1989 the old Czechoslovak Communist regime was only babbling incoherencies. Its policies were based on an ideology that was no longer relevent. During the 1989 revolution the mass media served only as a mirror of change. The influence that they are likely to regain is primarily as purveyors of entertainment and, through the presentation of advertisements and business information, as engines of economic change.

NOTES

1. "Report for the Czech Republic," *Balkanmedia* 2-3 (1993): 24.

2. Owen V. Johnson, "Newspapers and Nation-Building: The Slovak Press in Pre-1918 Slovakia," in Hans Lemberg et al., eds., *Bildungsgeschichte, Bevolkerungsgeschichte, Gesellschaftsgeschichte in den Bohmischen Landern und in Europa* (Vienna, 1988), 160-78.

3. Owen V. Johnson, "Unbridled Freedom: The Czech Press and Politics, 1918-1938," *Journalism History* 13 (Autumn-Winter 1986): 96-103.

4. See Thomas Marzik, "Czech Relations with the Slovaks: The Slavophile Writings and Activities of Karel Kalal" (Ph.D. diss., Columbia University, 1976).

5. Jan Oponcensky, *The Collapse of the Austro-Hungarian Monarchy and the Rise of the Czechoslovak State* (Prague, 1928), describes this "revolution."

6. H. Gordon Skilling, remark at conference on the East European media, Bloomington, Indiana, October 1983.

7. See Vojtech Mastny, *The Czechs under Nazi Rule: The Failure of National Resistance, 1939-1942* (New York, 1971).

8. Madeleine K. Albright, "The Role of the Press in Political Change: Czechoslovakia, 1968," (Ph.D. diss., Columbia University, 1976), overemphasizes the impact of journalism during the Prague Spring. The press had its greatest influence that year when it was used by politicians, not by journalists.

9. Jiri Hochman, "Words and Tanks: The Revival, the Agony, and Defeat," in Jiri Pehe, ed., *The Prague Spring: A Mixed Legacy* (New York, 1988), 27-40, estimates that a little over half the members of the journalists' union in 1968 left the profession, 180 emigrated, and 1,400 were expelled.

10. The difficulties the mass media were beginning to face in the early days of *glasnost* are evident in Zdenek Sumbera and Milan Kasik, "Ze petiletkou vyzkumu vlivu zurnalistiky na socialisticke spolecenske vedeni," (For the Five-Year Research of the Influence of Journalism on Socialist Social Leadership) *Sesity novinare* 21, no. 2 (1987): 91-121.

11. See Robert Dean, "Nationalism and Political Change in Eastern Europe: The Slovak Question and Czechoslovak Reform Movement," *Monograph Series in World Affairs* 10, no. 1 (1971-73).

12. Tomas Krystlik, "Masova media v Ceskoslovensku," Mass Media in Czechoslovakia *Zapad* 10 (Oct. 1988): 1.

13. *Zivot Strany*, no. 24 (1987): supplement.

14. "Otevrena politika, verejna informovanost," Open Politics, the Public Informed *Rude Pravo*, 19 July 1989, 3.

15. For a critical view of the party policy, see Rudolf Prevratil and Stanislav Perkner, "Nach der Euphorie der Freiheit die ganz normalen 'schwierigen Zeiten': Medien in der Tschechoslowakei" (From the Euphoria of Freedom to Ordinary 'Hard Times': Media in Czechoslovakia), *Media Perspektiven* 2 (1991): 77-78.

16. Peter Martin, "An Overview," *Radio Free Europe Czechoslovak Situation Report* 17 (21 Oct. 1988): 3.

17. Journalism students I spoke with in Prague in March 1989 were asking questions about the still relatively unknown playwright Vaclav Havel.

18. "Ukoly CSSN po zasedani UV KSC k ideologickym otazkam," (Tasks of the Czechoslavak Journalists after the Meeting of the Central Committee of the Communist Party of Czechoslovakia on Ideological Questions) *Novinar* 41, no. 2 (1989): 3, 9.

19. Part of the reason foreigners think CNN has such a tremendous effect is that it provides the only pictures and most of the news that the foreigners see, a view distinctly different from that available to the citizens of the country being watched.

20. Rasma Karklins and Roger Petersen, "Decision Calculus of Protesters and Regimes: Eastern Europe 1989," *Journal of Politics* 55 (Aug. 1993): 588-614.

21. Bernard Wheaton and Zdenek Kavan, *The Velvet Revolution: Czechoslovakia, 1988-1991* (Boulder, Colo., 1992), 52-54.

22. Ibid., 57-58.

23. Timothy Garton Ash, "The Revolution of the Magic Lantern," *New York Review of Books* 36 (18 Jan. 1990): 44.

24. Jan Obrman in *Radio Free Europe Czechoslovak Situation Report* 24 (8 Dec. 1989): 18-19.

25. *Svobodne Slovo*, 21 Nov. 1989.

26. Karklins and Petersen, "Decision Calculus," 597.

27. For a review of the development of Czech and Slovak journalism in the first year and a half of post-Communist rule, see Vladimir V. Kusin, "Media in Transition," *Report on Eastern Europe* 2 (3 May 1991): 5-19. For the following period, see Owen V. Johnson, "Whose Voice? Freedom of Speech and the Media in Central Europe," in Al Hester, ed., *Creating a Free Press in Eastern Europe* (Athens, Ga., 1994), 1-51.

Contributors

Jeffrey Brooks is professor of European history at the Johns Hopkins University. He is the author of *When Russia Learned to Read: Literacy and Popular Literature, 1861-1917* (Princeton University Press, 1985), which won the Vucinich Prize of the American Association for the Advancement of Slavic Studies in 1985. He has written widely on Russian and Soviet history. He is presently completing a book about Soviet public discourse, 1917-1953.

Jack Censer is professor of history at George Mason University. His published works include *Prelude to Power: The Parisian Radical Press 1789-1791*, *Press and Politics in Pre-Revolutionary France* (co-edited with Jeremy Popkin), and *The French Press in the Age of Enlightenment.*

Tim Harris, formerly a research fellow at Emmanuel College, Cambridge, is now an associate professor of history at Brown University, Rhode Island. His publications include *London Crowds in the Reign of Charles II* (1987), *Politics under the Later Stuarts* (1993), and (coedited with Paul Seaward and Mark Goldie) *The Politics of Religion in Restoration England* (1990). He has just finished editing a collection of essays, *Popular Culture in England, c. 1500-1850* (1994) and is currently working on a study of politics, power, and ideology in Britain during the 1680s.

Owen V. Johnson is associate professor of journalism and director of the Russian and East European Institute at Indiana University. He is the author of *Slovakia 1918-1938: Education and the Making of a Nation* (1985), and "The Press of Change: Mass Communications in Late Communist and Post-Communist Societies," in Sabrina Ramet, ed., *Adaptation and Transformation in Communist and Post-Communist Systems* (1992), along with many other works on Czechoslovak history and mass media.

Thomas C. Leonard is associate dean of the Graduate School of Journalism at the University of California, Berkeley. He is author of *The Power of the Press: The Birth of American Political Reporting* (1986), and *News for All: America's Coming-of-Age with the Press* (1995).

Stephen R. MacKinnon is professor of history and director of the Center for Asian Studies at Arizona State University. His most recent books include *China Reporting: An Oral History of American Journalism in the 1930s and 1940s* (1987) and *Agnes Smedley: The Life and Times of an American Radical* (1988). He is writing a study of the Chinese press as it interacted with the Western press during the 1930s, with special attention to the free press of Hankou, 1938.

Michael Mendle, associate professor of history at the University of Alabama, is the author of *Dangerous Positions* (1985) and a forthcoming study of Henry Parker. He is currently at work on "liberal" opposition to the successive parliamentary and army regimes of the 1640s and 1650s.

Jeremy Popkin is professor of history at the University of Kentucky. His publications include *The Right-Wing Press in France, 1792-1800* (1980), *Revolutionary News: The Press in France, 1789-1799* (1990), and numerous articles on the press during the period of the French Revolution.

Pierre Rétat is professor of literature at the University of Lyon II in Lyon, France, and director of the Center for Eighteenth-Century Studies. He has written or edited several works on the press of the Old Regime and the revolutionary period in France.

Jeffery A. Smith, an associate professor of journalism and mass communications at the University of Iowa, writes and teaches in the fields of communication law and history. He is the author of *Printers and Press Freedom: The Ideology of Early American Journalism* (1988) and *Franklin and Bache: Envisioning the Enlightened Republic* (1990).

Jonathan Sperber is currently professor of history at the University of Missouri, Columbia. His scholarly interests center on the social and political history of modern Europe, particularly nineteenth-century Germany. His major publications include *Popular Catholicism in Nineteenth Century Germany* (1984), *Rhineland Radicals: The Democratic Movement and the Revolution of 1848-1849* (1991), and *The European Revolutions, 1848-1851* (1993).

Mark W. Summers is professor of history at the University of Kentucky. His most recent books include *The Press Gang*, a study of the post–Civil War press and politics (1994), and *The Era of Good Stealings* (Oxford University Press, 1992).

Jeffrey N. Wasserstrom is associate professor of history and of East Asian languages and cultures at Indiana University. A specialist in modern Chinese history, his major publications include *Student Protests in Twentieth-Century China: The View from Shanghai* (1991), and *Popular Protest and Political Culture in Modern China: Learning from 1989* (1992), which he coedited with Elizabeth J. Perry.

Index
